CROCODILES

CROCODILES

Rodney Steel

CHRISTOPHER HELM

London

Acknowledgements

The author wishes to thank the following (listed alphabetically) for their assistance and advice during the compilation of this volume: Philip Chapman, City Museum, Bristol; Marilyn Holloway, British Museum (Natural History); Dr Barry Hughes; Ann Lum, British Museum (Natural History); Richard Luxmoore, IUCN Conservation Monitoring Centre; and Dr Colin McCarthy, British Museum (Natural History).

Special thanks are also due to the library staff of the British Museum (Natural History) for their helpful and enthusiastic assistance.

© 1989 Rodney Steel
Line illustrations by Tessa Lovatt-Smith
Maps by Robert Thorne

Christopher Helm (Publishers) Ltd, Imperial House,
21–25 North Street, Bromley, Kent BR1 1SD

ISBN 0-7470-3007-3

A CIP catalogue record for this book
is available from the British Library

Photoset by Paston Press, Loddon, Norfolk
Printed and bound in Great Britain by The Bath Press

Contents

Colour Plates

Figures

Maps

1.

Survivors of a lost world

Today, crocodiles cling only precariously to their tropical homelands. Lacking the appeal of fur-bearing mammals, they have a low popularity rating in conservation terms, and are still frequently treated only as dangerous vermin. Yet these largely unloved creatures are among the most remarkable of all so-called living fossils. Had they failed to survive into the modern world, their petrified bones would have been just as much a source of wonder and speculation as the skeletons of their close relatives, the dinosaurs.

Crocodiles are indeed the nearest thing to a living dinosaur that any human being will ever see, and throughout almost the entire age of reptiles, from about 200 million to 65 million years ago, there were crocodiles sharing the Mesozoic world with these now long-extinct giant reptiles. Some crocodiles that lived in those far-off days rivalled any contemporary reptile in size, and were obviously powerful enough to kill even the biggest plant-eating dinosaurs.

The most massive modern crocodiles attain only half the dimensions of these extinct Mesozoic creatures, and nowadays few individuals survive the hunter's rifle long enough to realise their full growth, but even so man-eating saltwater crocodiles occasionally run to 6 m (20 ft) or more. Such an animal would regard a man as an entirely suitable prey—in fact, an unwary human is a conspicuously vulnerable prospective victim for so powerful a reptile. The toll of human lives taken by crocodiles each year is almost impossible to ascertain, since many fatalities occur in remote areas and go unreported, but a figure of 2,000 deaths a year has been suggested.

The close relationship of crocodiles and dinosaurs is demonstrated by the presence in all these reptiles of two pairs of large openings in the skull, behind the eyes. These temporal openings are for the powerful muscles that open and close the jaws, the edges of the apertures offering a surface to which the muscles can attach themselves, while the opening itself provides accommodation for contracting muscle tissue as the mouth closes savagely and irrevocably on an unfortunate victim, exerting a pressure of up to 1,200 pounds per square inch.

This system of double-paired temporal openings is also found in a group of totally extinct reptiles called thecodonts which were widespread and, for a time, very successful some 225 million years ago during the early Triassic period. The original ancestors of the crocodiles, the dinosaurs, and the pterosaurs (extinct flying reptiles) are probably to be found among the thecodonts, and these groups are collectively known as archosaurs — the 'ruling reptiles' — so called because for over 150 million years they ruled the world. Only mass extinctions at the end of the Cretaceous period, 65 million years ago, brought their dynasty to an end, leaving only the crocodiles to compete (very successfully, in tropical climes) with the hordes of mammals that replaced the once-dominant reptiles.

Tracing the lineage of the archosaurs further back still, to the Permian period of 250 million years ago, leads to a group of small and not very well-known fossil reptiles with the characteristic double-paired temporal openings. Known as eosuchians, these obscure creatures may have been the progenitors of the archosaurs on the one hand, and of the other major group of living reptiles, the lizards and snakes, on the other. Collectively these 'two-arched' reptiles are all referred to as diapsids.

Today's crocodiles are regarded by many people as primitive, sluggish sprawlers, usually found lying in rivers, pretending to be floating logs so that they can snatch unwary animals coming to the water's edge for a drink. The truth is rather different. To begin with, crocodiles are far from primitive. Those alive today in the modern tropics have approximately the same outward appearance as the crocodiles of the Mesozoic, 150 million years ago, but this does not necessarily signify a primitive level of evolution. If crocodiles had acquired a successful combination of physical characteristics 150 million years ago that made them effective competitors with the mighty dinosaurs, why change a winning design? The tropics have shrunk since the warm, equable days of the Mesozoic, but between the longitudes of Cancer and Capricorn the rivers and lakes of South America, Africa and Asia still offer a lush, humid environment where the physical adaptations that enabled crocodiles to flourish along the shores of Jurassic water systems should guarantee their continued success in the modern world. Only man's arrival threatens the further perpetuation of the crocodilian line.

So crocodiles are not primitive, but magnificently adapted semi-aquatic predators. In the past, there have been groups of crocodiles that tried to break out of this mould, becoming either exclusively aquatic or seeking to spend all of their time on land. Although successful for a time, all these maverick offshoots ultimately became extinct. As a design for a water-dwelling reptilian hunter, the basic crocodilian configuration evolved 200 million years ago simply cannot be bettered.

Crocodiles have, for example, a secondary palate, functioning in much the same way as this structure in mammals, that enables them to breathe efficiently while holding their prey in their mouths: something that most other

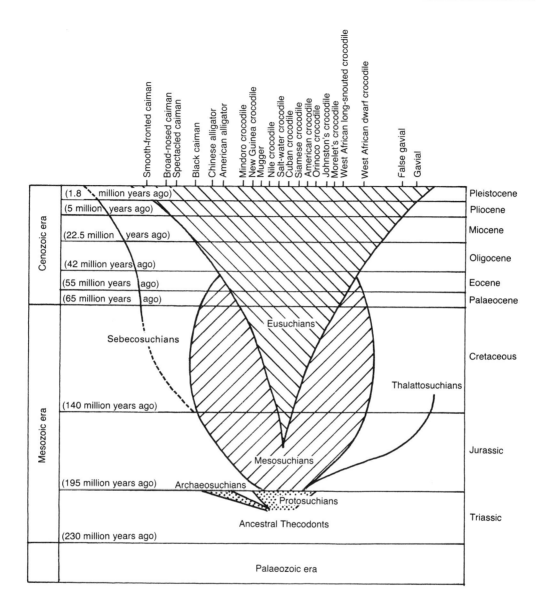

Figure 1   Crocodile origins

Mesozoic reptiles (including even the dinosaurs) never developed. They are therefore also able to breathe while floating with only the tip of the snout just above the water surface: because of the secondary palate, no water will enter the crocodile's lungs. The heart and the blood circulatory system have also become more sophisticated than is usual for reptiles, which normally have a three-chambered heart, with oxygenated blood from the lungs and oxygen-deficient blood from the muscles and internal organs passing into a common

3

ventral chamber, the ventricle. Theoretically, the two flows of blood remain separate in the ventricle, so that deoxygenated blood passes via the pulmonary system back to the lungs, while reoxygenated blood is directed to the body and head along the main arteries. In practice, some mixing of oxygenated and deoxygenated blood does inevitably occur in the ventricle, so that oxygen-deficient blood may be shunted back into the general circulation without being replenished through the lungs. In crocodiles, the heart's ventral chamber is effectively divided, so that oxygenated and deoxygenated blood are kept apart.

Living crocodiles fall into four broad categories, each of which is generally regarded as forming a subfamily. The typical crocodiles (Crocodylinae) include the huge saltwater crocodile, capable of attaining over 9 m (30 feet) in length, which owes its common name to a predilection for sea water, frequenting river estuaries and often ranging far out to sea, and the prolific Nile crocodile of Africa, together with a number of rather less familiar species, one of which (the broad-nosed West African crocodile) is only of small size — less than 2 m (6 ft 6 in) long when fully grown. Most of the members of this subfamily have moderately flattened skulls of typically crocodilian aspect, but the group also includes unusually broad-snouted species such as the mugger and slender-nosed reptiles like the West African long-snouted crocodile.

Alligators constitute a separate subfamily (Alligatorinae), the members of which typically have relatively broad skulls, although this is not a primary identifying feature of the group. The key to classification of a crocodilian as an alligator is to be found in the dentition, and specifically in the way the enlarged canine-like fourth tooth of the lower jaw is accommodated by the upper jaw when the mouth is closed. In crocodiles, the upper jaw is simply notched to make way for this tooth, which is therefore still visible externally even if the jaw is shut, while in alligators the fourth lower tooth fits into an upper-jaw pit so that it disappears from view. Today the group includes the two true alligators — one living in North America, one in China — and the caimans of South America, but in former times these crocodilians were more widespread, with fossil alligators also occurring in Europe.

Vying with the saltwater crocodile as the largest living crocodilian is the gavial of the Indian subcontinent and Burma, the sole existing representative of the subfamily Gavialinae. Although probably capable of attaining just over 9 m (30 ft) in length, the gavial is generally harmless to man and feeds almost exclusively on fish. It has a long, thin snout, sharply set off from the relatively short, broad cranium and provided with a multiplicity of peg-like teeth, which functions as a very efficient device for catching fish. This specialization has been developed on several occasions by crocodilians that became piscivorous, including an extinct group (the teleosaurs) that flourished in Jurassic times, about 150 million years ago. The fossil bones of these ancient fish-eating crocodiles were initially thought to be the remains of early gavials, but in fact they belong to a more primitive group, common during the age of dinosaurs, but now entirely defunct, that had the secondary palate less fully developed than modern crocodiles. The gavial seems to be of relatively recent origin, allegedly ancestral forms occurring only as far back as the Eocene, some 45 million years ago.

Another slender-snouted fish-eater, the so-called 'false gavial', is usually assigned to a separate subfamily named the Thoracosaurinae, after *Thoracosaurus*, an extinct relative of the living genus *Tomistoma*. The false gavial is found today in Thailand, Malaysia, Borneo, Celebes and Sumatra, and attains only half the size of the true gavial. Its narrow muzzle is not sharply demarcated from the rest of the skull in the manner of the gavial, and long nasal bones are retained (these elements are greatly reduced in the larger Indian reptile). Extinct false gavials have been reported from as far back as the Cretaceous period nearly 100 million years ago, and occur in South America, North America and possibly Africa, areas far from the group's present limited range in southeast Asia. Fossil remains of a huge crocodilian snout discovered in the Siwalik hills of the Indian subcontinent that may be attributable to a false gavial indicate a reptile possibly 18 m (59 ft) in length, and *Rhamphosuchus* (the name given to this inadequately-known mystery crocodile of 3 million years ago) is generally regarded as the largest crocodilian so far recorded.

Whether gavials and false gavials are closely related is unclear, but it is possible either that the former are descended from the latter or else that they both shared a common ancestry some time towards the close of the age of reptiles, subsequently evolving along similar but parallel lines and at one time ranging across most of the world's tropics. Their fish-eating specialization seems to have provided them with only a modest degree of success in competition with more conservative crocodiles, and their present restricted geographical range suggests that they were already in decline even before habitat destruction by human agencies threatened their further survival.

Crocodile myths and legends

Both feared and venerated by primitive peoples, crocodiles have been the object initially of worship and later of persecution at the hands of man. Today, no species of living crocodile is likely to survive for more than a short time longer without protection: hunters seeking hides and landowners who regard these reptiles simply as vermin would quickly eliminate them from every corner of their former ranges as the last tropical wilderness areas and rainforests come under threat of clearance and development.

At the dawn of civilization, Egyptian culture flourished along the banks of the River Nile, an area that had been one of the great crocodilian homelands for at least 75 million years. In early Palaeolithic times there was a huge lake in the Fayyum depression, to the southeast of the modern city of Cairo, in which the water level was 37 m (120 ft) above sea level. Crocodiles evidently swarmed there, and as civilisation prospered along the Nile the bizarre pantheon of Egyptian deities quickly came to include a crocodile god. Translated into English as Sebek (from the Greek 'Suchos'), this forbidding being was represented either by a crocodile-headed humanoid or simply by a

5

crocodile, and came to be regarded as the god of lakes and rivers. Sebek was one of the patrons of the 13th-dynasty kings (18th century BC), many of which were called Sebekhotep ('Sebek is satisfied'), and the worship of Sebek came to be centred on Shedet, in the Fayyum province, and at Ombos (later Kom-Ombo) in Upper Egypt, where there was a temple dedicated to Sebek.

The whole of the Fayyum province was supposedly under the protection of Sebek, with a specially constructed pool at Shedet (known to the Greeks as Crocodilopolis and to the Egyptians of Ptolemaic times as Arsinoë) where a sacred crocodile named Petesuchos ('He who belongs to Suchos') lived; the god Sebek was believed to be incarnate in this animal, which attendants adorned with gold rings and bracelets. Other crocodiles, in an adjacent pool, were believed to be the family of Petesuchos and received similar veneration. When any of them died, the body was carefully embalmed, and at Tebtunis, in the southern Fayyum, a whole cemetery of these mummified crocodiles has been discovered, each animal wrapped in old papyrus documents of the Hellenistic period; even eggs and recently emerged hatchlings were preserved. East of the Nile, the Egyptians apparently dug a canal straight out into the desert to join another canal running south from the Mediterranean through the Bitter Lakes to the Red Sea. This appears to have been in part at least a defensive measure, to keep unwanted immigrants out and possibly the Egyptians' own peasantry in, because the excavated spoil was heaped up into a rampart with fortifications at regular intervals. A contemporary picture from around 1300 BC shows that this canal system contained a substantial population of crocodiles, which must have made it an especially formidable barrier.

The water level in the Fayyum lake, known as Lake Moeris, fell steadily throughout the late Palaeolithic and by about 10,000 BC was some 4.6 m (15 ft) below sea level. During the Middle Kingdom, around 1950 BC, the Pharaohs widened and deepened the channel connecting Lake Moeris to the Nile, stabilising the water level at 55 feet (16.8 m) above sea level, and when Herodotus visited the area in about 450 BC the lake was 3,600 furlongs (725 km) in circumference and 50 fathoms (90 m) deep. Strabo (63 BC–20 AD), the Greek geographer, was a later sightseer at Arsinoë, when the city had become a tourist venue for prosperous Graeco-Roman travellers, and reported seeing the sacred crocodile fed by visitors with bread, meat, cake and honey wine: one of the priests would hold its jaws open, while another placed these delicacies in the creature's mouth. Presumably it was advisable to ensure that Petesuchos was always well fed and placid!

An early god in the Egyptian pantheon who also had crocodilian connections was Set, the son of Gib and the brother of Osiris and Isis. Set (or Seth) customarily symbolised the arid sterility of the desert, and was regarded by the Egyptians as a dark foreboding influence, despite being associated in the complicated pharaonic religious system with the Sun, and hence with Ra (whom he defended against the serpent Apep) and Amon. Gib divided Egypt between Set and Osiris, but Set wanted all of the country for himself and killed Osiris in the ensuing dispute. With Sebek's aid, Set took refuge in the body of a crocodile to escape apprehension and punishment. As a consequence, although crocodiles were venerated in some Egyptian provinces, because they were all believed to represent an incarnation of the ruling deity and killing any crocodile was regarded as a heinous crime, in other places the people regarded them as detestable creatures that should be hunted without mercy. Eventually the worship of Set was largely displaced by other religions, so that the cult became confined to Upper Egypt.

When Herodotus, the Greek historian and geographer, visited Egypt in the 5th century BC, vestiges of these beliefs lingered on in the valley of the Nile, and crocodile worship was still a feature of the area. After seeing captive crocodiles, Herodotus commented that in these reptiles the lower jaw was immovably fixed so that for the mouth to open there had to be a hinged upper jaw. Thus was established one of the earliest crocodile myths, to which was added, through subsequent centuries, an abundance of ill-informed anecdotes that eventually comprised an extraordinary catalogue of implicitly believed misinformation. In fact, all crocodilians have an entirely orthodox jaw articulation, but if the creature is in repose, with its head resting on the ground, it is inevitable that when the mouth opens it will be the snout that rises rather than the lower jaw that drops.

Another crocodilian myth that can be traced back to classical times is the assertion that crocodiles weep piteously to deceive sympathetic humans into approaching them, and, when the unfortunate victim has been seized and devoured, lachrymate copiously in sorrow for the deed. Belief in 'crocodile tears', meaning insincere remorse, became a firmly established feature of crocodile lore, with references occurring in Shakespeare and Spencer. Eyewitnesses such as John Sparke, a crew member with the notorious 16th-century slaver John (later Sir John) Hawkins, reported that the crocodilians of the Caribbean would 'cry and sobbe like a Christian body' to coax victims within range. Crocodiles do not, and cannot, cry, but the flesh around the eyes is so formed that the corner of each might with a little imagination, have the appearance of holding a tear.

Crocodilian legends, albeit of a rather less sophisticated sort than those prevalent in ancient Egypt, have also arisen among the tribes south of the Sahara. The Thongas of the Pongola River region in northern Zululand will often wear around their necks a crocodile tooth or claw, which came originally from a reptile they believed to have been responsible for widespread killings of domestic animals or people. Suitably anointed with potions by the local medicine man, these macabre relics are believed to ward off evil spirits and to confer on the wearer immunity to attacks by crocodiles. This tribe attributes supernatural powers to crocodiles, supposing them to be capable of bringing rain during a dry spell, and also claims that the reptiles possess the spirits of tribal ancestors which require to be appeased by appropriate sacrifices of chickens or goats at times of family illness or death. The Thongas believe crocodile liver to be a deadly poison, so that if a tribesman kills a crocodile he is obliged to present the liver to his chief for public burning to ensure that no-one can be poisoned by it (crocodile liver is toxic only if left to decompose before being eaten). Ointments and potions sold by the medicine man are often based on crocodile fat, which is also said to protect against lightning strikes, and desiccated crocodile brain used to be powdered and sprinkled in a river as a protection against attacks by these reptiles. Crocodiles were supposed to swallow stomach stones at the rate of one a year (at the beginning of the rains), so that they allegedly indicated the creature's age; crocodilian gastroliths are taboo to the Thongas, who use them in divination and to foretell the deaths of their chiefs (these worthies are obliged to swallow a suitably anointed stomach stone to ascertain their fate).

The Ashanti had an ancient tradition of crocodile worship, based on the belief that individual reptiles had formerly befriended ancestors of a given family. Sacred crocodiles were maintained in village ponds in many parts of tropical Africa, and these reptiles acquired a special significance on Madagascar, where the Zafandravoay ('sons of the crocodile') clan of the Antandroy people claim to be descended from the two sons of a woman who had married a crocodile. The Zafandravoay regard themselves as immune from attack by one of these reptiles, which they are at pains never to harm: their tribal dead are believed to turn into crocodiles after entombment and to go off to join their ancestors in the river. Other Madagascan tribes (the Antarkare, the Sakalava and the northern Betsimisaraka) all thought that the souls of their dead chiefs passed into the bodies of crocodiles, and in some places there was a tradition of human sacrifice — often a young man or woman, sometimes both — to placate these reptiles. The Sakalava used to feed the entrails of their dead kings to the crocodiles of Lake Komakoma, which were therefore regarded with special veneration, and the people who live near Lake Anivorano believe themselves all to be descended from one woman who long ago lived in a village on the site of the lake and offered a passing stranger a drink of water when all the other inhabitants had refused him: the visitor, it seems, was a mighty sorcerer who told his benefactor to remove her family to safety, and then caused the offending village to be swallowed up by water summoned from out of the earth, the wretched inhabitants all being transformed into crocodiles.

When the inevitable happened, and some poor Malagasy villager was taken by a supposedly sacred crocodile, it was the practice among the island's tribes to catch one of these reptiles with a baited hook and then kill it with fire-hardened poles (instead of spears, which were regarded as inappropriate for the execution of one of their saurian 'brothers'), simultaneously offering profuse apologies and lamentations for having to act in such a heinous manner. The animal's carcase would then be ceremonially buried, wrapped in silken cords, while the village women let down their hair in mourning.

Belief in crocodiles as 'familiars' was widespread in Africa, and it was imagined that sorcerers could either turn into crocodiles or else enter their bodies to use the reptiles' predatory capabilities for killing a rival or an enemy. In the Congo, crocodiles were regarded as harmless to people unless possessed in this manner, and if a crocodile seized a villager there was an immediate 'witch hunt' to find a human scapegoat. The Konde people of northern Lake Nyasa would punish anyone held to be a bewitcher of crocodiles by placing the unfortunate wretch in a fish trap and leaving him there until he was taken by a crocodile.

Elsewhere in the world, primitive societies also had their crocodile lore. The aborigines of northern Australia believe that the spirits of their forebears lived on in the crocodiles of the region (commonly the highly dangerous saltwater crocodile), and believed that in the past their ancestors had turned themselves into crocodiles by pushing a firestick up their rectums — the black blotches on the back and tail of a crocodile are allegedly scorch marks! In New Guinea, the Papuans who lived along the Sepik River employed crocodiles extensively in their decorative art — on drums, bowls and other utensils, as well as on the prows of canoes — and fashioned crocodile dancing masks, while the creation myths of the Kiwai tribe featured the crocodile as a father figure.

On the Indian subcontinent, many villages maintained sacred muggers in a nearby pool, and expected passing strangers to contribute towards their repast with offerings of food. The attendant fakirs and other hangers-on also, needless to say, profited from travellers' visits, obtaining pecuniary and other benefits from showing off their reptilian charges to itinerant bystanders.

In the mythology of pre-Columbian American civilisations, too, the crocodile seems to have had a prominent position. The Olmec cultures of 1,600 years ago occupied an area of low-lying tropical forests, tidewaters, lagoons and rivers in Vera Cruz and Tabasco, on the eastern coast of present-day Mexico, where crocodiles abounded. Much of the Olmecs' religious imagery seems to have been inspired by crocodiles, including some depictions previously regarded as 'were-jaguars'. Further back in time still, around 1500 BC, crocodiles probably provided the Indians of this region with a valuable source of meat and skins that were in all likelihood a major item of trade. T. Stocker, S. Meltzoff and S. Armsey suggested in 1980 that, as the Olmecs acquired ascendancy over hill tribes further inland, crocodile goods were widely exported, along with a religious cult that centred on crocodiles. To the Olmecs, crocodiles were apparently agricultural fertility symbols, the crocodile deity being illustrated with a 'flowering-vegetating' tail. It has been suggested that the Olmecs so depleted the local crocodile stocks that they were eventually unable to satisfy the demand for crocodilian regalia they had stimulated among their highland fiefdoms and for this reason gradually lost their influence and suffered cultural decline.

Subsequent Central American cultures maintained a crocodilian religious imagery. A were-crocodile with a cleft head (derived from the cleft between a crocodile's eye sockets) occurs at Teotihuacan (about 6th century AD), a stylised crocodile motif is repeatedly encountered at the Toltec site of Tula (about 10th century AD), and the Maya associated crocodiles with the Earth, the aquatic world (especially fish), subsistence crops (maize) and the water lily in their art. Aztec mythology (10th century AD to the Spanish conquest in the 16th century) seems to have retained some elements of crocodilian imagery in representations of the rain god Tlaloc, and the first of the 20 day signs in the Aztec calendar was Cipactli, the crocodile, which granted corn to men in return for blood or water sacrifices: it was believed that children born on days identified by this sign would become great tillers of the soil.

In South America, the Incas had special cages for caimans in their zoo at

Cuzco, and to this day in the Peruvian Montaña the wearing of a crocodile tooth is supposed to be a protection against poisoning, while scales and teeth are widely used as ornaments in Guiana, in the northern part of the continent.

The danger that large crocodiles pose to man is well attested, but early writers elaborated on this theme to an astonishing extent, and one William Bartram, who travelled the American southeast during the late 18th century, depicted astonishing scenes in an over-imaginative book published in 1791. Alligators (which Bartram referred to as crocodiles, regarding 'alligator' simply as a 'country name') were depicted 'rushing forth from the reeds . . . plaited tail brandished high . . . waters like a cataract descend from his opening jaws . . . clouds of smoke issue from his dilated nostrils . . . roaring terribly'. Stirring stuff for the folks back home, but a visualisation that owes more to legends of St George and the dragon than to the actual habits of any crocodilian.

Needless to say, neither alligators nor crocodiles spout water or smoke; and their nostrils, far from ever becoming dilated, are valvular slits that open only to a diameter of perhaps 2.5 cm (1 in) at most, and then only in very large specimens. So far as the 'clouds of smoke' are concerned, it is possible that this fiction owed its origin to a phenomenon witnessed in 1983 by Kevin N. Brewster, who saw large alligators (exceeding 3 m/9 ft 9 in in length) bellowing early in the morning at St Augustine Alligator Farm, Florida. Brewster described clouds of 'fog' emitted from the creatures' partly opened jaws that was briefly visible against a dark background in the relatively cool air. He surmised that this might be due to the vaporisation of water in the animal's lungs by sound waves generated during bellowing, or that it could simply be expelled carbon dioxide.

The myths publicised so luridly by Bartram were fuelled by a number of later writers, notably Thomas Ashe, who apparently navigated the Mississippi in 1806. Although crocodiles do have enlarged canine-like teeth, these two early writers promoted them to the status of tusks 'white as the finest polished ivory', and went on to perpetuate a legend that originated in Africa, thus transferring it to the American alligator: not the jaws so much as the tail were used by crocodilians to sweep prey off the banks into the water, or to thresh fishes within reach of the mouth. Up until the 1930s, this belief in the use of the crocodilian tail as a means of securing prey was universally accepted, further elaborated by accounts of crocodiles defending themselves or their nests by attempting to deliver blows with the heavily armoured tail.

Later observers have established that crocodiles customarily secure their prey and if necessary defend themselves by snapping or biting with the jaws. Any lashing of the tail is probably purely incidental, compensating for the animal's other movements, although premeditated offensive use of the tail cannot be altogether ruled out.

Strong-smelling emanations from a pair of musk glands beneath the lower jaw were reported by many writers, and these allegedly possessed a sexual function. Roaring bull alligators were claimed to eject copious 'sweet pungent-smelling' musk that scented the air and water for 'some hours'. Females were believed to excrete musk from a pair of cloacal glands as an attractant in the mating season. Early in the 20th century these beliefs were still being promoted, even in scientific publications. Such a prestigious writer as R. L. Ditmars stated as late as 1936 that when bull alligators roar the scent glands 'on the under surface of the chin' emit 'fine, steamy jets of a powerful musky-smelling fluid . . . the odour may be carried for miles.' Subsequent investigations have disclosed that juveniles do indeed evert the submandibular glands if alarmed, for example by being picked up, but no detectable emanation has been observed. The anal glands do produce an oily yellow secretion, however, and if the throat or anal glands are dissected out from a carcase, there is a faint odour detectable from perhaps a couple of feet away, but it certainly cannot be described as strong, and whether it is 'pungent' or 'musky' is largely a matter of personal interpretation. This seems to dispose of an ancient belief that cattle can detect the 'evil odour' of a crocodile when fording a stream. W. T. Neill suggested that in many cases the observers have in fact been smelling the normal odours of decaying organic matter in a swamp, which becomes particularly strong when a crocodile plunges into or out of the water and stirs up the mud and sediment. Structurally the 'musk glands' incorporate glandular cells containing numerous secretion droplets, with each gland enclosed in dense connective tissue (which divides it into lobes and lobules) and striated muscle, a large reservoir being additionally incorporated in the structure of the anal glands. When everted, 'musk glands' present a rosette-like appearance, ranging in colour from creamy-white to black.

Feared and detested, reviled and persecuted, crocodiles undoubtedly have a bad public image. But not only are they of outstanding interest to scientists as survivors from the age of dinosaurs, they are also an invaluable and integral part of the ecosystem in tropical lands. Their less than enviable reputation is due to aggressive predatory habits, but they are not simply ruthless killers. Crocodiles also scavenge carcases washed down rivers or lying in the shallows of lakes, and therefore perform a beneficial service, cleaning up corpses that would otherwise simply rot. In dry seasons, the wallows dug by crocodiles often contain the only available water for miles around, without which many other animals would die of thirst. They may also have much to teach medical specialists, for they are singularly resistant to disease and rarely develop tumours.

As the last of the ruling reptiles that once dominated the long-gone Mesozoic world, crocodiles surely now deserve to become better understood, so that their place in the natural world is appreciated and their future can be safeguarded.

2.

Anatomy of a living fossil

Reptiles were the first backboned animals to become effectively independent of the water. They had been preceded ashore by various invertebrates, which succeeded in establishing themselves on dry land as long ago as the Silurian period, 400 million years ago, but the amphibians that crawled out of Devonian lakes and rivers still had to return to the water for the purpose of breeding, as do their latter-day descendants.

Not so the reptiles: for they had evolved the amniote egg, which is laid on land and protects the embryonic animal from desiccation by enclosing it in a liquid-filled sac, the amnion. A second sac, the allantois, collects up the waste products generated by the developing embryo as it consumes the yolk which nourishes it during development to the hatchling stage, and the shell provides a barrier against the outside environment which is nonetheless sufficiently porous to allow the inward diffusion of oxygen and the egress of carbon dioxide.

It is true that many reptiles still spend a great deal of their time in water — crocodiles are a prime example — but they do just the same have the capability of living an independent terrestrial existence. The water, however, offers a ready source of food, concealment, protection, and body-temperature regulation, so it is not surprising that crocodiles have taken the easy option and remained semi-aquatic by inclination even if they have the physiological capability to adopt a more adventurous life style exclusively on dry land. In the past some crocodiles do, in fact, seem to have been more or less exclusively terrestrial, but these sebecosuchians were evidently considerably less successful in the long term than their stay-at-home cousins which remained in the water, and in due course they became extinct.

Metabolism and anatomy

Like all living reptiles, crocodilians are cold-blooded, which means that they have only a limited ability to control their own body temperature. Mammals, in contrast, are warm-blooded, and generate sufficient heat with their own metabolic processes to keep their internal temperature at an optimum level for functional efficiency (around 35°C, varying slightly from species to species), with an insulating layer of fur usually available to limit heat loss in cold conditions or provide insulation against excessive warmth. In order to achieve this thermal efficiency, mammals have to function at a far higher physiological level than cold-blooded reptiles. R. A. Coulson and J. D. Herbert of Louisiana State University found in 1981 that the metabolic rate of a shrew, weighing about 2 g, is some 60 times that of a 70-kg (11-stone) man, which is in turn some 60 times that of an alligator. By assuming that all three species were of 70 kg weight (i.e. that the shrew was 35,000 times bigger than it really is and the alligator substantially smaller), it was calculated that, whereas a man has a respiratory rate of 18 excursions a minute, the figure for a hypothetical 70-kg shrew would be 300 and for a 70-kg alligator only 0.3. Other measurements were worked out for blood flow (shrew 300 litres a minute, man 5 litres a minute, alligator 0.086 litres a minute), heart rate (shrew 1,200 beats a minute, man 70 beats a minute, alligator 3 beats a minute), water requirement (shrew 210 litres a day, man 26.5 litres a day, alligator 0.8 litres a day), survival time without oxygen (shrew 0.25 seconds, man 3 minutes, alligator 875 minutes), and survival without food (shrew 0.44 days, man 26.5 days, alligator 1,591 days). Size, it should also be noted, is a major factor in determining metabolic rates (more important than the identity of the species), and a very small alligator at 28°C would have a higher metabolic rate than a very large mammal at 37°C.

Crocodilians have an optimum body temperature, measured in the cloaca, of 30–35°C; below 5°C or above 38°C and they are in danger of either freezing to death or succumbing to heat prostration. Cold winters make markedly seasonal climes untenable for crocodilians, which are too large to hibernate in the tiny protected hideouts sought by temperate-zone snakes and lizards, so they are largely restricted to the tropics, with some species managing to colonise the warm-temperate zones. Because a large animal has a relatively small surface area relative to its volume, fully grown crocodiles of the larger species lose heat only slowly in cool conditions and take up heat in an equally tardy manner when it is hot. Size is therefore one factor that helps a cold-blooded animal to maintain its body temperature near the optimum figure, but additional measures are necessary to even out the disparity between daytime and night-time temperatures, even in the tropics. This requirement is one reason why crocodilians are essentially aquatic creatures, despite their theoretical independence of the water. A river or lake will warm up only slowly under daytime sunshine, and loses heat very gradually after sunset, so by taking refuge in the warm water at night a crocodilian can keep its temperature from falling during the hours of darkness, while by day excessive heat can similarly be avoided by remaining immersed. In between, the reptile emerges during the early morning from the now chilling water to bask in the sunlight on a bank or mudflat, returning to the water as the noonday sun gathers strength, and re-emerging in the evening to soak up more of the waning day's warmth before the thermometer begins to fall sharply again with the onset of darkness. There is some evidence of a circadian rhythm in this behaviour, experiments by J. W. Lang at the University of Minnesota in 1976 indicating that when captive juvenile alligators in outdoor pens moved into the water at sunset there was an accompanying decrease in body temperature, suggesting that this activity is not exclusively a warmth-seeking response.

Crocodilian cloacal temperatures must be treated with some caution. C. R. Drane, G. J. W. Webb and P. Hever of Sydney University found in 1977 that a saltwater crocodile basking in the sun sustained a more rapid temperature rise in the heart, the centre of the tail, the liver and the lungs than in the cloaca and along the lower surfaces of the body and tail. Probably the circulatory system provides a means of distributing warmth in a differential manner when a crocodilian is warming up, so that vital organs receive the quickest benefit from any temperature rise.

Reptiles in general are known to absorb warmth faster in hot conditions than they lose it in cool temperatures, and experiments reported by J. Scott-Turner and C. Richard Tracy in 1983 demonstrated that in crocodilians this differential heating/cooling rate is determined by blood flow to the extremities rather than a generalised perfusion of the skin. The tests involved restricting the blood supply to the limbs and tails of young American alligators (200–400 g/7–14 oz in weight) and then alternately warming and cooling them in a wind tunnel. It was found that preventing blood from reaching the extremities considerably reduced the capacity of these juvenile alligators to warm up in a hot-air flow, but had little effect on cooling rates in a cold-air flow. E. Norbert Smith of North-East Oklahoma State University had previously demonstrated in 1978 that alligators increase their cutaneous blood flow as a response to local warming and correspondingly reduce it under the influence of cooling. Unlike other reptiles, however, in these large ectotherms occupying a temperate climatic zone warming up one part of the animal led to heat loss and local vasoconstriction in areas of the body not subjected to heat. It was surmised that this is an adaptation to retain heat in an environment with a pronounced cool season: small alligators display less marked changes in cutaneous blood flow.

Crocodiles usually become torpid during the winter season or the dry period of the year (which in many tropical areas coincide), retreating to burrows or quiet bodies of water, feeding only rarely, to await the return of more favourable conditions: a process referred to as aestivation when induced by drought and hibernation if a response to winter cold, although crocodilians only become sluggish and do not enter into a prolonged comatose state. Smaller species and juvenile individuals are of course more vulnerable to both seasonal temperature variation and daytime/night-time temperature differentials because of their unfavourable surface area: volume ratio.

Crocodilians also lose water from their bodies in hot, dry conditions, work by J. E. Davis and his colleagues at State Univerity College, Buffalo, in 1980 indicating that most of this loss occurs through the skin (in the case of the American alligator, 36–54 per cent of it). The rate of evaporative loss is greater in small individuals than in large ones, owing to their larger relative surface area, and the rate of cutaneous water loss increases faster than that of respiratory water loss as the temperature rises. Small crocodilians are seldom seen to bask, whereas for large individuals this practice is an essential component of their heat-regulating strategy: with their thicker skin and body wall, they store more calories of heat for each degree rise in body temperature than their smaller brethren. Metabolism accounts for only 0.1 to 0.3 per cent of total energy exchange between crocodilians and their environment, while evaporation represents 1.8 to 2.8 per cent of heat loss at a body temperature of 28°C and an air temperature of 30°C. In small crocodilians, conduction and convection are significant temperature-control factors. G. C. Grigg and J. Alchin of Sydney University studied the relatively small Johnston's crocodile from northern Australia and reported in 1976 that the heart rate increases during heating, the convective transfer of heat through the body effected by the circulatory system far exceeding heat transfer by conduction alone. Localised warming promoted cutaneous vasodilation to promote the uptake of heat, whereas localised cooling led to vasoconstriction that enhanced heat conservation, but acceleration and deceleration of the heart rate and dilation and constriction of the blood vessels were seen as separate responses to heating or cooling at the surface: vasodilation and tachycardia increase blood flow and heat transfer from body core to the periphery, while vasoconstriction and bradycardia decrease heat flow.

Skeleton

An appraisal of a modern crocodile's skeleton leaves little doubt of its basically aquatic adaptation. The head is long and low, with the nostrils, eyes and ears high up in the skull so that the animal can float with only the tip of the snout and the eyes above water. Despite the antediluvian aspect of the group as a whole, a crocodile's skull has been considerably modified from the primitive diapsid pattern, with even the characteristic paired upper temporal openings sometimes becoming reduced in size or closing up altogether. A typical feature of all crocodilians is an elongate muzzle of varying breadth, the oldest known (Triassic) crocodiles still having a face of only quite modest length but all later forms possessing a considerably extended snout with the premaxillary bones (incorporating the external nostrils) at its tip and the paired maxillae (bearing all but the most anterior upper teeth) constituting the sides. Some exceptionally slender-nosed crocodilians (e.g. the gavials, and the extinct teleosaurs) have the maxillae meeting on top of the snout to the exclusion of the nasal bones, which normally form the muzzle's upper surface. Primitively a bar of bone separated the external nostrils, but this is frequently absent, and a facial opening (the antorbital fenestra) that is commonly found among archosaurs has been secondarily closed in most species. The skull table, overlying the brain case, is flattened and has no parietal foramen (associated with a light-sensitive organ in primitive reptiles), many of the bones in this area of the skull incorporating pneumatised air spaces for lightness. The lateral temporal fenestrae and the external opening of the ear are sunk below the level of the skull in modern crocodilians, and the skin is normally tightly adherent to the skull's sculptured surface (one group of extinct, totally aquatic marine crocodiles, the thalattosuchians, was exceptional in having smooth skull bones). The pterygoid and quadrate bones, which in primitive reptiles form a movable articulation with the brain case, are firmly fused to this structure in crocodiles to give the skull great rigidity, and the ear capsule is contained within the prootic, opisthotic and supraoccipital bones.

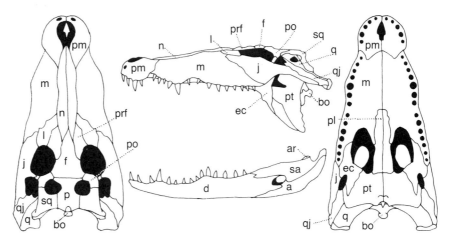

Figure 2 The crocodilian skull (*Crocodylus moreleti*). Abbreviations: a, angular; ar, articular; bo, basioccipital; d, dentary; ec, ectopterygoid; f, frontal; j, jugal; l, lacrimal; m, maxilla; n, nasal; p, parietal; pl, palatine; pm, premaxilla; ps, postorbital; prf, prefrontal; pt, pterygoid; q, quadrate; qj, quadratojugal; sa, surangular; sq, squamosal

The trunk is proportionately elongate, with relatively short limbs ending in slender-toed plantigrade feet, the front ones with five toes, the hind possessing only four digits (the fifth, or outer, toe in the back foot is represented simply by a vestigial metatarsal bone, having already been lost in ancestral crocodilians of the Triassic period, over 200 million years ago).

The bone structure of crocodiles has been found to exhibit a sequence of laminae from which J. M. Hutton deduced in 1986 that the age of individual animals could be determined. These alternating broad and narrow bands of bone deposition were detected throughout the skeleton, representing respectively warm seasons of rapid growth and cold seasons of negligible growth. Sections from limb bones or vertebrae can obviously be taken only from dead individuals, but Hutton, working in Zimbabwe with Nile crocodiles, found that even the bony scutes in the skin of the back display cortical stratification and under local anaesthesia it is possible to remove a 5-mm thick section from these elements to calculate the age of the individual, the operation site subsequently healing quickly providing the wound is packed with antibiotic powder. Hutton worked with captive animals whose ages were in fact already known, so age determination based on bone-laminae assessment could be checked. Some care was necessary in interpreting the results obtained from dermal scutes when dealing with breeding females, as in these animals the plates of the back armour seem to represent a reserve of calcium that can be drawn upon for incorporation into the developing eggs, resulting in considerable restructuring of the bone tissue.

Movement

Crocodiles float tail-heavy in deep water. When the animal starts to swim, it becomes horizontal under the influence of propulsive movements by the tail, which provides the main swimming effort, the limbs remaining for the most part pressed against the body (the limbs are not normally even used for steering, which is achieved by asymmetrical movements of the tail and bending of the whole body). The anterior part of a crocodile's tail bears a double crest of backward-pointed, sickle-like scales that are directed laterally (in alligators these crests are less well developed than in crocodylines), but the most flexible part of the tail (its distal end) bears only a single crest: this terminal region constitutes 60 per cent of the total tail length in alligators, but only 45 per cent in crocodylines. The principal muscle that bends the tail is the M. caudo-femoralis longus, which inserts on the fourth trochanter of the femur (a rugose area at the back of the bone) and originates from the haemal arches and the posterior region of each caudal vertebra. Contraction of this muscle also automatically flexes the knee joint and extends the tarsus through a series of interconnected tendons, as well as bending the tail and causing the vertebral column as a whole to flex laterally.

Although crocodiles do, when on land, spend a considerable time sprawled out on their bellies in indolent but wary repose, they are also capable of very rapid movement ashore. They will not infrequently employ what has become known as the 'high walk', in which the belly is lifted completely clear of the ground with the limbs supporting virtually the entire weight of the animal in fully terrestrial fashion. It is admittedly a relatively slow means of progression, and when alarmed on shore a crocodile will usually simply toboggan into the water on its belly, propelled by its legs. When seizing its prey or engaged in antagonistic behaviour, however, a crocodile is capable of extraordinary agility and energy. Anthony Pooley, the South African crocodile expert, witnessed a Nile crocodile in the Ndumu game reserve on the Mozambique border lying in wait for prey in shallow water at the foot of a steep bank down which nyala and impala would come to drink at Inyamiti Lake. Pooley recounted in 1982 how the crocodile moved so fast when a nyala came within range that the action seemed just a blur: the crocodile sprang upwards 'to a height of some two-thirds of his total length', propelled by the powerful hindlegs, seized its victim by the head, and fell back into the water, to re-emerge some minutes later still holding the drowned nyala in its jaws. Crocodiles floating almost submerged have also been seen to project themselves half out of the water to catch waterbirds flying just above the surface. A cold-blooded reptile does not have the same capacity for a sustained high level of activity that a warm-blooded mammal has, but crocodiles are nonetheless capable of moving with lightning speed on occasion.

Small species, and small individuals of large forms, will really gallop when in an urgent hurry on land. The crocodilian spine is constructed predominantly to allow for lateral movements, with ligaments uniting the backbone into a flexible column offering freedom of movement as well as stability. In the slow, symmetrical, trot-like walk, the thoracic and lumbar regions undergo lateral flexion under the influence of the iliocostalis and longissimus musculature, the limb girdles themselves swivelling to help lengthen the stride. When a crocodile gallops, however, the transverso-spinalis musculature comes into play to generate vertical thoracic-lumbar flexion, as C. Bornhuser and V. Ziswiler of the University Zoological Museum in Zurich demonstrated in 1983.

Respiration

The scales along the edges of the jaws bear conspicuous pigmented elevations that have a rich nerve supply and are evidently unusually well-developed organs of touch, but fleshy cheeks or lips are lacking, so it is not possible for a crocodile to exclude water from its mouth when underwater. If its nasal passages were of the normal primitive reptilian pattern, with the nostrils opening into the front of the palate, it could not breathe while floating with only the tip of the snout and the eyes above water. For air to reach the windpipe and hence the lungs, this unsophisticated construction would require the opening of the valve-like glottis (velum palati, or palatal valve) in the upper part of the throat which, in conjunction with a ventral basihyal valve (a muscular structure at the back of the tongue) seals off the pharynx; if the mouth is full of water, the lungs would flood and the animal must necessarily drown. In modern crocodiles the maxillary, palatine and pterygoid bones have been extended across the roof of the mouth to form a shelf of bone above which the nasal passages are carried to the back of the throat, eventually opening into the pharynx behind the slit-like glottis and the basihyal valve, immediately above the windpipe. With this secondary palate, modern crocodilians can continue to breathe when submerged with just their nostrils above the surface, even though the mouth cavity is full of water. If the animal dives, additional valves seal off the nostrils themselves, the musculature to effect this constituting much of the characteristic enlarged tip of the crocodilian snout: the posterior wall of each naris is pulled backwards by contraction of a large smooth dilator muscle to open the nostrils, closure being achieved when this dilator is forced to extend by the contraction of a circular smooth muscle that surrounds it, permitting the lips of the nostril to come together again and seal the opening. In addition, cavernous tissue consisting of blood vessels which dilate to press against the walls of the nasal vestibule provide an ancillary narial closure mechanism.

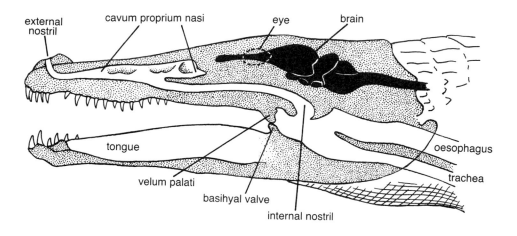

Figure 3 Semi-diagrammatic longitudinal section of a crocodilian head and lower jaw, showing the right-hand nasal passage and the structure of the throat. The tongue is non-protrusible

Crocodiles have developed a counterpart of the diaphragm, a muscular structure which in mammals divides the body cavity into two compartments (the lung cavity and the peritoneal cavity) and facilitates breathing by increasing and decreasing the capacity of the lung cavity. In crocodiles, the liver is attached to connective tissue that separates the pleural — or lung — cavity from the peritoneal cavity, with two diaphragmatic muscles connecting the liver to the pelvic bones. During exhalation there is an anterior shift of the liver effected by transverse abdominal muscles, inhalation being effected by contraction of the diaphragmatic musculature pulling the liver backwards to increase the capacity of the pleural cavity. Costal muscles further facilitate the air flow by shifting the position of the ribs, and in addition fix the flexible rib cage so that it resists the aspirating and compressing action of the so-called hepatic piston — the backward and forward movement of the liver. When a crocodilian's trunk is immersed, expiration becomes essentially passive, while inspiration requires increased muscular effort: the ribs do not change position but remain more or less fixed in place by the costal muscles, changes in the volume of the pleural cavity being achieved almost exclusively by movement of the hepatic piston.

It was shown in 1970 by K. A. Naifeh and his colleagues at the Texas Medical Centre, Houston, that there are ventilating periods in alligators and the South American caimans of from six to 22 seconds, with from one to five breaths, followed by apneic periods of from three to 13 minutes when active breathing ceases. The tidal volume in juvenile caimans was measured at 12 cc per kilogram of body weight. Each animal was found to display a widely varying respiratory sequence not just from one day to another, but from one cycle to another. J. C. Wright of Sydney University found in 1986 that oxygen consumption peaks at ambient temperatures of 30–33°C, regardless of whether the crocodilian is resting or active, and it seems probable that these reptiles are physiologically geared to generate mximum energy with optimum fatigue recovery within this relatively narrow temperature band.

An indication of how long a crocodile can remain submerged was provided by experiments carried out at Harvard in 1925 by G. H. Parker. In a procedure that modern researchers would probably find unethical, small caimans and alligators were kept underwater in a tank by lowering a net over them until they drowned. The caimans, 27 to 86 cm in length, died after only 34 to 72 minutes' submergence, but four alligators up to 26 cm long did not succumb until they had been underwater for from 5 hours 20 minutes to 6 hours 5 minutes. In a further series of experiments at Harvard reported by D. B. Dill and H. T. Edwards in 1931, it was found that a juvenile American crocodile began to accumulate lactic acid 6–10 minutes after respiration ceased, more than half the oxygen requirement being met after 25 minutes by lactic-acid formation.

It has been suggested that the oxygen consumption of a submerged crocodile may be reduced to below the level normal when the animal is resting on land. J. C. Wright of Sydney University, however, recorded in 1985 that the mean dive duration of saltwater crocodiles was only 4.3 to 6.6 minutes and that the reptiles resurfaced with no more than 30 per cent of their oxygen supply depleted, voluntary undisturbed submergence involving no reduction in oxygen consumption below normal resting levels. Furthermore, L. Y. Lewis and R. E. Gatten of the University of North Carolina found in 1985 that the standard metabolic rate of American alligators was not reduced when these animals dived of their own volition, their experiments also disclosing that oxygen consumption rose two to four fold during an hour of spontaneous activity and also increased significantly as body temperature was elevated.

Nutrition

Because crocodiles have a lower metabolic rate than mammals, they eat less frequently and take longer to digest their meals. The mammalian digestive tract shunts food through its convoluted tubes, with villi (tiny finger-like projections) to increase the surface area of the intestinal wall, in about 24 hours. A large crocodilian, on the other hand, probably eats its fill only once every seven days or so, and when gorged the meal is likely to require several days to pass through the digestive system.

C. O. da C. Diefenbach of Michigan University determined in 1975 that a caiman provided with 5 per cent of its body weight in food every day required about 100 hours to empty its digestive tract at a temperature of 30°C and approximately 315 hours at 15°C. Large and medium-sized crocodilians in this experiment in fact refused to feed at all when temperatures fell to 20°C, only small individuals continuing to take nourishment at a temperature of 15°C.

The crocodilian oesophagus is lined with long, straight, smooth-surfaced antero-posteriorly orientated folds and leads to a large, sac-like three-chambered stomach with a cardiac region (exhibiting few internal folds), a muscular-walled fundic region (somewhat resembling the gizzard of a bird) with an extensive internal network of thick rugae separated by short, deep random crevices, and a rear pyloric portion that has relatively few internal folds (an area corresponding to the pyloric antrum of mammals, containing small glands that incorporate gastrin and somatostatin cells). Apparently to assist the digestive process, crocodiles habitually swallow hard objects that act as gastroliths, churning around in the muscular, gizzard-like region of the stomach to help break down a carcase or its components in the presence of gastric secretions. Small pebbles are the most usual gastroliths, although charcoal and fragments of wood are also swallowed; modern artefacts that have been discovered in the stomachs of crocodilians include pottery, bottles, broken glass, cartridge cases, coins, a metal whistle, a thermos flask, and pieces of plastic — presumably any hard object will suffice, even if it is in fact of modern manufacture. Fossil gastroliths occur with the bones of extinct crocodiles and also with dinosaur remains.

It has been suggested that gastroliths are swallowed in order to reduce the creature's natural buoyancy and assist it to submerge, but they represent only about 1 per cent of the animal's body weight (the number and weight of gastroliths increase with age, their acquisition beginning towards the end of the first year of life) and this figure is such a small proportion of a crocodile's total weight that a digestive function seems more plausible, especially as objects are apparently chosen for their hardness rather than their weight. Accidental ingestion is effectively ruled out by the presence of gastroliths in crocodiles occupying habitats where suitable pebbles are notably scarce: the reptiles all still manage to acquire their requisite share of stomach stones, some of which have evidently come from far-distant locations and must have been systematically sought out. For instance, Nile crocodiles in Santa Lucia Bay, Natal, were found to contain water-worn pebbles from an Indian ocean beach a good many miles away, and examples of the same species shot in the extensive marshes at the junction of the White Nile and the Bahr-el-Ghazal all contained gastroliths despite the fact that pebbles were almost non-existent in the area.

In a particularly interesting experiment conducted in 1968 by A. W. Crompton, K. M. Hiiemae and M. Gibbons at the Yale Peabody Museum, a dead mouse was made radio-opaque by filling its abdominal and thoracic cavities with Lipiodol and the carcase was then fed to a caiman. Videotape was used to monitor a fluoroscopic image, and for 36 hours nothing very much happened, except that regular 15-minute scans revealed some blurring in the outline of the mouse; the gastroliths were clearly visible in the lower part of the stomach, reposing neatly in the folded lining. All of a sudden, however, in the experimenters' own words, 'all hell broke loose ... the gastroliths were moving like pebbles in a cement mixer and the mouse became invisible with the dispersal of the Lipiodol throughout the stomach.' These observations were not published at the time, but D. G. Darby and R. W. O. Jakangas mentioned them in 1980 when describing the occurrence of gastroliths in extinct sea reptiles (elasmosaurs).

The crocodilian small intestine, along the course of which digestion is largely completed, exhibits well-defined internal folds of a predominantly zig-zag pattern, although there are also transverse folds, protuberances, and other irregularities; more posteriorly the folds are taller, thinner and straighter, giving a wavy, ribbon-like pattern, and finally become lower, thicker and rounded to form compact waves. The colon has a generally smooth inner surface, although with low, broadly rounded and widely separated longitudinal folds, and leads to a cloaca, or vent, from which faecal matter is voided.

Hydrochloric acid is a major constituent of crocodilian digestive juices, with a pH value of as much as 2.0 after feeding as the stomach cells are stimulated to secrete it in copious quantities. Food is broken down into a gelatinous mass after about 24 hours, amino-acids being liberated from meat protein at around 2.5 $mmol/kg^{-1}h^{-1}$ in a temperature of 30°C (at lower temperatures of 25–28°C, digestion is slow and incomplete). A constant level of free amino-acid, not exceeding 3 mmol/kg, is maintained in the intestine, so absorption is evidently at a similar rate. Concentration of amino-acids in the blood plasma increases five fold after feeding, to a value of 15 mmol/kg or more, and is maintained at this figure for three to five days, with disproportionate increases in the levels of non-essential amino-acids (glutamine, glycine, alanine), while plasma chloride is slowly replaced by bicarbonate. Alligators have been found to consume 140 g of protein per kilogram of body weight per week, which is 10-20 times the value recorded in man. When food is not available, crocodiles lower their metabolic rate so that if necessary they can withstand a lengthy fast, oxygen consumption falling to only about half the normal rate. In addition, much of the food that is eaten during more plentiful times is converted with great efficiency into energy-dense fat on which the animal can draw during prolonged spells of deprivation.

There is no urinary bladder in crocodilians, but in males the cloaca, an oval bag closed anteriorly and posteriorly by strong sphincter muscles, also incorporates the copulatory organs: a pair of longitudinal ridges (the corpora cavernosa penis) in the ventral wall, composed of spongy fibrous tissue with an intervening groove, that become distended with blood during sexual excitation to turn the groove into a tube along which sperm from the long oval testes passes to a spongy glans penis at the outer end, which is protruded for insertion into the female's cloaca. The oviducts of the female crocodile carry the unfertilised eggs down from the flat, elongate ovaries.

Although many living species are essentially freshwater forms, crocodiles have throughout their long history demonstrated an ability to adapt to salt water. Some fossil groups (notably the thalattosuchians) evidently spent their entire lives in the sea, and the living saltwater crocodile is quite at home in a marine environment. This species, which ranges far out into the open ocean, has up to 40 complex tubular salt glands on its tongue that secrete a concentrated solution of sodium chloride when a saltwater crocodile is in saline surroundings. L. E. Taplin, G. C. Grigg and L. Beard used methacholine chloride to stimulate the lingual glands of various other species of crocodiles and reported in 1985 that all the members of the Crocodylinae which they tested had salt glands, which suggests either that this subfamily originated in a marine environment and subsequently colonized freshwater habitats or, conversely, that all the crocodylid subfamilies were of freshwater origin but only the Crocodylinae acquired a saltwater adaptation. Alligators and caimans do have minute pores (up to 200 in the American alligator) on the back of their tongues and in the palatal epithelia around the buccal valve, but it would seem that these are primarily salivary glands, although some sodium and potassium is excreted at a low rate. The alligatorine group may thus be more primitive than the Crocodylinae in this respect, lacking anything other than a superficial adaptation to salt water: F. A. Mazzotti and W. A. Dunson of Pennsylvania State University determined in 1984 that in *Alligator mississipiensis* the sodium influx exceeds efflux when the animal is in fresh water.

Senses

The crocodilian brain lacks the prominent cerebral development seen in mammals (and most notably in man), but these reptiles nonetheless exhibit complex behaviour patterns not all of which can simply be ascribed to instinct. Very little investigation has been undertaken to determine the learning capacity of crocodilians, but the manner in which severely hunted populations become shy and furtive as a survival strategy clearly indicates an ability to interpret cause and effect. Witnessing the deaths of colleagues and assimilating the manner of their demise, survivors learn to take precautions that will minimise the chance of their suffering a similar fate. They will even learn to associate having a light shone in their eyes at night with attempts to capture them, and they become 'light shy'. An imitated distress call has been used to call muggers at their pool, but although initially responding these creatures quickly realise that it is only a ruse and the deception rarely works at the second attempt: evidence of at least rudimentary deductive powers. Work by J. M. Verlander at the University of Houston in 1974 showed that the electro-encephalograph of a submerged spectacled caiman displays frequent bursts of high-voltage spikes and spindles with periodic lowering in the amplitude of higher frequencies, but the significance of these observations has not been determined.

Crocodiles, like all major predators, must have acutely receptive senses if they are to capture their prey successfully. The eyes of these reptiles offer some 25 degrees of binocular vision, which assists the animal in judging distance and hence striking accurately at an intended victim, and there is a nictitating membrane (a 'third eyelid') containing a cartilage with two folds of tissue on the outer surface which closes across the eyeball underwater to facilitate vision while submerged and is lubricated by a special gland opening through a duct on the inner surface. Crocodiles frequently hunt at night or in the

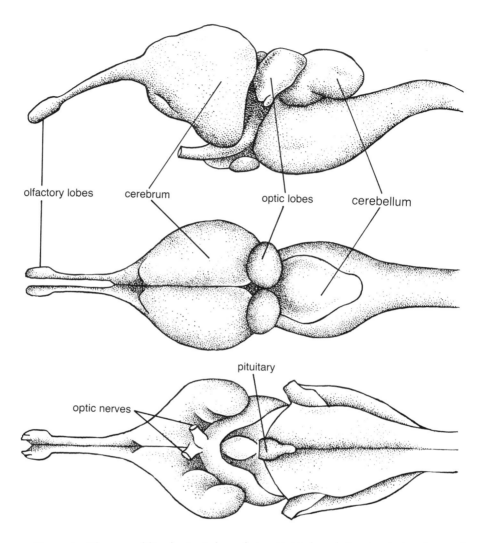

olfactory lobes   cerebrum   optic lobes   cerebellum

pituitary

optic nerves

Figure 4 The crocodilian brain, in lateral view (*top*), dorsal view (*centre*) and ventral view (*bottom*)

subdued light of evening, and rhodopsin ('visual purple'), a protein combined with a carotenoid pigment related to vitamin A, occurs in the rods of the retina when the eye has adapted for vision in faint light. The iris becomes a vertical slit in bright conditions, a feature characteristic of nocturnal animals that nonetheless like to emerge in sunlight: a slit-like opening is easier to close effectively than a circular one, and so gives better protection to a retina that is basically adapted for vision in low levels of illumination.

Closure of the eye is apparently achieved primarily by movement of the upper lid, which contains a bony ossicle, whereas in other living reptiles occlusion is effected by the lower lid (this lacks any bony support in

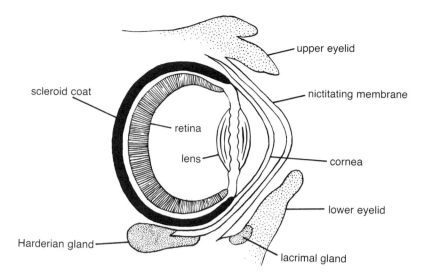

Figure 5 The crocodilian eye, showing the outer scleroid coat (which contains the eyeball), the retina, the lens and its protecting cornea, and the nictitating membrane. The lacrimal gland's secretion, rich in acid mucins, lubricates the cornea; the harderian gland produces a secretion containing abundant proteins but with few acid mucins (its function is obscure)

crocodiles, although containing an ossified tarsus in most reptiles). The eyeball is nearly spherical, with a cornea that subtends an angle of about 128 degrees. Modern crocodilians never have the bony scleral rings in the eye socket that occur in birds and many other reptiles and which apparently help to maintain the inward convexity of the junction where the cornea (in front of the lens) meets the scleral coat (the outer investment of the entire eyeball), thus assisting the ciliary body to exert pressure on the lens and change its curvature for close vision. The crocodilian ciliary body, with just over 100 processes, extends from the ora serrata to the equator of the lens, but the eyes of these reptiles seem to be focused primarily for seeing in air, and inability to accommodate their eyes sufficiently to the different refractive index of water means that they are acutely farsighted when submerged and use other senses to catch subaqueous prey.

The lens consists of over 900 radial lamellae, displaying great regularity in their disposition but with poorly defined sutures of only limited extent, and shares with the lenses of some birds' eyes the substantial presence of a soluble protein, epsilon crystallin. Between 20 and 50 per cent of the wet weight of a vertebrate lens is accounted for by crystallins, all vertebrate eye lenses containing alpha crystallin and the related beta and gamma crystallins, while reptiles typically also include delta crystallin in their lenses. The epsilon crystallin is characteristic of certain birds (predominantly those which hunt or fish through or near the water surface or at high altitude) and crocodiles. Up to 23 per cent of the total crocodilian lens protein may be epsilon crystallin, which G. J. Wistow, J. W. M. Mulders and W. W. de Jong reported in 1987 had virtually identical amino-acid sequences in the lenses of ducks' eyes to the glycolytic enzyme lactate dehydrogenase (LDH); in other tissues (e.g. the heart muscles), LDH drives the conversion of pyruvate to lactate during the production of chemical energy. Birds and crocodiles apparently shared a common ancestry some 240 million years ago, and the acquisition of epsilon crystallin presumably dates from this time, but it is rather unexpected to find that this lens constituent has retained its LDH-like structure when located in the eye, a site where it is probably valuable for its structural stability in the presence of repeated long-term exposure to light during the animal's lifetime.

C. R. Braekevelt of Manitoba University determined in 1977 that the retinal epithelium consists of a single layer of cuboidal pigmented cells with extensive basal (scleral) infoldings and numerous apical (vitral) processes enclosing photoreceptor outer segments. As well as rod cells, the crocodilian retina also contains cone cells, which are primarily to provide acuity of vision, but the rods are far more numerous. There is, however, an elongated horizontal area near the centre of the retina, above the optic papilla, which exhibits a fine mosaic of visual cells, suggesting that it is a focal point for high visual resolution.

Experiments suggest that accommodation of the crocodilian eye to changes in the intensity of light are slow and of limited extent. Within the retina, however, the rods expand in light conditions and contract in the dark, exhibiting a total range of movement amounting to around 4 mu, while cones extend in darkness and contract in the light over a range of about 2 mu.

A tapetum layer, outside the retina but internal to the choroid layer, incorporates guanine, which reflects light back to the visual cells to enhance vision in dim light. According to Braekevelt, who worked with caimans, no melanosomes are present in the central tapetal area, so the tapetum is non-occlusible, although guanine crystals and melanosomes occur in cells around the tapetal margins. The tapetum is responsible for the reddish crocodilian 'eye shine' reflected back down a flashlight beam after dark. Of special interest is the fact that visual cells in the tapetal area have undergone a form of transmutation, with cells exhibiting rod-like outer extremities acquiring cone-type footpieces.

Extra-retinal photosensitivity seems to be an additional feature of the crocodilian sensory array. M. Kavaliers of Colorado State University reported in 1980 that hatchling alligators display sensitivity to light that is not attributable to the eyes and may be traceable to the brain's diencephalon or the area of its third ventricle. The youngsters demonstrated maximum sensitivity to light in the red 580–670 nanometres region of the spectrum, and response seems to be temperature-related: at low temperatures only a low level of energy was required to generate a reaction.

Crocodilians lack either a pineal organ or a parietal organ, structures which develop from the roof of the brain in primitive vertebrates and are apparently sensitive to light. The characteristic secretion of the pineal body is melatonin, a hormone synthesised principally during the hours of darkness which influences an animal's behaviour in response to the duration of illumination: lengthening spring days, for example, result in reduced melatonin production which causes mammals to lose their winter coats and come into breeding condition, while the shortening days of autumn cause an upsurge in the nightly output of melatonin, making winter coats grow and some species prepare for hibernation. There is a constant low level of melatonin present in the blood of at least some crocodilians (notably alligators), and M. Kavaliers and C. L. Ralph of Colorado State University determined in 1980 that alligators kept in either continuous darkness or continuous light still exhibited a stable, free-running 24-hour circadian rhythm, i.e. activity normally associated with daylight was still engaged in at what would have been the appropriate time, even though the subject was in total darkness. Melatonin will probably prove to be present in all crocodilians, with an established circadian rhythm governing their alternating diurnal/nocturnal behaviour to a greater or lesser extent. J. J. and E. C. Roth and their research colleagues at St Augustine's Alligator Farm, Florida, suggested in 1980 that, as all the extinct ruling reptiles — dinosaurs, pterosaurs, thecodonts — also apparently lacked pineal organs, this structure was lost during the Mesozoic era when a stable, equable climate prevailed, with little or no seasonal variation that would have required these reptiles to make provision for hibernation during an inclement winter.

Little is known concerning the acuteness of a crocodile's sense of smell, but the nasal cavities are remarkably complex, suggesting a sophisticated level of olfactory function. The vestibulum behind the nostrils is a short tubular structure, lined by a stratified squamous epithelium, that opens into the main nasal chamber (the cavum proprium nasi), the lateral walls of which incorporate three projections (the preconcha anteriorly, the concha itself, and the postconcha posteriorly) composed of cartilage covered by mucous membrane, which bulge into the basal cavity (other living reptiles possess only a single conchal projection, and these structures are rather simpler in crocodylines than in alligatorines). Opening into the nasal cavity on each side are a number of membrane-lined recesses and paranasal sinuses.

Olfactory epithelium, comprising ciliated cells supplying sensory impulses to the olfactory nerves, is restricted in crocodiles to the posterior and upper region of the cavum proprium and to the dorsal part of some of the paranasal sinuses. There is, however, no evidence of Jacobson's organ in adults, a vomero-nasal organ which in other reptiles apparently enables the animal to receive olfactory stimuli from food in the mouth; embryonic crocodiles, it has been claimed, still display some vestigial evidence of a Jacobson's organ, but only at a very early developmental stage. Most aquatic reptiles have retained a Jacobson's organ but seem to have a regressed olfactory epithelium. Crocodiles display the exact reverse of this situation; furthermore, their olfactory epithelium includes not only mucous and ciliated cells but also (in the ventro-lateral parts of the cavum) sero-mucous cells forming small glands. Probably the presumed common ancestor of crocodiles and birds was a terrestrial form that had already lost any previous aquatic specialisations, the crocodilians' subsequent return to the water leaving them with a somewhat anomalous olfactory adaptation for living on land. As a probable substitute for Jacobson's organ, however, crocodiles have acquired a hypertrophied lachrymal duct, forming a large naso-pharyngeal gland, the lumen of which is lined by mucous and ciliated cells, and taste buds are present in the mucous membrane covering the pterygoid region of the palate.

The external ear, located just behind the eye, consists primarily of two valve-like folds of skin which normally lie flush with the head and conceal the tympanic membrane — the ear drum — upon which sound waves impinge, its vibration in response to these waves being transmitted via the stapedial bone and a cartilaginous extrastapes to the inner ear, where auditory stimuli are registered by the auditory nerve and transmitted to hearing centres in the medulla oblongata of the brain. Primitive extinct reptiles had a pair of open otic notches at the rear corners of the skull table which accommodated the ear drum, but in advanced forms like crocodiles the ear opening forms a closed ring providing attachment for the tympanic membrane around its entire circumference. Of the two folds protecting the external ear, the lower one, continuous with the tissues of the cheek region, is the smaller; the larger upper fold, covered with scaly skin, overlaps the lower one and is held firmly against it by contraction of a slender muscular band attached to the squamosal bone anteriorly and to other musculature (the mandibular depressor and the dorsal axial musculature) posteriorly. A small slit-like aperture at the front of each flap is normally kept open when the animal is out of the water and apparently constitutes the normal route for auditory perception. Closure of the lower ear flap when submerging is apparently triggered by closure of the lower eyelid: L. D. Garrick and E. I. Saiff discovered in 1974 that squirting water in the eye of an immobilized caiman elicited blinking and concomitant shutting of the inferior ear flap. Crocodiles are the only living reptiles with external ear flaps, and allegedly vibrate them rapidly up and down when frightened or angered, two small muscles for this purpose being present at either end. Pooley witnessed small crocodiles using a hindfoot to remove foreign objects from the external ear in a most delicate fashion, but it is not known if full-grown individuals of large species retain this dexterity.

The tympanic cavities of the crocodilian ear are more fully enclosed by bone than is the case in other living reptiles, and the structures traversing them evince a greater degree of compartmentalisation. There is a simple but elongate cochlea duct, comprising a single loop that extends from a perilymphatic cistern behind the fenestra ovalis (the opening in the inner wall of the middle ear against which the sound-transmitting stapedial bone is apressed) to a 'round window' or fenestra pseudorotunda, an aperture opening back into the middle ear chamber which provides an exodus for impulses transmitted down the cochlea from the fenestra ovalis at the other end of the system. Enclosed within the loop of the cochlea is an extension of the lagena (only a very small structure in the more primitive representatives of the Reptilia) and its attendant basilar papilla. The lagena is itself an outgrowth of the sacculus, one of two conjoined sac-like structures (the other is the utriculus, with its semicircular canals arranged in three separate planes) which provide vertebrate animals with their sense of balance, registering the creature's changes of direction or orientation, or in the speed of its movement.

The basilar papilla is an area of hair cells coverd by a common gelatinous membrane which registers the sound vibrations being transmitted down the perilymph of the cochlea from the fenestra ovalis to the fenestra pseudorotunda. To achieve this in crocodilians, the basilar papilla and the lagena have become elongate in conjunction with the extended cochlea, the basilar papilla being contiguous with the distal section of the cochlea's loop, while the lagena lies against the proximal part of this structure.

Mammals have a far more elaborate cochlea which takes the form of a spiral to conserve space, but the arrangement found in crocodilians resembles that of their close relatives, the birds, and represents an intermediate level of refinement, in advance of that seen in other living reptiles but less sophisticated than the mammalian ear structure, which has not been directly derived from the crocodilian type of construction: the mammalian 'round window' is deemed to be a true fenestra rotunda, that of crocodiles an independently evolved fenestra pseudorotunda. This has led some commentators to postulate a crocodilian ancestor for birds, or alternatively a common ancestor among the ancient Triassic thecodont stock that gave rise to both the birds (usually regarded as dinosaurian descendants) and the crocodiles.

The middle ear cavity and eustachian tubes of crocodilians are complex, with an inner and an outer eustachian tube issuing from the ear on each side, the inner pair joining to form a single median tube that exits from the base of the skull through the basisphenoid foramen (just behind the internal nares), while the two outer tubes emerge from smaller apertures on either side of this median foramen. Ultimately all these eustachian tubes unite to form a common duct that opens on the mid-line of the pharynx.

Crocodilians have acute hearing and will evince an unmistakable response to even the faint sound of a small animal jumping into a pool on the edge of which they are lying, apparently dead to the world.

Experiments by E. G. Wever and J. A. Vernon at Princeton University, reported in 1957, demonstrated that juvenile spectacled caimans 20–50 cm (16–20 in) in length have cochlear potentials of 20 to 6000 cycles, with greatest sensitivity at 100 to 3000 cycles (closure of the external ear flap reduced sound transmission by 10–12 db). The American alligator, in comparison, had previously been shown to have cochlear potentials of 50 to 4000 cycles, with peak sensitivity between 400 and 1000 cycles.

There is some evidence that crocodilians, like many other animals, have a sophisticated navigational capability—something that exists in man only vestigially, if at all. In 1984, G. H. Rodda of Cornell University published the result of some experiments on homing behaviour in juvenile American alligators, which apparently make use of short-term geomagnetic changes to find the way back when transported outside their home territory. Very young individuals probably never range far, and can orientate themselves by simple route-based ability, sensing the different distances and directions which they have travelled from their starting point. If in difficulty, juvenile alligators seem to have a water-seeking orientation which brings them quickly to the nearest river or lake, a reasonably safe haven for a young crocodilian and infinitely preferable to wandering about lost on land. Older animals range further afield, and Rodda's research suggested that they use multi-coordinate navigation to return home: a method that requires the animal to detect at least two divergent large-scale geomagnetic gradients at both its home and its present location, inferring the homeward direction from differences in the values sensed. Rodda's alligators apparently detected differences between the dip angles at the time and place of their initial capture and those prevailing at the location and time when the homeward journey was initiated.

In experiments reported in 1985, Rodda dispersed 285 young Florida alligators up to 1 m (3 ft 3 in) long, each tagged with two coloured plastic neck bands, for distances up to 20 times the diameter of the creatures' normal home range, using automobiles, airboats or motor boats, some subjects being transported in opaque containers while others were given visual access to the open sky during the journey. At least 46 of the alligators returned to their previous home, and 27 more were last seen heading in the direction of the original capture site; only one individual of the 285 made no attempt to home (it in fact travelled a short distance in the opposite direction), and that animal had been re-located to a particularly favourable habitat and obviously knew when it was well off.

Additional work on crocodilian navigation was undertaken by P. A. Murphy of the Savannah River Ecology Laboratory in Florida, who concluded in 1981 that juvenile alligators used celestial cues (solar, stellar or possibly lunar) to seek the landward end of the Y-axis (an axis perpendicular to a familiar shoreline), although Rodda's work failed to reveal any indication that the alligators he transported with visual access to the sky homed any better than those denied this facility (those carried in automobiles were, however, statistically under-represented among successful 'homers').

The circulatory system

The blood circulatory system of crocodilians is more sophisticated than that of other living reptiles, approaching the refinement seen in the warm-blooded birds and mammals. In fish, there is a relatively straightforward system pumping deoxygenated blood from the trunk out of a simple heart to the gills, where metabolic waste products (notably carbon dioxide) are exchanged for oxygen, the blood then passing into dorsal arteries that supply freshly oxygenated blood to the head and body. Reptiles have lost their gills, and as terrestrial vertebrates (albeit of aquatic habits) they rely for respiration on lungs, which have developed complex internal subdivisions and a system of alveolar pockets, this spongy structure providing additional respiratory surface compared with the much simpler structure found in many other modern reptiles. The blood vessels running to and from the crocodilian lungs are modifications of the ones that in fish supply the gills, with deoxygenated blood returning from the body into the right auricle of the heart while oxygenated blood from the lungs enters the left auricle. In amphibians there is only a single ventricle, which means that the two blood streams — deoxygenated and oxygenated — tend to mix as they are pumped out to travel via what used to be the sixth aortic gill arch back to the lungs and through the modified third and fourth gill arches to the head and body. It is obviously inefficient to shunt already oxygenated blood back to the lungs, or to return deoxygenated blood around the body, and in mammals there are two separate heart ventricles, the left one collecting oxygenated blood from the left auricle and pumping it to the head and body while the right ventricle takes deoxygenated blood from the right auricle and returns it to the lungs. Birds have arrived at a similar system to that seen in mammals, although apparently by a different evolutionary route, but crocodiles display an intermediate situation, with a single ventricle divided internally to effect separation of venous and arterial blood. There are three efferent vessels leaving the ventricle: one leading to the pulmonary arch (supplying the lungs with deoxygenated blood from the right side of the heart), one supplying the left systemic arch (apparently carrying venous blood that is then returned to the body, notably to the stomach and intestines), and one feeding oxygenated blood through the right systemic arch to the carotids (for the jaw region and the brain) and the dorsal aorta.

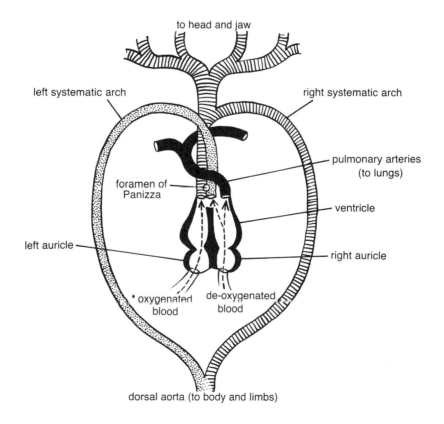

Figure 6 Diagrammatic representation of the crocodilian heart and blood circulation

31

Thus deoxygenated venous blood flows through the right side of the heart and oxygenated blood traverses the left auricle and ventricle: the potential inefficiency of a retained left systemic arch, which may shunt venous blood into the dorsal aorta and thence back to the body, is avoided in the crocodilians' more sophisticated relatives, the birds, by elimination of this arch, leaving only two efferent vessels exiting from the heart's ventricle. Nevertheless, the crocodilian blood circulatory system, with a heart featuring a divided ventricle, is physiologically more advanced than that of any other living reptiles. Some of the crocodilians' extinct cousins, the dinosaurs and pterosaurs, may have been warm-blooded, and it is interesting to speculate on whether they retained a crocodilian pattern of three blood vessels leaving the heart or had attained an avian level of specialisation with only two efferent vessels. Some research has suggested that in fact the crocodilian circulation is functionally double, with the foramen of Panizza (located between the roots of the two systemic arches) conveying blood from the right arch to the left-hand one (except, apparently, when the animal is diving), so that both the right and the left systemic arches feed oxygenated blood to the dorsal aorta.

When diving, crocodilians may exhibit a substantial degree of bradycardia, the slowing down of the heart's beat being more pronounced when they are forced to dive from alarm than when making a more leisurely spontaneous dive. Undisturbed alligators at rest have a heart rate of 25–35 beats per minute at 30°C (for a 2-kg/4.4 lb individual, 34 beats per minute at 28°C and 29 beats per minute at 25°C), and E. N. Smith, R. D. Allison and W. E. Crowder determined in 1974 that pronounced bradycardia (31–32 beats per minute) occurred when a submerged alligator was approached by man, although short voluntary dives at night failed to produce any such reaction. High-level activity, such as rapid swimming, can produce heart rates of up to 60 beats per minute, and the heart rate of small alligators exceeds that of large animals by a factor of about ten.

The vascular system of crocodilians evidently functions not only as a transport system for oxygen and the waste products of respiration, but also as a major aid to temperature regulation. There seems to be a significantly greater consumption of oxygen when a crocodilian is being cooled, and it has been found that during heating the heart rate at 20°C is twice that pertaining during cooling.

There seems to be no modification of the circulation to the musculature and the tail in crocodilians when they are submerged, but C. J. Weinheimer and his colleagues at the State University College, Buffalo, determined in 1982 that the peripheral blood flow is quite variable, being sensitive to noise, sudden illumination, shutting off of the light, or handling by an experimenter. The muscles and skin are minimally perfused when the animal is at rest, but voluntary movement stimulates an increased blood flow.

The normal blood structure of crocodilians, determined in 1971 by U. Srisomboon from animals in Bangkok zoo, is approximately 600,000 white corpuscles per cubic millimetre, 500,000 red corpuscles per cubic millimetre, 25–28 per cent haematocrit, and 7 g of haemoglobin per 100 millilitres. Crocodilian haemoglobin has an intrinsically high oxygen affinity, but

C. Bauer and W. Jelkmann of Regensburg University discovered in 1977 that when one of these reptiles engages in energetic activity an antagonism apparently arises between the carbon dioxide that this activity generates and the oxygen-binding mechanism of the haemoglobin. As a result, oxygen is more readily liberated from haemoglobin to fuel the animal's energy requirements.

The fact that crocodiles frequently display complete healing of a wound site even after loss of the end of the tail (which regenerates with a short, cartilaginous tip) or a limb and part of the adjacent body wall suggests that their blood must incorporate an efficient haemostatic and wound-repair mechanism. C. L. Arocha-Piñango, S. J. Gorzula and A. Ojeda reported in 1982 that progressive anti-thrombin is present in caiman blood, which displays low thromboplastic activity and very high concentrations of plasma fibrinogen, but no fibrinolytic function.

Gaping

Resting with the jaws wide open ('gaping') is a characteristic crocodilian habit that remains unexplained. An individual lying out on a river bank or a mudflat will for no obvious reason suddenly open its mouth and leave it open, gaping widely. The practice has been familiar to observers of crocodilians from the earliest times and elicited some exceedingly bizarre explanations. The writings of Herodotus and Pliny repeated the then current belief that Nile crocodiles left their mouths open until the buccal cavity had filled with insects, then snapped their jaws shut on a tasty meal. This account was accompanied by a piece of unalloyed fiction which alleged that sometimes an ichneumon would jump down the throat of a crocodile lying with its mouth gaping and would eat its stomach, thus killing the reptile. The idea of insectivorous crocodiles as an explanation for gaping duly spread to other species besides the Nile crocodile, but it is not regarded by modern authorities as a likely reason for this curious habit. More sophisticated hypotheses have suggested that crocodiles gape as a means of temperature control, evaporation from the moist lining of the mouth helping to reduce temperature — in the nature of an analogy with an overheated, panting dog, although the crocodilian tongue is not protrusible in the manner seen in canines. Crocodilians have, however, been regularly witnessed gaping early in the morning when temperatures are still low. Alternatively, it was suggested that gaping kept just the head region cool while allowing the rest of the body to continue soaking up the sun's heat. A widely repeated explanation is that crocodilians open their jaws so that birds can clean vestiges of meat from between the reptiles' teeth, the story originating with Herodotus (who identified the bird as the 'trochilos' and claimed that it was removing leeches from the crocodile's mouth). Pliny repeated this account, although suggesting that the birds were seeking left-over scraps of food, and it became a more or less accepted item of crocodile lore, ornithologists identifying the 'trochilos' as either the Egyptian plover (*Pluvianus aegypticus*) or the spur-winged plover (*Haplopterus spinosus*).

33

First-hand accounts of such behaviour seem to be sparse, although C. A. W. Guggisberg did report in 1972 seeing a marabou stork steal a complete fish from out of a crocodile's mouth, and cited Alfred Edmund Brehm (a 19th-century German naturalist), Col. Richard Meinertzhagen (the ornithologist) and Sir Harry Johnston (the African explorer) as eyewitnesses of plovers apparently cleaning the jaws of Nile crocodiles. Birds do, in fact, habitually wander among basking crocodiles, apparently possessing an instinctive appreciation of when these potentially dangerous predators are slumbering peacefully and can be approached with impunity, but the teeth of crocodiles are widely spaced and it seems unlikely that shreds of food would regularly become lodged between them, particularly as the act of devouring a prey is accompanied by vigorous head-shaking that would be likely to dislodge any adherent morsels of food. Furthermore, Anthony Pooley reported seeing crocodiles removing detritus from their teeth with a hindfoot. Algae and fungae will readily parasitise crocodilians if given the chance, and the suggestion has been made that gaping dries the mucosa of the jaws and prevents these organisms from colonising the mouth cavity.

Conceivably, however, gaping is merely a response to a real or imagined threat, the widely open mouth with its formidable teeth being calculated to deter any prospective interloper. Crocodilians have very sharp hearing and probably excellent eyesight and an acute sense of smell, so individuals seen gaping may well have become conscious of some intrusion into their neighbourhood of which the observer was unaware: perhaps the observer's presence itself promoted the gaping response.

Vibration or fluttering of the gular region frequently accompanies gaping, but it has been demonstrated that this is associated with olfactory-lobe activity and K. H. Naifeh and his colleagues at Texas Medical Centre, Houston, concluded in 1970 that gular activity probably draws in air for olfaction, the glottis being closed when it occurs. C. Gans and B. Clark of the University of Michigan determined in 1976 that buccal oscillation did indeed fulfil this function, by flushing the internal nares: as the larynx is adpressed to the internal nares, the posterior buccal chamber is excluded from the path of air flowing in during ventilation and so does not contribute to respiratory dead space.

The endocrine system

Research on the endocrine system of crocodiles indicates that the adrenal glands, situated adjacent to the kidneys, are sites of steroidogenic activity. Y. M. Gouder and V. B. Nadkarni of Karnatak University, Dharwar, India, determined in 1976 that the inter-renal cells have the potentiality to produce sex steroids besides corticosteroids, while the adrenomedullary cells are sites of catecholamine synthesis. Chitaru Oguro and Yuichi Sasayama of Togama University, Japan, reported in 1976 that *Caiman crocodilus* possessed two to six parathyroid glands embedded in the thymus (one to three on either side of the body). These structures maintain normal levels of serum calcium and phosphorous concentrations: the number is evidently variable, and in individuals with a full complement of six the smallest pair may be regarded as accessory parathyroids. Embryos of *Crocodylus porosus* (the saltwater crocodile) have two pairs of parathyroids, but in adults these are reduced to a single pair.

Parasites and diseases

Parasites of crocodiles commonly include black leeches which attach themselves singly or in groups at the junction of scutes, between the toes, and around the eyes. Tabanid horseflies are known to attack crocodilians in South America, settling on the head, back, limbs and tail, while in Africa the tsetse fly (*Glossina palpalis*) is to be found feeding on the blood of crocodiles, acting as a vector for *Trypanosoma gambiense* (the cause of sleeping sickness in humans), *T. grayi* (harmless to man) and the haemogregarine *Hepatozoon petiti*. Helminths are regular internal parasites, including nematodes (in the stomach and small intestine) and trematodes, but seem to be well tolerated by their hosts; pentastomes, on the other hand, cause bleeding and tissue destruction in the lungs. Diseased crocodiles in the wild would quickly be eliminated from the population by predation or inability to compete with their healthier brethren for food and are in consequence rarely seen, but even in captivity crocodiles seem to be remarkably free of disease. Small juveniles held in pens are prone to respiratory ailments that can cause widespread mortality—the bacterium *Shigella* is found at post-mortem in the spleen (which is usually ruptured), being spread from infected faecal matter by flies or by attendants passing through the enclosures—and leptospirosis is also responsible for some juvenile deaths, but otherwise crocodiles seem astonishingly resistant to pathogens. However, W. T. Hornaday, who travelled widely in the Far East during the late 19th century, reported two 7-ft (2.1-m) muggers in an overcrowded pool in Ceylon that had developed an extensive epidermal necrosis, and an alligator in San Diego zoo was reported in 1981 to have required surgery for the removal of pedunculated tumours from the fifth toe of its left forefoot which proved to comprise whorls and arcades of glistening white connective tissue encased by thick keratinised epithelium (a similar case occurred in the Bronx zoo, New York, in 1900).

Many crocodilians carry potential pathogens without developing any clinical symptoms, of course, but it has been found that the stress induced when wild individuals are captured or zoo animals are translocated may lower the reptile's resistance and allow infection to become active. R. W. Gorden and his colleagues at the University of Southern California discovered in 1979 that *Aeromonas hydrophila*, a ubiquitous and normally harmless bacterium of wild alligators (occurring in the oral cavity, on the exterior of the jaws and in the tissues) which causes red sore disease in fish, was responsible for the sudden deaths of nine recently captured alligators. Post-mortem disclosed the presence of *A. hydrophila* in the livers, lungs and kidneys, accompanied by tissue damage similar to that induced by lytic

35

toxins. It would appear that stress, possibly allied with high water temperatures of 20°C or more that favour proliferation of the organism, can result in a fatal epizootic.

3.

Man-eaters, rarities and dwarfs: the central crocodilian stock

Modern crocodiles can be grouped in four subfamilies, none of which is with certainty traceable further back in the fossil record than the closing stages of the Cretaceous period, about 75 million years ago.

These four subfamilies (the alligators, the gavials, the 'false gavials', and *Crocodylus* and its relatives) may be included in the family Crocodylidae, which is itself part of the suborder Eusuchia, a major grouping that includes not only the living species, but also a number of extinct forms that share certain characteristic anatomical features with their extant cousins but themselves failed to survive into the modern world. Some were very early, apparently ancestral forms, others bizarrely adapted to specialised life styles that made their continued existence impossible when the environment in which they once prospered underwent irrevocable change.

The Eusuchia are all distinguished by the presence of a fully developed secondary palate, the air passages running from the external nostrils back to the throat being separated from the mouth cavity by a long bony floor composed not only of the premaxillary bones (at the front), the maxillae and the palatines, but also by the two pterygoid elements. This extensive development means that the breathing passages are carried far back into the pharynx. In the earlier part of the Cretaceous and during the preceding Jurassic period (extending back to a time some 195 million years ago), before the eusuchians had appeared, the crocodilian dynasty was represented by a less advanced suborder known as the Mesosuchia. In these the secondary palate was not so comprehensively developed: the pterygoid bones made little or no contribution to its construction.

This apparently quite small anatomical difference nonetheless marked a significant evolutionary watershed in crocodilian evolution and clearly distinguishes the modern eusuchian crocodiles and their extinct relatives from the totally defunct mesosuchians, the last survivors of which died out before the end of the Eocene period, 40 million years ago, and two aberrant groups of extinct crocodiles (the wholly aquatic thalattosuchians and the apparently largely terrestrial sebecosuchians) which have also disappeared without leaving any living descendants.

Additionally, eusuchians demonstrated some advances in the structure of their vertebrae, the neck bones usually possessing prominent ventral keels while the centra throughout the presacral column are of a procoelous type: the front end forms a socket into which the convex posterior termination of the preceding vertebra fits (mesosuchian vertebral centra have both ends slightly concave, an arrangement which offers a much weaker articulation). Eusuchians also have the post-orbital bar (a vertical pillar of bone behind the eye socket) buried well below the outer surface of the skull where it joins the jugal bone at its lower end, and their dermal armour plates are never interlocked by the peg-like articulations seen in the bony scutes of many mesosuchian fossils.

Collectively, the living Eusuchia constitute a well-established and quite tightly knit natural assemblage, which the protein analyses by L. D. Densmore of Louisiana State University demonstrated in 1983 is a monophyletic grouping, all the constituent forms being descended from a common ancestry. Just what that universal forebear was is still a matter for speculation.

The oldest eusuchian so far discovered appears to be *Hylaeochampsa*, which comes from the Hastings Sand of Sussex, a Lower Cretaceous deposit of Wealden age dating back some 125 million years. The specimen was found by the famous 19th-century physician, Dr Gideon Mantell, who had, in 1825, announced the discovery of *Iguanodon* (only the second dinosaur to be scientifically described) from strata of similar age in the same region of southern England. Unfortunately, the remains of *Hylaeochampsa*, contained in a nodule of ironstone, comprise only a dozen or so vertebrae that seem to be of the characteristic eusuchian procoelous type, together with what looks like part of the cranium. It is not certain that the vertebrae and the fragmentary skull belong to the same animal, and the palatal structure cannot be elucidated to find out if the pterygoid bones contribute to formation of the secondary palate.

Also of Lower Cretaceous age is a single procoelous vertebral centrum discovered in New South Wales which is probably crocodilian and hence eusuchian. Very little, however, can be deduced from a solitary, rather questionable specimen, beyond accepting it as evidence of modern-type crocodiles in the antipodes 125 million years ago, a time when this island continent still retained land connections with other elements of the former conjoined southern supercontinent, Gondwanaland (composed of South America, Africa, India and Antarctica, as well as Australia).

The most successful modern crocodiles are without doubt the members of the subfamily Crocodylinae. Essentially broad-faced forms, although one or two species have relatively slender snouts, these reptiles include among their number the Nile crocodile (*Crocodylus niloticus*) and the estuarine or saltwater crocodile (*Crocodylus porosus*)—two wide-ranging species that even today are still the largest predators in their tropical homelands, far exceeding in size any of the carnivorous terrestrial mammals and as meat-eaters rivalled for bulk only by some of the biggest sharks and toothed whales.

The mugger or swamp crocodile (*Crocodylus palustris*) of southern Asia, the Orinoco crocodile (*Crocodylus intermedius*) and the American crocodile (*Crocodylus acutus*) are also animals of some size, attaining a length of around 4.5 m (15 ft), but they are not considered to be anything like as dangerous as their two huge relatives, and the subfamily additionally includes a number of relatively small forms that do not exceed about 3 m (10 ft) in length: Johnston's crocodile, Morelet's crocodile, the Cuban crocodile, the long-snouted West African crocodile, the New Guinea crocodile and the Siamese crocodile. All of these species belong to the genus *Crocodylus*, but the subfamily additionally incorporates a second living genus, *Osteolaemus*, a relatively tiny crocodile from West Africa that never grows more than 1.83 m (six ft) long.

There are a number of fossil crocodilians that carry the history of the Crocodylinae back to the Cretaceous period, over 70 million years ago, so it is evident that although rather unspecialised they have nonetheless been highly successful animals over a substantial span of time. Throughout the long ages during which the mammals have evolved and proliferated as the dominant terrestrial vertebrate life forms, culminating their ascendancy with the appearance of man, the Crocodylinae have had no difficulty in maintaining their status as major predators in tropical swamps and watercourses, more than holding their own in competition with mammalian carnivores until the advent of modern man, equipped with firearms, decimated their numbers in less than a century.

All crocodylines have their upper jaws notched to receive the enlarged fourth lower tooth, in contrast to alligatorines which characteristically accommodate these canine-like fangs in sockets. There are four or five pairs of teeth in the premaxillae, with 11–19 in the maxillary bone of the upper jaw and 14–26 in each ramus of the lower jaw. The nasal bones extend forward down the top of the muzzle to reach the premaxillae, sometimes reaching as far as the openings for the nostrils, and the mandibular symphysis (where the two halves of the lower jaw are joined at the front) is relatively long to give strength and rigidity.

Nile crocodile

The typical crocodyline type is exemplified by the Nile crocodile, *Crocodylus niloticus*, which is not by any means restricted to the river that gave this reptile its common name. At one time this powerful predator ranged almost the entire length and breadth of Africa, from the Nile delta in the north to the Cape of Good Hope in the south, and also apparently occurred in Asia Minor (in fact there is still a river, near Caesarea, officially called the Nahr es Zerka or Wadi Zarga, that is known locally as the Crocodile River). Only the barren deserts of the north and the Kalahari in the south lacked populations of this ubiquitous crocodilian, and in prehistoric times when the Sahara enjoyed a less desiccated climate there were Nile crocodiles to be found even there, with survivors lingering on in the dwindling lakes of the Wadi Iherir in the central Sahara's mountainous Tassili-n-Ajjer region until the 1930s and other remnant populations persisting in the Menake swamps south of Aïr, in the Ennedi mountains of the southern Sahara, and in Lake Galula, Mauretania. There were once Nile crocodiles in the Seychelles, those on La Digue surviving until 1810 and on Mahé until 1819, and there have also been occasional reports of them reaching the Comoros. The species still exists in Madagascar (where the population was at one time held to constitute a separate species, *Crocodylus madagascariensis*), and in the northern part of the island these reptiles take refuge from hunters in the Ankarana caves, which penetrate deep into the Middle Jurassic limestone: Philip Chapman, of Bristol Museum in the west of England, reported sighting juveniles in the Ambatoharanana cave, through which the River Mananjeba runs for some 2 km (1¼ miles), with slide marks and footprints visible on mud banks up to about 1 km (1100 yards) inside the cave, and also in the Styx River cave (the source of the Antenankarana River); the testimony of local people indicates that the crocodiles take refuge in the caves when river levels begin to fall at the start of the dry season, and remain there for four or five months until the beginning of the rains.

Since the beginning of the 20th century, the Nile crocodile has declined precipitately in numbers and its range has been·drastically reduced. Treated as vermin and indiscriminately hunted to supply a flourishing trade in crocodile skin for shoes, handbags and other luxury goods, the species had no chance of survival anywhere near Africa's burgeoning European settlements. By the late 18th century it had already vanished from its best-known habitat, the Nile delta, and in another hundred years it was rare below the river's first cataract. Since the beginning of the 20th century it has been systematically exterminated from the Nile below the second cataract, and although substantial populations persisted on the Victoria Nile between Murchison Falls and the Lake Albert delta into the 1950s these, too, dwindled rapidly. Elsewhere in Africa the story has been the same, as this once common reptilian is driven out of one area after another.

In the extreme south of the continent Nile crocodiles still occur in the River Limpopo and in the Nduma and St Lucia game reserves, but they have long since vanished from the Keiskamma River, near East London, and the Umkomaas River, just south of Durban. The present range of the Nile crocodile extends from the River Senegal, Lake Chad, Wadai and the Sudan south to the Okavango and Cunene Rivers, Ngamiland, the northern Transvaal and Natal, with a population still persisting in Madagascar's low-lying southern and western regions, including Lake Itasy, 1270 m (4170 ft) up in the hills 80 km (50 miles) west of Tananarive.

The Nile crocodile has a relatively smooth skull, with a flat forehead and no ridges occurring in front of or between the eyes, or down the centre of the snout. There are five pairs of premaxillary teeth (the common number in *Crocodylus*, although old individuals of some species sometimes have only four pairs), and 13 or 14 maxillary teeth, opposed by 14 or 15 pairs in the lower jaw. The anterior nuchal plates on the back of the neck are well

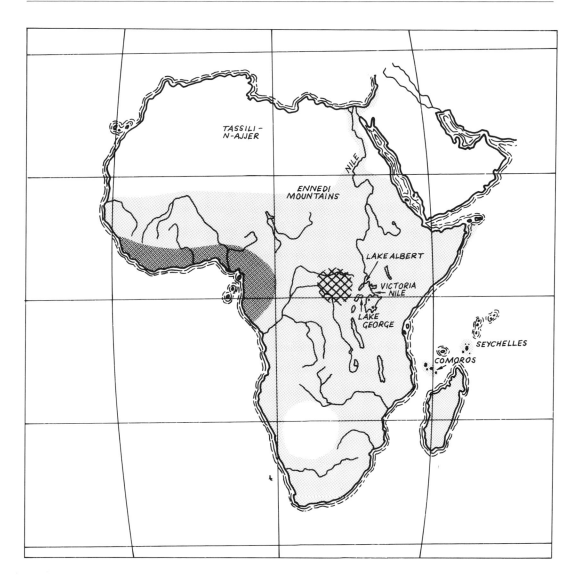

Map 1

 The range of the Nile crocodile (*Crocodylus niloticus*) before European colonisation

The range of the West African dwarf crocodile (*Osteolaemus tetraspis tetraspis*)

The range of the Congo dwarf crocodile (*Osteolaemus tetraspis osborni*)

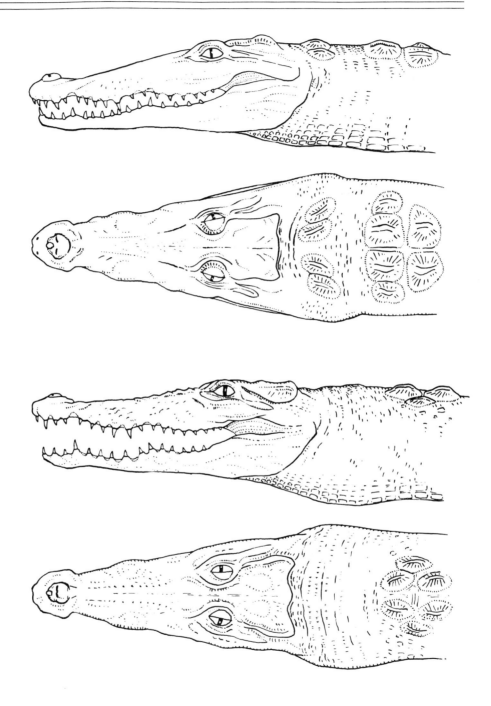

Figure 7 Top, the Nile crocodile (Crocodylus niloticus); Bottom, the saltwater crocodile (Crocodylus porosus)

developed, and adults are a uniform dark olive colour; juveniles at hatching exhibit poorly defined black or grey cross-bands on green-coloured dorsal surfaces, with some 10 or 12 blotchy, broken rings around the tail, the ventral regions being pale hued. The maximum size attained by the species seems to be about 6 m (20 ft), an official record having been set in 1953 when a member of the Uganda Game and Fisheries Department took a 19½-ft (5.94 m) specimen on the Simliki River, this example having a belly girth of 7 ft 4 in (2.24 m). Other records of large Nile crocodiles include an alleged 21-ft (6.4-m) example shot near Nungwe on the Emin Pasha gulf of Lake Victoria in 1948 by a professional hunter named Erich Novotny; an animal known as Kwena, killed by another professional hunter, Bobby Wilmot, in the Okavango swamp of Botswana in 1968, that measured 19 ft 3 in (5.87 m) between pegs with a belly girth of 7 ft (2.13 m); and an example 21 ft 4 in long (6.5 m), shot by the Duke of Mecklenberg near Mwanza, Tanzania, in 1905. Males become sexually mature at about 3 m (9 ft 10 in), while the smallest breeding females measure just over 2 m (6½ ft), representing an age of nearly ten years. In some areas, so-called 'pygmy' Nile crocodiles occur, those of the Aswa River in northern Uganda attaining a length of only 1.8 m (6 ft) with disproportionately large heads. These dwarfed individuals live in an unfavourable environment, with a long dry season during which they retire to holes dug in the river bank. Evidently they must be regarded as runts that have failed to show a normal annual length increment.

Throughout its range the Nile crocodile is essentially an inhabitant of river courses, although populations also occur in freshwater marshes and along coastal areas in estuaries and mangrove swamps. They are sometimes present in very isolated bodies of water, such as Lake Chula at the foot of Kilimanjaro, but in East Africa are surprisingly absent from such prospectively excellent habitats as Lake Edward, Lake George and Lake Kivu, having apparently failed to get past the falls south of Lake Albert that bar the Semliki River on its way from Lake Edward or to traverse the turbulent cataracts of the Ruzizi between Lake Tanganyika and Lake Kivu. Fossil remains found at Lake Edward indicate that crocodiles did once live there, but presumably they perished in a prolonged dry spell and have never recolonised the area.

Full-grown adults are catholic feeders, taking virtually any prey they can overpower and also eating carrion if the opportunity occurs. Within the stomachs of Nile crocodiles have been found remains of zebras, hippopotamuses, river hogs, domestic sheep, goats and cattle, antelopes of various kinds, marsh mongooses, porcupines, numerous types of mice, cane rats, baboons, guenons, pangolins, toads, frogs, turtles, monitor lizards, snakes, waterbirds (cormorants, pelicans, herons, ducks), doves, plovers, an abundance of fish (constituting up to perhaps 70 per cent of an adult individual's food intake, and including elephant fish, characids, dace, catfish, eels, killifish, cichlids and sharks), crabs, shrimps, snails and clams. In addition, the stomach contents of adult Nile crocodiles usually include a wide variety of insects, but most or all of these will be present as a result of secondary ingestion, having first been swallowed by a frog or other small animal that was later taken by the crocodile. Small juvenile individuals, however, may well catch insect prey at first hand.

The favourite hunting ground of adult Nile crocodiles is the water's edge, where prey, particularly mammals, can be seized while drinking. Antelopes, zebra, warthogs and domestic animals are usually grabbed by the muzzle and hurled off balance by the weighty crocodile's initial onslaught. This sometimes breaks the victim's neck outright, but more frequently the unfortunate creature is simply dragged into the water, shocked and still struggling feebly, where it drowns. Whether or not Nile crocodiles use their tails as offensive weapons seems to be a contentious issue, although individuals that find themselves in a hazardous situation seem to accompany loud exhalations of breath, calculated to warn or deter an enemy, with tail-lashing. The belief that Nile crocodiles will bury carcases or store them in underwater caverns beneath river banks is widespread, but there is little evidence to substantiate these accounts, although a crocodile may drag a carcase to a relatively secluded spot to devour it free of interference from others of its kind and will spend several days in the vicinity if the victim is a large animal, defending the corpse against interlopers and dining off it regularly. On the other hand, these reptiles have frequently been seen dismembering a carcase by fastening their jaws in a limb or a mass of muscle and then rotating in the water like a revolving shaft until a piece of meat or a joint is torn loose and can be swallowed. A crocodile has also been seen tearing at the body of an antelope with its jaws while holding the carcase with a clawed foot.

Very large mammals, including hippopotamuses, giraffes, rhinoceroses, buffaloes and even apparently the occasional lion, also sometimes fall victim to crocodiles. Juveniles of all these species would certainly be vulnerable to attack by crocodiles, and it is possible that the hippopotamus population in some areas was in fact controlled by crocodile predation on young animals. Taking on large mammals can, however, be a hazardous affair: a crocodile that seized a young giraffe by the muzzle at a Kruger National Park water hole was dragged abruptly from the water as its intended victim jerked its head up, and was left hanging in mid-air until it relinquished its hold, the aggrieved and still thirsty giraffe stalking back into the bush. There are numerous accounts of crocodiles that met their deaths trampled under the feet of enraged elephants; the body of one Nile crocodile was found bitten in two just in front of the hindlegs, apparently by a hippopotamus; and on several occasions crocodiles that tried to appropriate the kills of lions while the rightful owners were temporarily absent found themselves becoming victims of the angry lions — two such injudicious crocodiles in the Kruger National Park were themelves eaten by the lions, and a crocodilian corpse 2.5 m (8 ft 2 in) long reported in 1980 by A. Whateley of the Natal Parks Board on the Black Umfolozi River had been savagely bitten on the neck and forelimbs. On the Tana River, in Meru National Park, Kenya, a 1.8-m (6-ft) Nile crocodile was observed in mortal combat with a 4.5-m (15-ft) python, its jaws locked in the snake's body: the contest lasted for two hours, the antagonists threshing and rotating in the water between intervals of lying quiescent to regather their strength, until finally the crocodile was crushed by the python and killed. Occasionally Nile crocodiles die in bizarre circumstances, such as the subadult found dead on Lake St Lucia with a large terrapin stuck in its throat.

The capture of fish by Nile crocodiles is often achieved simply by pursuit in open water, the reptile thrusting its head above the surface or emerging on to the bank as soon as a victim has been seized, killing it with a swift bite or beating it against the ground or a rock, and then manipulating the carcase so that it can be swallowed head first. Barbel are frequently taken (Nile crocodiles probably act as a major population control on these cyprinids), and because they have awkwardly barbed, plated heads they are neatly decapitated before being swallowed. Sometimes a crocodile will simply lie in wait to capture fish as they swim by, and occasionally a whole group of Nile crocodiles will act in concert, notably when fish are migrating, as Anthony Pooley witnessed at Lake St Lucia when a group of crocodiles formed a semicircle across a narrow section of the water channel and systematically snapped up the densely packed mullet with sideways bites of their jaws, each crocodile maintaining its position without contesting its neighbours' captures to maintain the integrity of their ambush. Nile crocodiles have also been seen to swim slowly along a river close inshore with the tail curving towards the bank so that small fish fleeing through the shallows from the water disturbed by the trailing tail can be seized with a sideways lunge of the jaws.

Immature Nile crocodiles necessarily have to seek less ambitious prey than their seniors. Subadult animals over two years old of 1–3.5 m (3¼–11½ ft) in length, which seem to constitute about 60 per cent of the total crocodile population, subsist very largely on fish: these juveniles tend to occur in twos and threes, although sometimes in groups of up to 20, and do not mix with fully grown adults. The larger subadults do eventually begin to integrate with the full-grown animals by surreptitiously edging their way into the fringes of established adult communities, which usually have their favoured hauling-out areas along river banks and lakeshores. Customarily, however, there is a very large dominant male in each of these groups who will periodically employ splash displays and slap the water noisily with his head to demonstrate his ascendancy. Youthful tyros stay well clear of him, keeping to the least favoured basking spots on the edge of the colony's established site. The overlord bull is usually the first crocodile to leave the water in the morning and selects a prime spot for sunning himself before lesser animals emerge, with the subadults inevitably having to accept peripheral locations; the latter, if challenged by a larger crocodile, indicate submission by raising their heads almost vertically, exposing the throat. The dominant male will, however, acquiesce more readily to the approach of young females, and, in order presumably to impress them with his size and strength, fills himself with air and then submerges his nostrils to generate two powerful jets of water that spout for five or six seconds; he may also, in a further display ritual, raise his head, neck and tail above the water, curving his tail around in a semicircle so that just the tip touches the water, then submerge his snout and allow bubbles to escape from his partly open jaws.

Yearling individuals less than 1 m (3 ft 3 in) in length keep well out of the way, possibly because cannibalism is not unknown among Nile crocodiles. They are active principally at night, and frequent feeder streams and protected river embayments, where they can hide under fallen tree trunks and branches in the shallows, or seek safety in offshore reedbeds or beneath rosettes of *Potamogeton* weed. Quite a lot of their time seems to be spent on land, possibly because a substantial proportion of their diet consists of beetles and other insects, and they also take large numbers of frogs and toads. These youngsters are disinclined to wander far from their safe havens until well enough grown to be relatively safe from predation.

Hatchlings initially have no need to forage, as they can live for several weeks on the remnants of their yolk sac, traces of which are still discernible six months after hatching. However, they quickly acquire dexterity in catching insects or other small prey, living mostly ashore and often travelling substantial distances from the lakes and rivers on whose shores they hatched; 50-cm (about 1¾-ft) long hatchlings have been found in marshes a mile (1.6 km) or more from the banks of the Victoria Nile, apparently seeking seclusion in thick vegetation.

Most of the breeding females in Nile crocodile communities will mate with the dominant male, the favoured time for copulation being early afternoon when these reptiles are returning to the water after a morning of basking. Females display by arching their body above the water with the head and tail submerged, then raising the head with the jaws opened in an attitude of submission. Males respond by rubbing the underside of the jaw and throat backwards and forwards across the female's neck, both partners emitting warbling growls. The male then mounts the female, throwing a hindfoot over her rump and a forefoot across the back of her neck, gripping with his claws while they copulate for about two minutes, with tails entwined and mouths partly open. An individual male can mate several times in a single afternoon, at intervals of about an hour.

Female Nile crocodiles excavate their nests with their hindfeet along sandy shorelines, in dry stream beds, or even atop relatively high river banks perhaps 15 m (50 ft) above the water level, individual animals frequently returning each year not just to the same breeding ground but also to the same nest site. A major hazard to the eggs is flooding, so deposition of the clutch at the start of the dry season should minimise the risk of this occurring during the three-month incubation period that precedes hatching. As a result, this species lays its eggs in November on Tanzania's Ulanga plains, from November to mid-December in the eastern Transvaal, in early December on the Upper Victoria Nile and Lake Kioga, over the New Year period on the Lower Victoria Nile and Lake Albert, in January and February in Sierra Leone, between April and August in the Ruzizi valley, in late August and early September in the Bangweolo marshes, at the beginning of September on Lake Mweru and on the rivers Luangwa and Kafue, and from September to October in Madagascar. There appear to be two breeding seasons on Lake Victoria (August–September, December–January) marking periods when the water level falls, while in Zululand the Nile crocodile is seemingly obliged to breed during November–December, which is in fact the wet season: low temperatures during the southern winter months in this area probably make the dry season too cold for hatchlings, so nesting during the warmer but wetter summer is a lesser risk, although substantial losses of nests and juveniles occur in particularly wet summers.

The eggs of the Nile crocodile usually measure about 90 mm by 60 mm ($3\frac{1}{2}$ by $2\frac{1}{2}$ in), and occur in clutches of from 25 to nearly 100, the average being 45–55. Very young females tend to lay fewer, smaller eggs than fully mature matriarchs. Usually the eggs are deposited in two or three tiers, the hindlegs being used to guide the eggs gently into position and shovel in sand or soil to separate the different layers of eggs. When the clutch is complete, the nest is covered over to leave the uppermost eggs buried some 10–40 cm (4–16 in) deep; nests in the cool silt of a dry river bed will be shallow, while those in the hot white soils of St Lucia Bay or the black clays of the Pongola River are much deeper. Excessive heat and evaporation can kill the developing embryos as readily as can flooding, or the bacteria and fungi that proliferate in excessively damp soil during an unusually wet rainy season.

Favoured breeding sites often accommodate numerous nests, with each female assiduously guarding her eggs either by lying right on top of the nest or by watching it during the heat of the day from an adjacent pool or the shelter of nearby shady vegetation. The male will usually not be far away, and his mate will greet interlopers with threatening displays that include loud exhalations accompanied by raising the head-and-shoulder region and partial opening of the jaws, progressing to rapid snapping of the jaws, tail-lashing and the utterance of a low, threatening growl.

The most notorious predators on Nile crocodile eggs are monitor lizards (*Varanus niloticus*), which excavate as many as a third of the nests in some areas and carry off the eggs one by one to a secure distance, where the shells are broken and the yolks swallowed. Monitors have been seen to work in pairs, with one decoying the female crocodile off the nest so that its companion can raid the eggs, the decoy rejoining its companion after eluding the pursuing crocodile. Other animals reported to prey on crocodile nests in Africa include spotted hyaenas, olive baboons, honey badgers, white-tailed mongooses, Egyptian mongooses (in Egypt), water mongooses (in southern Africa), warthogs, bushpigs, and sometimes servals, while previously disturbed nests are further pillaged by marabou storks, black kites, palmnut vultures, grey herons, goliath herons and sacred ibis. In addition, cocktail ants (*Crematogaster*) will burrow through the soil into crocodiles' nests and use their pincers to bite through the shells and inner membranes of the eggs so that they can gain access to the eyes, ears, mouths and nostrils of the embryos within, quickly killing and devouring them. Once a nest has been exposed, Nile crocodiles apparently make no effort to re-bury the eggs, and any embryos that have not been devoured will speedily perish in the hot sun. Probably about two-thirds of nests are lost, and not more than about 2 per cent of eggs produce hatchlings that will eventually grow to full maturity.

Incubation is normally for about 11–13 weeks, although the lower temperatures prevailing in Zululand mean that eggs in that region may not be ready to hatch for as long as 14 weeks. Full-term embryos give croaking, grunting calls or yelps that alert the mother to the imminence of their hatching. She clears the sand and soil from around the eggs with her forefeet so that, when the youngsters have forced their way through the shell's tough inner integument (using the caruncle on the end of the snout) and broken out of the softened shell, they will not find themselves buried alive. The female and her mate will also take eggs that are about to hatch into their mouths and roll them on their tongues for up to 15 minutes to crack the shells gently and to aid the hatchlings to escape: the membrane and empty shells are subsequently swallowed, as are infertile or rotten eggs when the shell has been cracked to disclose the unviable contents. The hatchlings are about 28 cm (11 in) long and 100 g (3½ oz) in weight and, although immediately capable of defending themselves fiercely with their powerful jaws, their small size makes them highly vulnerable to predation by marabou storks, herons, ibis, fish eagles, ravens, eagle owls, ground hornbills and genets; even if they reach the relative safety of the water, there are voracious pelicans, otters, turtles (*Trionyx triungis*), hinged terrapins (*Pelusios sinnatus*), tiger fish and catfish waiting to seize them. Weaklings (such as those that develop umbilical abscesses) or congenitally deformed individuals (blind in one or both eyes, or with twisted spines or jaws, for example) quickly succumb to predators.

With this multitude of hazards surrounding them, the juveniles need maternal help if they are to have any hope of initial survival, and the female will speedily gather up her brood. Each hatchling will be delicately picked up by the adult's massive jaws and slipped into a gular pouch in the floor of her mouth, where they can be heard making low chirruping calls. Youngsters wandering near the nest site will try to attract the mother's attention by yelping continuously and flicking their tails from side to side until they are found and safely installed in the gular pouch for transportation to the safety of the nearest pool or river, where their arrival may be greeted by a welcoming chorus of roars from adult denizens of the site. The belief that Nile crocodiles cannibalise their young was at one time widely asserted, and there can be little doubt that the practice of females carrying their brood from the nest in their mouths led to this misconception—not, perhaps, surprisingly, since crocodiles were not credited with such sophisticated patterns of social behaviour. With their close relationship to birds, whose nesting practices and care of their young are so well known, the discovery that crocodiles also display parental concern for their offspring should not be so surprising. There is substantial evidence that their extinct cousins, the dinosaurs, guarded their nests and cared for the newly emerged young in a similar manner.

During at least their first few weeks the hatchlings are shepherded by their mother, who alerts them to possible danger by rapid vibrations of her flank muscles: this warning response is elicited by, for example, circling herons, storks or fish eagles, and prompts the juveniles immediately to jump into the water and submerge. Generally speaking, the wet season breaks soon after hatching is complete, which means that marshes, stream beds and lakes quickly fill with floodwater to provide a safe refuge for the youngsters, with an abundance of food in the shape of insects, tadpoles, frogs, crabs and fish fry. The tiny crocodiles are to be found exploring the shoreline and the shallows, learning to hunt but still remaining together as a group, any individual that becomes isolated yelping loudly until re-united with its companions by their answering calls. In between energetically clambering among the reeds, mangrove roots and water-lily pads, they bask and sleep, often on the back or head of their mother. The juvenile distress call will quickly bring any nearby adult to the threatened youngster's assistance.

First-year juveniles make little or no growth during the cold season, and indeed often go without food when temperatures are particularly inclement. They are able to excavate burrows in which they lie up on cold days, biting their way into river banks and carrying mouthfuls of mud back to the stream, where they submerge, shaking their heads, to disgorge the mud, which is then scraped backwards into the current with the hindfeet. Where the burrows reach above water level, they soften the earth by splashing water on to the sides of the tunnel with their tails.

Older crocodiles also dig these refuges during the winter, each tunnel opening into a large upper chamber where a number of animals can accommodate themselves, tightly wedged in layers, having worked together to complete the excavation as a communal effort, digging normally being a nocturnal activity. A large individual will sometimes become the solitary occupant of a burrow, defending its primacy against potential intruders of smaller size. In some areas, Nile crocodiles dig themselves into the mud of dried-up river courses during the dry season, excavating holes up to 1.5 m (5 ft) deep to reach the remaining moisture. At this time of the year, they are also known to travel substantial distances across country in search of water. Normally these migrations take place at night, the creatures hiding up in thick bush during the day: 10 km (6 miles) a night is well within the capabilities of an adult animal.

As the largest and probably the most abundant predator in Africa, frequenting the very rivers and lakes where human habitations are most often sited, it is not surprising that Nile crocodiles have an unhealthy reputation as man-killers. When Africa was still a wilderness from coast to coast, and these reptiles swarmed in the tropical watercourses, the human toll must have been substantial: a figure of 3,000 deaths a year has been estimated. Although no records of most such fatalities exist, accounts by early European explorers of fatal crocodile attacks give lurid details of the manner in which victims were seized: usually by an arm or leg, although in one instance, on the Omo River, an especially large crocodile caught up an African across the middle of the man's body and vanished into deep water, carrying the unfortunate wretch 'like a fish in a heron's beak'. Some places acquired a particularly evil reputation for crocodile attack, among them the lower Pongola River, the Juba River, and Sesheke on the Zambezi. Conversely, the Nile crocodiles of Amatongaland and Lake Baringo (in Kenya) were believed to have no propensity whatsoever for attacking man, and allegedly constituted no threat to bathers or fishermen.

With the greatly reduced crocodile populations of today, and fewer individuals surviving to full maturity, attacks on humans are much reduced in frequency. They do, nevertheless, still occur, and, even when the victim is rescued from the crocodile's jaws, getting him or her to a doctor from some still remote bush outpost may take hours or possibly days. Even the claws of a crocodile can leave severe gashes on a human victim, and the sharp teeth of these reptiles inflict lacerating punctures, frequently carrying infection deep into the flesh, so that irrigation of the wounds and treatment with tetanus toxoid (or human antitetanus globulin) and broad-spectrum antibiotics is essential (gangrene and tetanus are ever-present risks). The strength of the jaws frequently splinters the bone and may make limb amputations inevitable even if infection is staved off, while severe loss of blood can be fatal in its own right as well as leaving the patient doubly vulnerable to infection.

Typical crocodile-bite injuries were suffered by two of the rescuers who in May 1987 saved a 15-year-old South African boy from a Nile crocodile in the Zambezi. Jeremy Lloyd was seized while swimming, but Rupert Novis, a 20-year-old British Coldstream Guards army officer, jumped into the water to wrestle with the reptile, accompanied by the boy's father (Hugh Lloyd) and a 20-year-old British student, Alexander Shaw. The boy was dragged below the surface, and Novis was up to his neck in the water before Hugh Lloyd plunged his arm into the crocodile's mouth, allowing Novis to drag Jeremy, severely bitten on an arm and his buttocks, to safety. It cost Hugh Lloyd his arm, however, bitten off at the elbow, and Shaw had his forearm bones broken by the reptile's savage bite. Rupert Novis subsequently received the Royal Humane Society's silver medal for his courage, with bronze medals for the other two rescuers.

A human victim's only real chance of escape if alone when seized is to try and jab at the creature's eyes (with a finger if no weapon is available), or failing that to stab at the nostrils at the tip of the snout. With a weight of perhaps a ton, a large crocodile can easily drag a full-grown man into the water, and it appears that the sense of shock is so great that there is little feeling of pain: those who have been rescued at the last moment cannot usually recall suffering pain from their injuries as they were pulled under.

Attacks on small motor boats have often been reported, notably on those once used to ferry passengers out to flying boats on the River Gambia, and appear to be incited by the sound of the vessel's engine, which possibly resembles the challenging bellow of a rival bull (described as a series of short, sharp guttural grunts not unlike the noise of an outboard engine). When flying boats were widely used in Africa for passenger transport, servicing engineers noticed that Nile crocodiles would frequently bellow when they heard an engine being run up.

Whether the Nile crocodiles of Africa represent a single homogeneous population has been questioned, and a division into seven subspecies may be advisable: *Crocodylus niloticus niloticus* is from the Nile, Ethiopia and the Sudan, *Crocodylus niloticus suchus* is the Central African crocodile, *Crocodylus niloticus chamses* is the West African Nile crocodile, *Crocodylus niloticus pauciscutatus* is the Kenya crocodile, *Crocodylus niloticus cowiei* is the South African crocodile, *Crocodylus niloticus africanus* is the East African crocodile, and *Crocodylus niloticus madagascariensis* is the Madagascan form. The species as a whole has a quite lengthy fossil history in Africa, and *Crocodylus niloticus* stock has obviously been established on the continent for many millions of years: it occurs in the Pleistocene of Ethiopia and the Pliocene of Uganda, and fragmentary fossil remains of either this or a very similar species are present in the Lower Miocene of East Africa.

A possible ancestor of the Nile crocodile is *Crocodylus pigotti*, from the Lower Miocene of Rusinga Island, which was a rather small form with a low, flat skull. There is a permanent 14th pair of maxillary teeth in this fossil species, a rare feature in the living form and indicative of a less advanced evolutionary level in *Crocodylus pigotti*. Lower-jaw remains from the Lower Miocene of Al-Sarrar, in eastern Saudi Arabia, also probably belong to *Crocodylus pigotti*, which some scientists believe to have evolved in parallel with *Crocodylus niloticus* to fill a similar evolutionary role, rather than being an actual ancestor of the Nile crocodile. *Crocodylus pigotti* was named after D. B. Pigott, a young British government officer in East Africa during the early 1900s. Despatched to Karungu, on the eastern shore of Lake Victoria, in 1909 on a fossil-collecting expedition, Pigott had the considerable misfortune to be eaten by a crocodile on the return journey. His fossils arrived safely at their destination, however, and as some recompense for Pigott's regrettable demise a fossil species was in due course named in his honour: that it should be a crocodile, and possibly an ancestor of the one which ate him, was perhaps unintentional irony on the part of the scientist who described the small skull on which it was based.

Saltwater crocodile

The Nile crocodile is occasionally encountered in marine environments, and has been seen nearly a dozen kilometres out to sea, but it is not so well adapted for life in a saline environment as its even more massive relative, the estuarine or saltwater crocodile (*Crocodylus porosus*). Capable of existing more or less indefinitely in saline conditions, the saltwater crocodile has a vast geographical range that extends from Cochin on the west coast of India to Ceylon, Bangladesh, the southern Malay peninsula, Indonesia (Sumatra, Borneo, Java, Labuan, Sulawesi, the Moluccas, the Riau archipelago, Ambon, Ternate, Flores, Timor where it is misleadingly known as the jacare, Batjan, Simeulue etc.), the Philippines, the Palau Islands, New Guinea, northern Australia (by whose population it is often referred to as an alligator), the Bismarck archipelago (a 3.8-m/12½-ft male caught on Ponape in 1971 had in its stomach several crabs, an eel, the remains of a small green turtle, and a piece of mangrove wood), the Solomons, the New Hebrides, and Fiji. Saltwater crocodiles have frequently been sighted far out to sea (one was observed 48 km/30 miles north of New Zealand's North Cape), and their tolerance of saltwater conditions has evidently facilitated the phenomenal spread of this species. A solitary individual even found its way to the Cocos (Keeling) Islands, 970 km (600 miles) from the nearest land, another specimen migrated 1100 km (690 miles) across the Indian Ocean from the Andaman Islands to the Krishna sanctuary in Andhra Pradesh, and there are records of former occurrences in the Burmese portion of the upper Malay peninsula and in southern China.

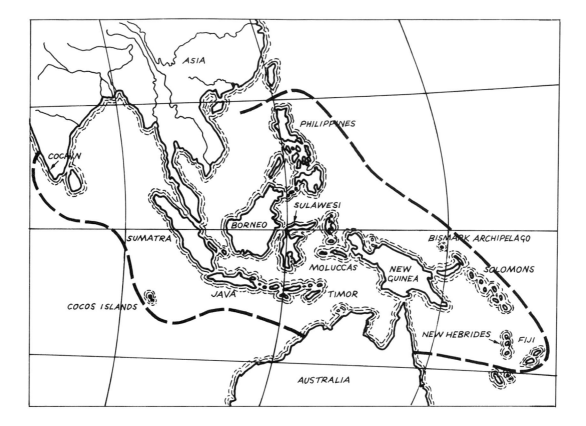

Map 2

The extensive range of the saltwater crocodile (*Crocodylus porosus*) which has often been seen far out to sea

This species is usually regarded as the largest of living crocodiles, and can with reasonable certainty be said to attain 9 m (30 ft) in length, although it is unlikely nowadays that any individual would escape a hunter's bullet long enough to achieve such dimensions. A crocodile of this magnitude would compare favourably in size with the largest known carnivorous dinosaurs: the mighty *Tyrannosaurus rex*, regarded as the largest flesh-eating land animal that ever lived, probably measured about 12.5 m (40 ft) from nose to tail (figures of 47 ft were based on an initial over-estimate of the number of caudal vertebrae), while such formidable raptors as *Megalosaurus* and *Eustreptospondylus* from the Jurassic were not much more than 7 m (23 ft) in length, and *Daspletosaurus* (a late Cretaceous relative of *Tyrannosaurus*) only about equalled the biggest saltwater crocodiles in size.

Many claims for gigantic specimens of *Crocodylus porosus* prove on investigation to be spurious, such as the alleged 27-ft (8.2-m) animal shot in the Phillipines by Paul de la Gironiere in 1823 at Jala Jala, near Lake Taal, on Luzon. The skull of this creature is today in the Museum of Comparative Zoology at Harvard, and is readily identifiable by the damage to the palate caused by musket balls which Gironiere had fired into the animal's mouth. This skull measures 25½ in (64.77 cm) from snout to occiput, from which it can be deduced that the entire crocodile would have been only about 6 m (20 ft) long. It was nevertheless a formidable reptile that had acquired an unsavoury reputation as a man-eater. Gironiere and his party trapped it in a small river but required six hours to kill it, finally achieving their objective by severing its spinal column with a lance thrust. To beach the body apparently required the efforts of 40 men, and when the stomach was opened it was found to contain the body of a horse (in seven pieces) and 150 lb (68 kg) of pebbles ranging in size from the dimensions of a walnut to those of a man's fist.

Similar over-estimates of total length have evidently been made in respect of a supposed 25-footer (7.6 m) killed in the Hooghly River of Alipore, Calcutta, with a skull (now in the Indian Museum, Calcutta) measuring 75 cm (29.53 in) from snout to occiput which could not have exceeded 22 ft (6.7 m) overall, and a claimed 33-ft (10.1-m) reptile killed in the Bay of Bengal during 1840 whose skull (in the British Museum of Natural History) measures 65.5 cm (25.8 in) and would therefore have been only 19 ft 4 in (5.89 m) in total length.

Nonetheless there is some indirect evidence of 9-m (30-ft) saltwater crocodiles existing down to modern times. In the early part of the 20th century, the Seluke people of the Segama River in North Borneo venerated a giant crocodile which they believed to be 200 years old. On one occasion this giant was shooed off a sand bank (seemingly an act of either remarkable bravery or astounding foolhardiness) so that the impression in the sand could be measured. It proved to be 32 ft 10 in (10 m). The Seluke regarded their huge neighbour as the father of the devil, and threw silver money into the river to placate him. No-one, it seems, ever shot the monster.

One huge saltwater crocodile that was killed fell to a .300 H. & H. magnum bullet fired from the rifle of Mrs Kris Pawlowski on MacArthur Bank, Norman River, in the southeastern Gulf of Carpentaria, during July 1957. Mrs Pawlowski's husband, Ron, was present, but there was no means to hand of dragging the body off the tidal flat where it lay, and even the head was too heavy to lift. The crocodile apparently measured 28 ft 4 in (8.64 m), but the photographic evidence of this outsize kill has now seemingly been lost, the pictures not having been seen since 1968. The Pawlowskis were experts on saltwater crocodiles, and had previously examined over 10,000 examples, none of which exceeded 18 ft (5.5 m).

A 6.5-m (20-ft) example of *Crocodylus porosus* would weigh about 3 tons (3050 kg), which agrees well with an estimated weight of 7 tons (7110 kg) for a 12.5-m (40-ft) *Tyrannosaurus*, and a male exceeding 7 m (23 ft) in length was reported to be living in the Bhitarkanika sanctuary of Orissa, India, in the late 1980s. It is extraordinary to reflect on the continued existence in the 20th century of carnivorous reptiles as large as all but the most gigantic flesh-eating dinosaurs. As their habitats are steadily destroyed by encroaching farms, settlements and industrial development, the opportunities for studying saltwater crocodiles in their natural environment are diminishing rapidly. And so little is really known about these huge relics of the dinosaurian age.

Saltwater crocodiles are by no means restricted to a marine habitat and also range far up rivers, occurring as much as 1130 km (700 miles) inland in New Guinea, although more numerous in coastal locations. Generally lethargic creatures, when in offshore waters they seem to be averse to coping with strong wave action or engaging in unnecessarily vigorous swimming, preferring simply to drift with the tide in relatively calm water. Juveniles and subadults customarily take themselves off to side branches of the main streams and there spend their early years, hiding up in vegetation-choked pools by day and venturing into the river proper only after dark.

The back of *Crocodylus porosus* is protected by long, oval-shaped scutes, but the dermal armour of this species has been substantially reduced. The post-occipital plates are often poorly developed or even absent, although the claim that these elements occur only in the Ceylonese saltwater crocodile population (which has therefore sometimes been regarded as a separate subspecies) was demonstrated by S. K. Kar to be inaccurate: working in the Bhitarkanika wildlife sanctuary in Orissa during 1975–79, he found that even a single brood includes some hatchlings with post-occipital plates and some completely lacking them, with a few exhibiting an intermediate condition of incipiently formed post-occipitals. Loss of heavy protective scales may indicate a greater degree of aquatic adaptation in *Crocodylus porosus* than is exhibited by any other living crocodilian species.

The snout is relatively slender, with a bony ridge extending forward from the eye socket on each side, and there are 13 or 14 pairs of maxillary teeth opposed by 14 or 15 pairs of teeth in the lower jaw. Adults are olive-brown above, with conspicuous black spots, the undersurfaces being pale-coloured, although a population in the tidal mangrove creeks of the Bhitarkanika wildlife sanctuary was reported by S. K. Kar and H. R. Bustard in 1982 to have a light, unpigmented ground colour that eventually tends to dull to the normal shade, except for the face which always stays white (these animals are known locally as sankhua). D. Kirshnev of Sydney University reported in 1985 that saltwater crocodiles have an ability to change their dorsal coloration to match the environment in which they live: hatchlings raised in a black tank had a dark ground colour, while individuals placed in a white tank became pale-hued, even the dark spots eventually being affected. If the animals were changed over (dark-coloured individuals placed in a white tank, and vice versa), the coloration gradually reversed over a period of several months.

This species is without doubt one of the most successful — perhaps the most successful — of all living crocodilians. Of potentially enormous size and enjoying a vast geographical range, *Crocodylus porosus* has acquired a notorious reputation as a man-eater. The most spectacular human mass killing by crocodiles was attributed to the saltwater species when, in February

1   Along the top of a crocodile's tail there are two scaly crests anteriorly, which merge to form a single ridge-like projection (*Crocodylus johnsoni*)

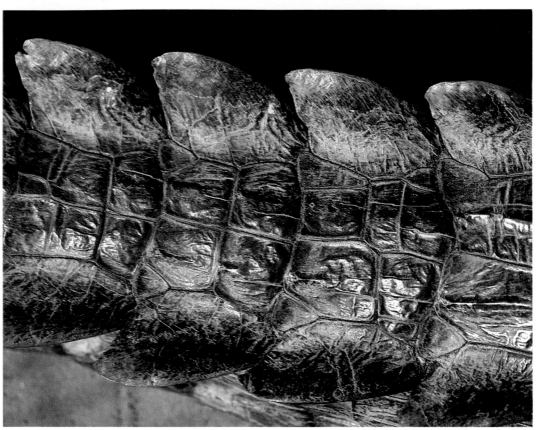

2   The paired rows of crested scutes present along the top of a crocodile's tail anteriorly (*Crocodylus niloticus*)

1944 during the Second World War, allied troops surrounded between 400 and 800 Japanese soldiers on Ramree Island, in the Bay of Bengal. During the night, saltwater crocodiles emerged on to the island and allegedly butchered the beleaguered Japanese piecemeal until in the morning only a handful of survivors supposedly remained to surrender. There seems to be some doubt as to the veracity of this frequently quoted account, however, and David Finkelstein concluded in 1984 that in fact the majority of the Japanese troops escaped to rejoin the rest of their army.

In December 1975, over 40 people were attacked and eaten by crocodiles, presumably *Crocodylus porosus*, when a holiday boat sank in the Malili River of central Celebes, and a Palau Island fisherman was killed at 3 a.m. one day in 1965 — the crocodile hacked off one arm and part of the other, a lung, and his liver. In April 1981, a 23-year-old Australian named Hilton Graham was badly mauled by a saltwater crocodile at Channel Point, 112 miles (180 km) southwest of Darwin, Australia. Graham was accompanying 12-year-old Peta-Lynn Mann on an airboat trip around the nearby swamps when he was seized while trying to retrieve his pistol from the shallow water where he had dropped it. In three separate attacks the 4-m (13-ft) crocodile successively seized his left arm, his right thigh and his right buttock, but its efforts to pull Graham below the water by spinning over and over were frustrated when the little girl rushed into the swamp and grasped his right arm. With her help, Graham succeeded in preventing the crocodile from dragging him into deeper water, although at one stage his face was below the surface, and suddenly the crocodile gave up the struggle, retreating to float watchfully offshore as the girl helped Graham up the bank to a safe refuge and then ran across country to fetch a truck. Despite her youth, she had learnt to drive and returned to pick up the stricken man. At Channel Point, Graham still had sufficient strength to call a homestead 19 miles (30.5 km) further down the track while Peta-Lynn dressed his gaping wounds with antiseptic powder. She drove him on towards Darwin, another vehicle meeting them to rush Graham the rest of the way to the city hospital, where in due course he made a complete recovery. His injuries included a double fracture of the left forearm and massive lacerations 9 in (23 cm) long in his right thigh. Eighteen months later, Peta-Lynn Mann was presented with the Royal Humane Society of Australia's Clarke Gold Medal by the Queen for what the society described as 'the country's most outstanding incident of bravery during 1981'.

During the southern hemisphere summer of 1986–87, there was a series of fatalities in northern Australia. Some were tourists who seemingly failed to realise just how dangerous the local saltwater crocodiles are, with the result that in March 1987 Mrs Fay Meadows, an American on a launch cruise off Queensland, elected to swim from a dinghy to the launch while it was moored in the mouth of the Prince Regent River and was seized by a crocodile estimated to be about 3.7 m (12 ft) long; she was never to be seen again. A few weeks earlier, during Christmas 1986, Mrs Beryl Wruck was taken by a crocodile while wading in Barratt Creek, 950 miles (1530 km) north of Brisbane, what were believed to be some of her fingernails, toenails and bones subsequently coming to light in the stomach of a 4.6-m (15 ft) saltwater crocodile trapped a few weeks later. Other human fatalities in this area during 1986–87 included Lee McLeod, who was taken while asleep in his camp outside a fishing village in September 1986, only his severed legs being left uneaten (McLeod's presumed remains were found inside a 4.6-m/15-ft crocodile killed a few days later), and a fisherman whose foot was discovered inside a crocodile shot in 1987. While all this was going on in Australia, a professional hunter, Jukin Sin Tapaling, was trying to negotiate a fee of £105,000 to shoot a giant saltwater crocodile in the Lupar River of Sarawak that had been killing the local natives for years. Believed to be 7.6 m (25 ft) long, with a distinctive white patch on its back, the so-called 'King of Crocodiles' was regarded as being imbued with supernatural powers. In the event, it seems that the money was not forthcoming, and the 'King' remained unmolested.

The Batang Lupur River of Sarawak acquired a singularly unsavoury reputation for fatal crocodile attacks that extended back for decades, and when these incidents were analysed by R. Stuebing, G. Ismail and K. Sallih in 1985 it was found that the area between Lingga and Bijat was a prime breeding habitat for saltwater crocodiles, which became aggressively territorial as the monsoon changed over. Unfortunately this period also coincided with the local prawn-fishing season, and as a result the months between May and September regularly witnessed a succession of human tragedies as fishermen and breeding crocodiles came into unwitting conflict. S. K. Kar and H. R. Bustard reported in 1982 that in Orissa, India, there had been only four attacks by saltwater crocodiles on people in a period of ten years, two of which were by the same crocodile (subsequently killed) three years apart: this particular reptile could have taken a man about once every two weeks had it wanted, so there seems little reason to believe that crocodiles become 'man-eaters' with an acquired taste for human flesh. Nor do they seem to become habitual cattle-killers.

Like the Nile crocodile, the saltwater species is a catholic feeder. In the Indian subcontinent it is known to kill cheetal (*Axis axis*), rhesus monkeys (*Macaca mulatta*), sambhar (*Cervus unicolor*) and wild boar (*Sus scrofa*), with kangaroos and feral buffaloes added to the diet in northern Australia, but any unwary mammal is likely to be seized by a well-grown saltwater crocodile — even cattle and horses, not to mention humans. Sharks and turtles are frequently taken, along with various species of fish (e.g. archer fish, barramundi, mullet, mudskippers), mangrove snakes, cormorants and magpie geese. Juveniles feed mainly along the water's edge or among the mangroves at high tide and prey on crustacea (especially crabs), insects, small fish, and occasionally the hatchlings of monitor lizards.

The saltwater crocodile mates during February–March in eastern India, with nest-building and egg-laying through May and June, but the breeding season in Australia coincides with the November–May wet season, maximum reproductive activity occurring before the turn of the year. Copulation is preceded by courtship displays that include snout-lifting, circling, head contacts, bubbling and periodic submergence, copulation eventually occurring in shallow water. Nesting sites are necessarily varied, in view of the extensive range of wetland habitats where *Crocodylus porosus* makes its home, but mangrove swamps are widely used, while in Arnhem Land, Australia, the banks of main streams and tributaries in the Liverpool–Tomkinson river system are favoured locations, together with the margins of floodplain billabongs or spring-fed freshwater marshes. On New Guinea, this species has become increasingly wary owing to hunting by man, and may nest in dense forest up to 50 yards (46 m) from water, September to January being the chosen time, although large females allegedly also nest in the exceptionally rainy months of February to April. In Ceylon, the species breeds during July–September, with hatchlings appearing at the beginning of the rains, and in India and the Andaman Islands nesting occurs from April through September (coincident with the onset of the southwest monsoon).

Vegetation mixed with soil is piled up to build the nest, ferns (*Acrostichum aureum*, Kharakhari) or hental (*Phoenix paludosa*) being favoured in Orissa (the former in swampy areas, the latter on higher ground), leaves from standing or creeping canes in the Andaman Islands, grass and small branches in Java, and tall grass and herbaceous water plants in the Philippines. The rather loosely assembled structure reaches a height of 50–90 cm (1½–3 ft) with a width of 1.5–2.50 m (about 5–8 ft). Nests are usually about 10 m (32½ ft) apart on beach breeding sites, rather closer in swamps, and there are often several adjacent wallows in which the guardian parent lies.

In New Guinea, nests are frequently on mats of floating grass (beneath which the water may be up to 4 m (13 ft) deep), or in the shade of trees, the egg chamber being covered by about 25 cm (10 in) of nesting material. Internal nest temperatures range from 27° to 33°C, the variation being caused by the process of vegetable decay in the nesting material, evaporative heat exchange, and convection; low humidity has been found to weaken embryos in commercial breeding units, while excessive temperature fluctuation causes abnormalities to appear.

Floating mats of vegetation are also used as nesting sites along the Finniss-Reynolds River, in the Darwin area, but the saltwater crocodiles of the freshwater Malacca swamp have to deposit their eggs in low-lying shaded areas that are very vulnerable to flooding. The mean clutch size in this region is just over 50 eggs, but G. J. W. Webb, G. C. Sack, R. Buckworth and S. C. Manolis of the University of New South Wales determined in 1983 that only 31.6 per cent of the eggs laid produce live hatchlings, flooding killing 36.3 per cent in the Malacca swamps and 40.6 per cent along the Finniss-Reynolds River; between 3 and 6 per cent were infertile, and from 0.6 per cent to 2.4 per cent were damaged by adult crocodiles, but dehydration and predation were not recorded. In India, H. R. Bustard and B. C. Choudhury estimated in 1980 that as few as 3.3 per cent of saltwater crocodile eggs ever hatched, 80 per cent of nests being lost through flooding.

Nests in low-lying locations, especially beside rivers, are inevitably at risk from floodwater. Eggs will survive brief tidal flooding, but laboratory tests conducted by W. E. Magnusson of Sydney University in 1982 indicated that immersion for 8–13 hours would prove fatal. In northern Australia, monitor lizards (*Varanus indicus*) and a rat (*Rattus colletti*) allegedly prey on the nests, and aboriginal hunters pilfer riverside nests, although eggs laid at swampy sites frequently escape detection by human agency; nests of the Indian and Ceylonese saltwater crocodile populations are sought by the kabaragoya (*Varanus salvator*) and to a lesser extent by *Varanus flavescens*. Fungus infestations and extremes of temperature fluctuation also take their toll of saltwater crocodile eggs, but flooding is undoubtedly the main cause of clutch mortality. On the Liverpool–Tomkinson river system in Australia, eggs laid during the annual floods of February and March have scant prospects of survival.

Female saltwater crocodiles take about seven days to build a nest, working at night and sometimes constructing additional 'trial' nests in which no eggs are laid. About a month elapses after fertilisation before laying takes place, deposition of the 20–90 hard-shelled white eggs, each measuring 50–95 mm (2–$3\frac{3}{4}$ ins) in length, 35–60 mm ($1\frac{1}{2}$–$2\frac{1}{2}$ in) in diameter and weighing 50–150 g ($1\frac{3}{4}$–$5\frac{1}{4}$ oz), taking perhaps a quarter of an hour.

Incubation requires up to 90 days. Full-term embryos will croak in response to a bump on the nest or a loud noise, and the female then opens the nest and carries the emergent juveniles in her mouth to the relative safety of the water. The hatching process may take as long as three or four days, especially if the clutch is a large one, all the empty egg shells apparently being eaten by the parent. Females have been observed to maintain a fruitless guard over nests flooded by up to 3 m (nearly 10 ft) of water for as long as four days. If all the embryos are dead, no attempt is made by the parent to excavate the nest, and in the absence of parental assistance only one or two hatchlings from viable clutches are likely to succeed in digging their own way out: some will succumb without even breaking the shell of their imprisoning egg, whereas others just manage to force their snouts through the shell but get no further.

The juveniles, about 30 cm (12 in) long, vocalise to maintain contact and seem usually to swim near their mother's head, presumably so that they can quickly receive warnings of possible danger and if necessary scramble back in her gular pouch. In the absence of the parent, they scatter and fail to maintain the original family group, but normally hatchlings will be protected by the mother for up to $2\frac{1}{2}$ months. Small saltwater crocodiles are vulnerable to predation by varanid lizards, birds and sharks, and the vicissitudes of their early lives are demonstrated by the frequency with which they sustain injuries of one sort or another: 80 per cent evince wounds or scars, over 50 per cent of which are to the tail, some 20 per cent to the body, and 10 per cent to the head. In addition, about 0.5 per cent are deformed, with misaligned jaws, missing legs or tail, no eyes, etc., and either quickly succumb to predators or fail to thrive. Overall mortality in the first two months of life, however, is probably no more than about 15 per cent.

Hatchlings have no apparent requirement for fresh water to drink, and flourish in salinities as high as 45‰ (one saltwater crocodile population, in Mungardobolo Creek, northern Australia, lives in water that has 60‰ salinity, but appears to be composed of itinerant individuals, and specimens up to 2 m/$6\frac{1}{2}$ ft long have been reported in salinities of 70‰). Very young animals live mostly on marine crustaceans (crabs, shrimps, etc.), which are electrolyte rich, but G. C. Grigg, L. E. Taplin, P. Harlow and J. Wright of Sydney University discovered in 1980 that juvenile saltwater crocodiles nevertheless maintain homeostasis of plasma electrolytes along a salinity spectrum of 0–35‰. From a survey conducted in the Liverpool–Tomkinson estuary at Meningpride, Northern Territory, G. C. Grigg concluded in 1977 that the blood plasma of adult saltwater crocodiles displays excellent ionic and osmotic homeostasis throughout the salinity gradient.

The saltwater crocodile is unable to produce urine that is hyperosmotic to the blood, liquid and solid fractions of urine excreted by individuals in a saline environment containing only negligible sodium. Insoluble nitrogenous wastes predominate, as the ammonia and bicarbonate excretion typical of fresh water (in a clear solution containing small amounts of white precipitated solids, with high concentrations of calcium and magnesium) is replaced by production of urea, creatinin, and uric acid and its salts in a creamy fluid containing a high proportion of solids which then becomes a major route for the excretion of potassium as well as calcium and magnesium.

It has also been determined that this species possesses 30 or 40 multi-lobed glands in the mucous membrane covering the back of the tongue, each lobule containing scores of tightly packed tubules which secrete a concentrated solution of sodium chloride: these glands are osmoregulators that permit *Crocodylus porosus* to live in strongly saline environments like that of Mungardobolo Creek, even hatchlings being able to survive and grow in sea water.

G. C. Grigg and M. Cairncross determined in 1980 that the blood of saltwater crocodiles has a high oxygen capacity and is able to cope with a large build-up of blood lactate after a dive or a burst of energy, but that it also seems to have a much lower oxygen affinity than the blood of the American alligator.

On New Guinea, the saltwater crocodile allegedly digs a den during the dry season that extends down to the water level of the shrinking lagoons and comprises a series of chambers that each accommodate one or two of these animals (sometimes associated with turtles), interconnected by a series of tunnels. No winter dormancy has been reported among saltwater crocodile populations in northern Australia, however, and by and large this species seems to spend most of its time lying in shallow water, the preferred daytime body temperature being 28–30°C, with a night-time minimum of between 25–27°C.

Saltwater crocodiles seem to be territorial, to judge from the behaviour of animals in crocodile farms, priority being established on a size basis: this behaviour is apparent all the year round, but intensifies during the breeding season. Juveniles up to 1 m (3 ft 3 in) in length are accepted by adults, but larger animals will be excluded from breeding areas by their peers, sexual maturity being reached at a length of about 2 m (6 ft 6 in) in the case of females and 3 m (9 ft 9 in) for males, corresponding to an age of 10–15 years. Males therefore grow faster than females and can eventually be distinguished by their proportionately thin bellies and long tails, females being bulkier with shorter tails. All juveniles demonstrate higher growth rates in the wet season than in the dry season (in the case of hatchlings, twice as fast), and will reach a length of 45 cm (18 in) in the first year. Individuals less than 2 m (6½ ft) in length have been observed to gallop when on land, and an example measuring 45 cm was timed at 48.9 kph (30.4 mph) over a very short distance by G. R. Zug of the National Museum of Natural History in Washington in 1974.

Fossil remains of the saltwater crocodile occur in the Plio-Pleistocene of Australia, but the species does not appear to have a long palaeontological history.

Swamp crocodile

Less massive than either the Nile crocodile or the saltwater crocodile, and nowhere near as dangerous to man, the mugger or swamp crocodile (*Crocodylus palustris*) of the Indian subcontinent does not exceed about 5 m (16¼ ft) in length and has a short, broad snout with a concave forehead and no development of bony facial ridges. The dentition includes 13 or 14 pairs of teeth in the maxillary bones and 14–15 pairs in the lower jaw. There are normally four longitudinal rows of dorsal plates running along the back (two each side of the midline, the two inner rows being distinctly broader than the two outer rows), with four large nuchal shields on the nape of the neck, accompanied by a pair of lateral scutes and preceded by four smaller post-occipital scutes immediately behind the head. The population in Ceylon (Sri Lanka), however, has six longitudinal rows of dorsal scutes (all of similar width) and throat scales broadened to give the appearance of collars. These Ceylonese reptiles may represent a separate subspecies, *Crocodylus palustris brevirostris*, which is sometimes alluded to as *Crocodylus palustris kimbula*, considerable taxonomic confusion having arisen because when Franz Werner described *Champse brevirostris* in 1933 he thought that his type specimen came from Africa, whereas it was in fact a Ceylonese mugger; the name *Crocodylus palustris kimbula* was not proposed until three years later, when it was published by P. E. P. Deraniyagala. At least one population of Ceylonese muggers, at Wilapalawewa water hole in Yala National Park, is allegedly of an unusual red colour at certain seasons of the year owing to the fact that the skin is covered in red ostracod eggs.

Seemingly a somewhat timid animal, the adult mugger is of a rather uniform dark colour on its upper surfaces and normally subsists mainly on fish (especially catfish), amphibians, aquatic mammals, small terrestrial mammals and occasionally birds, with large individuals sometimes taking ungulates as large as sambhar (*Cervus unicolor*) or gaur (*Bos gaurus*). It is essentially a freshwater form, preferring lakes, rivers or swamps, but occasionally occurs in brackish coastal marshes, the geographical range extending from Sind and Baluchistan to Assam and (at one time) Burma, with Ceylon marking the southerly limit of its distribution. The lakes and streams in this type of habitat tend to evaporate during the dry season, and muggers allegedly wander extensively on land in search of ponds or rivers still containing water; failing this, it is claimed that they will excavate burrows 8–10 m (26–32½ ft) deep in which to shelter during extremes of summer and winter temperatures. The species is particularly adept at colonising artificial lakes (e.g. village ponds, irrigation reservoirs), and substantial populations of these reptiles occur in Ceylon around the water tanks constructed there between the 5th century BC and the 13th century AD, while Hirlan Lake, a reservoir in Gujarat, supports what is probably the largest concentration of *Crocodylus palustris* still remaining anywhere.

Mating takes place in spring (January to April), and nests are usually dug in sand banks above the water line, often preceded by several trial excavations. About 10–50 eggs, measuring some 60 mm by 45 mm (2½ by 1¾ in), are laid from February to May (some females have been known to breed twice in a season, at 40-day intervals) and covered over with earth and sand, the resulting mound being 1.5–2.15 m (5–7 ft) in diameter and 60–90 cm (2 or 3 ft) high, with a base of twigs and leaves. A mugger's nest is not easy to discern at a casual glance, but the eggs are nonetheless subject to predation by monitor lizards, mongooses, jackals, sloth bears, pigs, and the local native population. The female guards the site during the 50–75 days' incubation period, and one or other parent excavates the clutch when it is due to hatch (the young grunt from within the egg). If the male carries out this task, the female remains in the nearby water to receive her brood when they are delivered by her consort, carrying them carefully in his gular pouch. The parent opening the nest aids hatching by rolling full-term eggs in the jaws to crush the shells, juveniles that have already made their escape attracting attention by vocalising, lifting their heads and twitching their tails until the adult notices them and picks them up for transportation to the waterside.

High nest temperatures apparently produce a preponderance of male hatchlings, as has been demonstrated in the case of the American alligator; presumably, low temperatures result in a largely female brood. Newly emergent young are about 25 cm (10 in) long, weigh 60–100 g (2–3½ oz), and have dark spots on the sides of the body, with dark cross-bands around the tail; they feed mostly on small fish, toads, frogs and insects. As in the case of the Nile crocodile, the juvenile distress call brings adults hurrying to the scene, and the young animals apparently keep in touch with each other by emitting grunting sounds. For the first two years, they will grow at the rate of about 6 cm (2½ in) per month, and attain sexual maturity at the age of six (females) to ten (males) years.

No doubt muggers, like crocodiles in general, will readily eat carrion, and they have been accused of consuming human bodies floating downstream from the burning ghats of India, where the local Hindu population cremate their dead. Perhaps they do, but the evidence seems to be only hearsay, and there is no proof at all that muggers which thereby acquire a taste for human flesh become man-eaters.

Muggers rarely if ever bellow. According to R. and Z. Whitaker in a 1978 report, however, they make 'gurgling growls' during threat displays and mating, the submissive individual raising its head as a gesture of appeasement and emitting a grunt.

Fossil remains of *Crocodylus palustris* are not uncommon in the Indian subcontinent, occurring in the Pleistocene of the Narbada valley, the Siwalik beds, and deposits dating back to the Upper Miocene in Tripura.

American, Orinoco, Cuban and Morelet's crocodiles

Approximately the same size as the mugger, and of a similarly timid disposition, the American crocodile (*Crocodylus acutus*) ranges from southern Florida down through Central America (from southern Sinaloa on the Pacific shore and Tampico on the Caribbean), thence along the northern perimeter of South America to Ecuador and northern Peru in the west and Venezuela in the east, with a probable initial centre of distribution in the West Indies, where it still occurs on Cuba, Jamaica, the Isle of Pines and Hispaniola (pre-Colombian fossils have been found in the Bahamas). Occasional individuals, but not breeding populations, occur on the Tres Marias Islands, 35 miles (56 km) out in the Pacific, and on Trinidad and the Cayman Islands.

The American crocodile has a more limited range of temperature tolerance than the American alligator (in water at a temperature of less than 65°F the animal will sink to the bottom in a torpid state and drown) and even in its heyday, before hunting or habitat destruction reduced its distribution, *Crocodylus acutus* probably never occurred further north in Florida than Sanibel Island on the west coast and West Palm Beach in the east. There were, however, populations living all along the Florida Keys, right down to Key West, although it seems never to have been common on the lower Keys. Elsewhere in its range it is also becoming scarce, and in many areas where it was once fairly abundant it is no longer to be found.

The present distribution of *Crocodylus acutus* and a paucity of fossil remains suggest a Caribbean origin of fairly recent date, but despite the short period of time available and its narrow temperature tolerance this crocodile has nonetheless already passed through the area of strongest caiman influence (northern South America), although it has not colonised the regions populated by *Crocodylus intermedius* (the Orinoco crocodile) or *Melanosuchus niger* (the black caiman); indeed, these three forms occupy contiguous but non-overlapping ranges which have apparently been established as a result of direct competition, since there are no evident physical barriers between them. *Crocodylus acutus* has invaded the Magdalena and similar rivers along the northern coast of South America, and in the Rio Chucunaque of Panama and the Atrato of Colombia it was known to feed on caimans, which in consequence retreated to drainage creeks and lagoons. Subsequently the crocodile population was largely eliminated by hide-hunters, and in the 1950s the caimans had replaced it in all the large rivers of the area where the current is relatively weak.

The American crocodile exhibits a high tolerance of marine environments, and like the saltwater crocodile possesses prominent salt glands on the tongue (20–40 in number) which enable it to regulate the salt content of the blood by excreting hyperosmotic sodium/potassium solutions. T. M. Ellis of Miami

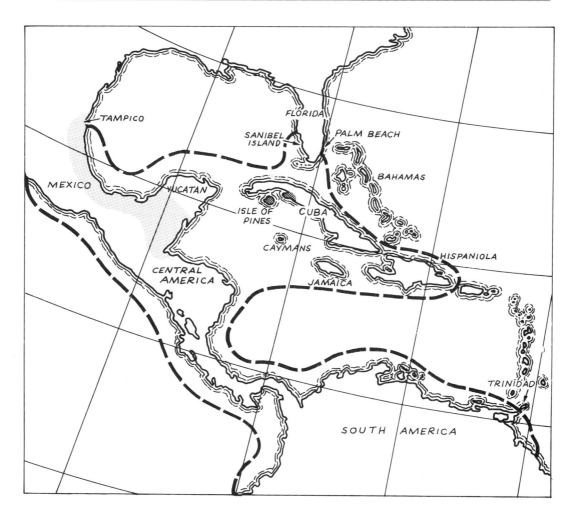

Map 3

The range of the American crocodile (*Crocodylus acutus*) is demarcated by the broken line

 The Cuban crocodile (*Crocodylus rhombifer*) occurs in Cuba and on the Isle of Pines

Morelet's crocodile (*Crocodylus moreleti*) is a Central American species

University determined in 1981 that examples of *Crocodylus acutus* captured in sea water had plasma sodium concentrations similar to those of animals taken from fresh water, and corresponding to those of freshwater reptiles in general. However, a sodium chloride loading of 1 mmole Na/100 g body weight evokes an elevated concentration of sodium in the blood coupled with an apparent reduction in cloacal flow rates.

63

This relatively slender-snouted species will grow to about 5 m (16¼ ft) in length, individuals from the South American region having a markedly narrower muzzle than those from further north; in an area where broad-nosed caimans predominate, a thin snout possibly allows *Crocodylus acutus* to exploit an ecological niche not already pre-empted by the indigenous caimans. The muzzle bears a distinct median ridge extending along up to half its length, and the maxillae accommodate 13–14 pairs of teeth, with 15 pairs in the lower jaw. Four large nuchal plates are usually present, disposed in the form of a square with a smaller pair lateral to the anterior elements, while the dorsal plates along the back are arranged in four to six longitudinal rows, comprising 15 or 16 transverse series. The second and third toes of the front foot are slightly webbed, and in the hindfoot the outer toes are all united by a well-developed membrane. Adult animals are blackish-olive in colour above, with yellowish underparts.

Despite its evident affinity for saltwater or brackish environments, the American crocodile ascends far up the major river systems and is often found in large freshwater lakes. The principal prey seems to be fish, but crabs, birds and small mammals (including dogs) are also taken.

The breeding season is in the northern spring, eggs being laid from mid-March to mid-May, with April the peak time, so that most hatchlings appear in late July or early August—the rainy season. Nests, generally located above beaches among hardwood thickets or shrubs or in mangrove stands, are built up from sand or gravel, usually heaped up into a mound about 30–45 cm (12–18 in) high and 3–3.7 m (10–12 ft) across, with an excavation in the top to accommodate about 35 eggs, each of which is 60–70 mm (2½–2¾ in) long and 40–50 mm (1¾–2 in) wide. Sand is scooped back to cover the eggs, using the hindfeet, and the female will then guard the nest against such would-be intruders as raccoons, black bears, or possibly jaguars. In some areas, where the sand is hard packed, nests will be almost flat, dug down into the firm substratum and then covered with what little loose sand can be scraped up. American crocodiles are shy creatures today, possibly as a result of ruthless hunting, and the female will not defend her nest against a human intruder with any determination, quickly backing off and seeking refuge in nearby water.

When the eggs are ready to hatch after about 85 days' incubation, the nest is opened and the emergent young are carried to the water by the brooding female. They are about 24 cm (9½ in) long and of greenish-grey colour above, usually patterned with blackish cross-bars (often broken up into spots) that number four to five on the body and eight to ten on the tail, although the Cuban population of this species apparently lacks any black markings. The juvenile distress call is voiced by imperilled youngsters and quickly brings adults to their rescue, but older juveniles may be tempted to prey on newly emerged animals under certain circumstances: a 62.8-cm (24.7-in) specimen in Venezuela's Pueblo Viejo dam was found trying to eat a 26.7-cm (10.5-in) specimen, admittedly in an area where food was scarce and the aggressor had in consequence become somewhat emaciated. During the first month of life, hatchlings grow to about 30 cm (1 ft) in length, thereafter adding something like 20 mm (1 in) a month. They have a low sodium intake and drink selectively from the low-salinity brackish-water lenses that accumulate after showers, surviving quite satisfactorily even if opportunities to drink occur only once every week or so. For three or four months they grow rapidly and by October–December, when the dry season begins, they are large enough to tolerate immersion in 35‰ salinity sea water.

At four years of age the species has normally attained 1.2–1.5 m (4–5 ft) in length and begins to employ the adult roar, which in reality is a series of loud hisses, usually expressed with the head high out of the water and the tail arched and waving, this behaviour often being accompanied by jaw-banging. The largest American crocodile whose size has been reliably documented was a specimen 15 ft 2 in (4.62 m) long, with an estimated 6 in (15.2 cm) of its tail missing, that was killed in 1875 by C. E. Jackson and W. T. Hornaday at Arch Creek (this area is now part of north Miami). There is an old record of a 23-ft (7-m) specimen shot in Venezuela, and the American Museum of Natural History in New York has in its collection a skull 72.9 cm (28.7 in) long, suggesting an overall length of about 6 m (20 ft).

Further south still in the western hemisphere, the crocodyline assemblage is represented by the Orinoco crocodile (*Crocodylus intermedius*), a long-snouted species coloured olive above and yellow below that occupies the lower elevations of the Orinoco basin, extending westwards along the Meta River to Colombia. This reptile attains a similar length to the American crocodile (about 5 m/16¼ ft) and, in the opinion of some experts, may be very closely related to the more northern form, perhaps even only a geographical race of *Crocodylus acutus*. The Orinoco crocodile is characterised by a slender and relatively deep snout, devoid of ridges but exhibiting a median elevation, together with a concave profile and an unossified nasal septum; there are 13–14 pairs of maxillary teeth and 15–16 pairs in the lower jaw, the mandibular symphysis extending posteriorly to the level of the sixth, seventh or eighth tooth. American crocodiles also sometimes have snouts equally as slender as those of Orinoco crocodiles, and occasionally possess a concave nasal profile, while the six enlarged nuchal plates of *Crocodylus intermedius* are sometimes matched in *Crocodylus acutus*. The mandibular symphysis in the American crocodile, however, never extends back beyond the fourth or fifth lower teeth, and the Orinoco crocodile is generally regarded as a distinct species, albeit a possible descendant of *Crocodylus acutus*, derived from immigrant American crocodile stock that penetrated as far as the mouth of the Orinoco before evolving into *Crocodylus intermedius* (Figure 8, p. 66).

South America is a caiman stronghold and these broad-snouted forms seem to have effectively filled all the ecological opportunities for crocodiles of this configuration, effectively barring South America to broad-snouted crocodylines. The slender-nosed Orinoco crocodile has obviously been able to exploit a vacant niche for a crocodilian of this sort, and apparently preys principally on fish and capybaras. It is said to seize natives occasionally, but the average-sized adult nowadays is only about 3 m (9 ft 10 in) long, the largest specimen recorded in the 20th century measuring just under 13 ft (4 m). Alexander von Humboldt and Aimé Bonpland, however, claimed to

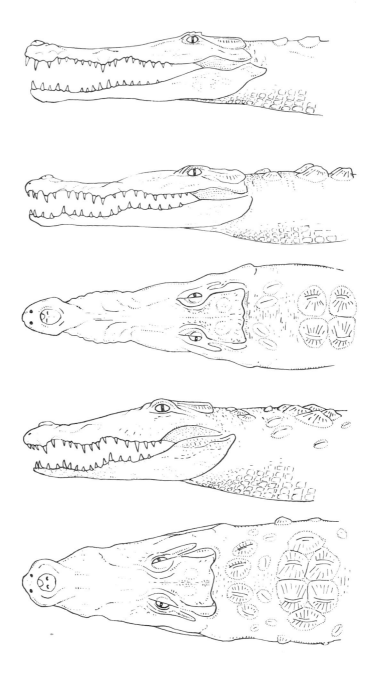

Figure 8 Top, the Orinoco crocodile (*Crocodylus intermedius*); *Centre*, the American crocodile (*Crocodylus acutus*); *Bottom*, the mugger (*Crocodylus palustris*)

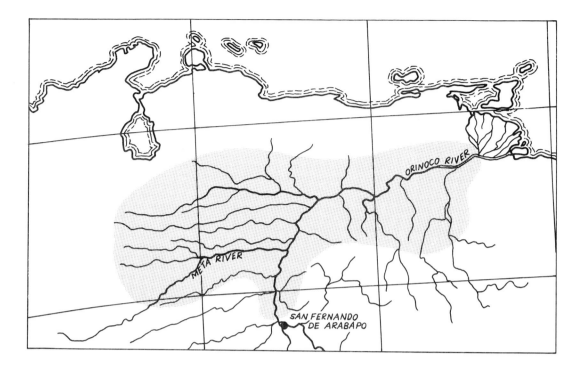

Map 4

The Orinoco and the Meta rivers are the home of the Orinoco crocodile (*Crocodylus intermedius*)

have shot two examples in 1800, while exploring the Orinoco, that measured 22 ft (6.7 m) and 17 ft 2¾ in (5.25 m) respectively, so these reptiles apparently have the potential to achieve a considerable size, quite large enough to represent a real hazard to humans.

The Orinoco crocodile may wander considerable distances overland in the rainy months to find still lakes or pools, and in the dry season favours wide deep rivers (in some areas, such as Arauca and Casanare, it allegedly aestivates during the arid months in water-eroded caves under steep river banks). It apparently excavates a nest in sand banks, well above water level, during January and February, and then covers the clutch of 15–70 eggs in much the same way that the American crocodile does (they are subject to predation by the great tegu, a large teiid lizard, and by the South American black vulture). Hatchlings emerge in late February-late March and are initially protected by the female.

Crocodylus intermedius is declining rapidly owing to hunting, for the skin of this relatively large crocodyline is more saleable than the hide of the caimans that are the other crocodilians resident in the Orinoco basin (these alligatorine species are not only smaller, but usually have bony platelets in the ventral scales, which reduces the value of the skin). The future of the Orinoco crocodile must be regarded as bleak, and it is likely to remain an enigmatic species since opportunities to observe flourishing wild populations are now almost non-existent. No adequate explanation has been offered for its absence from the Amazon basin: the Orinoco crocodile has never been reported further upstream than a point just beyond San Fernando de Atabapo in Venezuela, close to the mouth of the Rio Guaviare. The Casiquiare channel connects the upper Orinoco with the Rio Negro and hence the Amazon itself, but it seems that this southerly representative of the Crocodylinae never succeeded in finding its way far enough south to take advantage of the link. The Orinoco crocodile is essentially a freshwater form, although isolated specimens have been reported from Trinidad, having apparently arrived from the mouth of the Orinoco by passive migration, perhaps on drifting rafts of vegetation.

Two rather smaller crocodyline species are also to be found in the New World. The Cuban crocodile (*Crocodylus rhombifer*) exhibits a number of peculiarities which suggest that it is possibly the most terrestrial of all living crocodilians. Attaining a length of about 3.5 m (11½ ft), and of yellow and black coloration patterned with small spots, the Cuban crocodile has a relatively short, broad snout and is a powerfully muscled reptile protected by well-developed dermal armour, including greatly enlarged scales shielding the legs and six rows of plates along the back merging anteriorly with a series of six large nuchal plates. The brain case region of the skull is deep, and bears a pair of prominent bony crests formed by the squamosal bones extending back from just behind and above the eyes (which have darkly pigmented irises) to the outer corners of the cranial table. The forehead has a convex configuration and the muzzle bears a pair of converging bony ridges that almost meet towards the end of the snout. The dentition is inclined somewhat outwards, with 13–14 pairs of maxillary teeth and 15 pairs in the lower jaw, the mandibular symphysis extending back to the fifth inferior tooth.

With strong legs and short-toed feet possessing only vestigial webbing, the Cuban crocodile is very much at home on land. It adopts the 'high walk' more frequently than any other species and often squats on its haunches with the forelimbs fully extended, a posture sometimes adopted by other crocodiles, but usually only when they are immature.

The nesting habits of *Crocodylus rhombifer* are obscure, but a hole is allegedly dug in the ground to receive the eggs, which measure about 75 mm by 50 mm (3 in by 2 in), and is then covered over. Juveniles emit a characteristic crocodilian distress call when threatened (a repetitive series of high-pitched grunts), which brings adults hastening to the scene.

As its common name implies, *Crocodylus rhombifer* is essentially restricted to the island of Cuba, with a small population in the Lanier swamp on the nearby Isle of Pines. Even on Cuba itself, the reptile is seemingly limited to Las

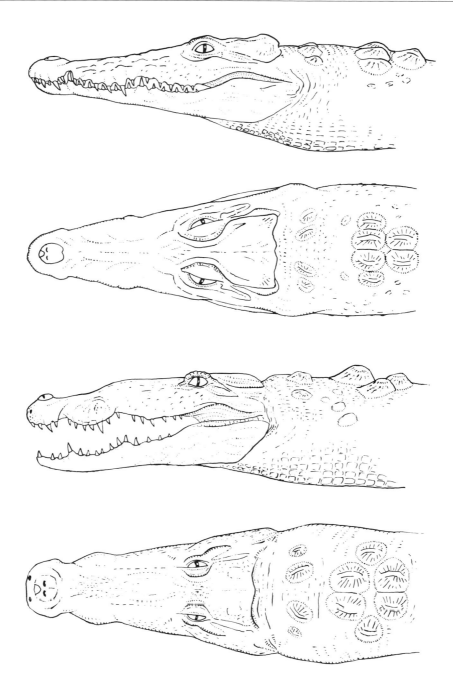

Figure 9 Top, the Cuban crocodile (*Crocodylus rhombifer*); *Bottom,* Morelet's crocodile (*Crocodylus moreleti*)

Villas province (formerly Santa Clara province) on the island's south coast towards its western extremity. In former days the Cuban crocodile was apparently an inhabitant of freshwater marshes, thus avoiding competition with the Cuban population of American crocodiles, which preferred saline environments. Subsequently, hide-hunters decimated the local stock of *Crocodylus acutus*, with the result that *Crocodylus rhombifer*, whose extensively armoured skin is not of much use to the hide trade, moved into coastal areas formerly occupied by the larger American crocodile. There has been some interbreeding between *Crocodylus rhombifer* and *Crocodylus acutus* in Cuba, and hunters claim that a proportion of the crocodiles on the island are *mixturados* or *cruzados*, hybrids intermediate in character between the Cuban crocodile and the American crocodile.

The present-day prey of the Cuban crocodile is uncertain, although fish, waterfowl, pigs and turtles have been suggested, along with dogs (occasionally perhaps) and people. Children might be vulnerable, and this reptile is certainly a particularly aggressive crocodile, but few Cuban crocodiles nowadays exceed 2 m (6 or 7 ft) in length and animals of this size are not likely to tackle a full-grown man.

In the past the Cuban crocodile evidently had a wider range, fossil remains occurring at Casimbas de Jatibonico and Ciego Montero in conjunction with the bones of extinct ground sloths (huge relatives of the sluggish arboreal edentates found in Central and South America today, that were far too large to climb trees like their modern cousins). The Cuban crocodile has very prominent 'canine' teeth combined with a rather stout, blunt posterior dentition well adapted for crushing bones, and in ages past *Crocodylus rhombifer* may well have preyed extensively on these massive ground sloths, some of whose fossilised bones bear the unmistakable marks of crocodile teeth.

Crocodilian remains from the Cuban Pleistocene seemingly indicate crocodiles of the *Crocodylus rhombifer* type, but evincing slightly less specialisation than the living representatives of this population, and it is believed that some fragmentary skull bones (described as *Crocodylus antillensis*) from Cueva Lamas, a cave on the north Cuban coast near Santa Fé, in La Habana province, may represent the actual ancestors of the living Cuban crocodile.

Still occupying a fairly extensive range in Central America is Morelet's crocodile (*Crocodylus moreleti*), which occurs along the Caribbean coast of Mexico from Tampico in the north to Campeche in the south, and thence across the base of the Yucatan peninsula to Belize and northern Guatemala. Attaining a length of about 3 m (9¾ ft), this freshwater species is primarily a denizen of savannah ponds and lakes, also occurring in rainforest areas although avoiding large permanently flowing rivers and seeking out swampy stretches of marshland or intermittent streams that break up into isolated pools in the dry season. Morelet's crocodile, named after P. M. A. Morelet, a 19th-century biological collector who secured the first example of this form to be scientifically examined, is a rather generalised species of crocodyline. Adults are a drab, uniform greyish-brown colour on their upper surfaces,

3   A crocodile can move with lightning speed when lungeing at its prey. This Nile crocodile was evidently not quite quick enough

4   Although often seen and photographed sprawled in repose, crocodiles can move with the belly clear of the ground, using the 'high walk' (*Crocodylus niloticus*)

5 The function of gaping, with the jaws widely open, is uncertain (*Crocodylus niloticus*)

6 The Nile crocodile (*Crocodylus niloticus*) is a typical, relatively unspecialised, modern crocodile

pale-coloured ventrally, and exhibit a longitudinal median elevation along the top of the muzzle that extends almost to the nostrils. There are 13–14 teeth in the maxillary bone, which in old individuals is unusual in having an angulate swelling to accommodate the tenth upper tooth rather than the rounded eminence more usual in crocodiles; the dentition of the lower jaw comprises 15 pairs of teeth.

The breeding habits of Morelet's crocodile are poorly known, although captive females in Atlanta Zoological Park, Georgia, built nests of peat moss, dry leaves and gravel in May–July, using their back feet (while facing away from the site) to pile these materials into a mound. Eggs (20–45 in a clutch) were laid early in July, a back foot being used first to position them as they appeared at the rate of one per minute and finally to cover the nest. R. H. Hunt reported in 1975 and 1980 seeing full-term clutches being dug out by the female, which then carried the 17-cm (7-in) hatchlings in her mouth to the water (sometimes assisted by the male), where the yellow-and-black spotted juveniles were subsequently to be observed basking on the back of the resident dominant male. One of them, however, was devoured by a female, although adults normally leave hatchlings alone. Juveniles over a year old are chased away by brooding females, and a 68-cm (27-in) specimen in whose jaws Hunt taped a vocalising hatchling was pursued and killed by a female guarding a brood of 37 youngsters. Newly emerged youngsters catch roaches and crickets at the water's edge, but the natural food of fully grown Morelet's crocodiles is open to speculation: presumably fish, amphibians, reptiles, waterbirds and small mammals make up a large part of the diet; the more posterior teeth of *Crocodylus moreleti* are relatively stout and blunt, suggesting adaptation to the crushing of turtle shells or possibly molluscs. In some ways, this species resembles the brown caiman (*Caiman crocodilus fuscus*), and the two forms do in fact favour similar habitats, although the crocodyline species is restricted to the Caribbean coast of Central America and the alligatorine form to the Pacific drainage of the region: they appear to be mutually exclusive, and do not mix.

At one time, Morelet's crocodile was regarded as something of a myth, the original specimen, collected from Lake Flores in what was then Yucatan but is now Guatemala, having been shipped from Cuba in conjunction with some molluscs which had been collected on the island but wrongly labelled as having originated, like the crocodile, on the mainland. When it was discovered many years later that the molluscs had been assigned an incorrect locality identification, it was assumed that the crocodile had also been inaccurately attributed to Yucatan: presumably it came, like the molluscs, from Cuba, and if so merely constituted an example of the Cuban crocodile (*Crocodylus rhombifer*). In 1924, K. P. Schmidt of Chicago's Field Museum satisfactorily demonstrated the separate identity of *Crocodylus moreleti*, the more easily because the species was at that time exceedingly abundant around Belize City, literally hundreds of these reptiles being visible from the causeway that linked the town with the nearby higher ground. Regrettably, Morelet's crocodile is now quite rare, hide-hunting and habitat destruction having decimated its numbers. The northern and southern populations seemingly exhibit significant distinguishing characteristics, but some reports of this species may be attributed to misidentified American crocodiles.

New Guinea, Mindoro and Siamese crocodiles

Across the Pacific Ocean, in southeast Asia and on the Philippine Islands, the Sulu archipelago and New Guinea, there is a group of three freshwater crocodiles which may represent surviving populations of what was once a single widespread form that occupied the rainforest swamps, sluggishly flowing streams and shaded pools of the western Pacific region before the first waves of human immigrants arrived. The best known of this probably quite closely related trio is the New Guinea crocodile (*Crocodylus novaeguineae*). To begin with, it was assumed that only a single species of crocodile, the saltwater crocodile (*Crocodylus porosus*), inhabited the island. Two small crocodile skulls obtained in New Guinea by anthropologist George A. Dorsey in 1908 eventually found their way to the Field Museum in Chicago, but excited very little interest, the assumption being that they were simply immature examples of the saltwater crocodile. There were nonetheless persistent rumours of a small freshwater crocodile on the island, and in 1928 Dorsey's two skulls were described by K. P. Schmidt as a new species, *Crocodylus novae-guineae* (the hyphen was later dropped). Not until the mid-1930s was Schmidt able to convince the doubters (or at any rate most of them) that his new species was valid, and it required an expedition to New Guinea to do it: over 20 skulls and four complete specimens (two of them shot by expedition members) were collected by Schmidt from the Sepik River area. Subsequently, W. T. Neill spent some time in the region during 1943–44 and made extensive observations on this hitherto obscure species.

Attaining a length of about 3 m ($9\frac{3}{4}$ ft), the New Guinea crocodile is a dull greyish reptile, with 13–14 pairs of maxillary teeth and 15 pairs of lower teeth. There are eight longitudinal rows of dorsal plates, with two pairs of large nuchal plates flanked by two small subsidiary scutes, and the anterior part of the tail bears a double crest of 20 paired projecting scales, merging posteriorly to form a single terminal series of 18 median scutes. Two major populations are present, a northern and a southern, distinguished by features of squamation and cranial morphology, and separated geographically by the Owen Stanley mountains, the Central mountains and the Wandammen mountains. The species occurs throughout Irian Jaya as well as in Papua New Guinea, and has been introduced to the Palau Islands, but its alleged occurrence on the Aru Islands was stated in 1986 by C. A. Ross of the Smithsonian Institution to have been based on an immature specimen of the saltwater crocodile.

The favoured habitat of this species seems to be small overgrown lakes and deep sluggishly flowing channels, although at the mouth of the Fly it is found in brackish water. Inland, the New Guinea crocodile has been reported 600 m (1970 ft) above sea level in the upper reaches of the August River (West Sepik). This species rarely basks in direct sunlight, preferring shady spots

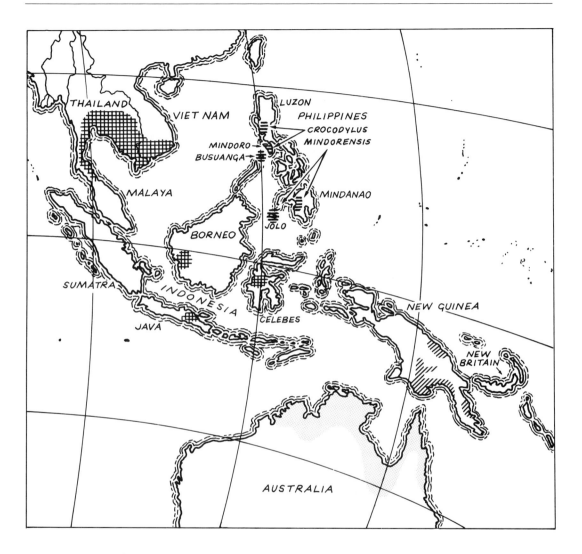

Map 5

Ranges of the freshwater crocodiles of southern Asia and Australasia:

Siamese crocodile (*Crocodylus siamensis*)

Mindoro crocodile (*Crocodylus mindorensis*)

New Guinea crocodile (*Crocodylus novaeguineae*)

Johnston's crocodile (*Crocodylus johnsoni*)

73

when on shore, and spends much of its time in the water, floating with the body at an angle of about 45 degrees to the surface, the head being bent forward on the neck so that the eyes and nostrils are above the water. The animals use their legs to steer themselves while floating in this manner, and display considerable submarine dexterity; for rapid swimming, the tail is the primary means of propulsion, as is customary among crocodilians. Small individuals prefer to stay close inshore, taking advantage of cover provided by emergent vegetation, fallen trees and overhanging branches.

New Guinea crocodiles apparently feed extensively on waterbirds (notably gallinules and coots), as well as fish, amphibians and small reptiles; observing at night, W. C. Neill saw one individual, fortuitously illuminated by an electric light, leap from the water to seize a lizard from a reed. The species seems to be territorial, normally occurring only singly, and becomes sexually mature at eight to ten years of age, at a length of about 1.4 m/4 ft 7 in (females) or 1.5 m/5 ft (males).

The main breeding season is September to December, and D. Jelden claimed in 1985 that along the Sepik the freshwater crocodiles nest two months earlier than *Crocodylus porosus*, before the onset of the rains; like the saltwater crocodiles of this area, however, it is alleged that large females will also nest in the very wet months of January to April. During the mating period, dominant males challenge would-be usurpers by head-slapping on the water, but at other times of the year New Guinea crocodiles seem relatively tolerant of conspecifics, although some degree of social hierarchy is apparently maintained more or less permanently. Nests are approximately 1 m ($3\frac{1}{4}$ ft) wide and 60 cm (2 ft) high, located in shady positions (about 30 per cent of them on floating grass mats), and constructed of scraped-up plant debris (*Pandanus* leaves, sticks, reeds etc.) mixed with mud. Clutches, laid approximately 70 days after mating, comprise 23–45 eggs, each about 75 mm (3 in) long and 50 mm (2 in) in diameter, which are deposited at the top of the nest in a chamber lined with a soft, dry material (grass, leaves, and strips of the bark that falls naturally from curly-bark trees). Internal nest temperatures are about 96°F (35.5°C).

Females guard the nest for 80–90 days while eggs are being incubated, facing up to intruders open-mouthed and hissing, with lashing tail, but usually backing off and scuttling back to the water if a human adversary advances upon them. In the Lake Murray region of Papua New Guinea, about 13 per cent of nests are lost owing to flooding or predation, with some 87 per cent of the nests located on land hatching successfully as opposed to 78 per cent of those on mats (which are probably susceptible to water seepage from below).

Hatchlings are olive-yellow above, whitish below, with five or six blackish cross-bands on the back, broken into rows of spots, and further small rounded dark spots on the flanks which continue along the sides of the tail; the distal two-thirds of the caudal appendage have a brown-hued undersurface, and is encircled by seven or eight blackish broken bands. If threatened, youngsters emit a loud, shrill distress cry that quickly summons adults to the scene.

Initially, hatchling New Guinea crocodiles still possess a residual yolk sac in an unscutellated mid-ventral protuberance, so that for the first two to 14 days they have no need to feed, digestion of the yolk in the small intestine possibly being aided by the maintenance of an unusually high body temperature (around 33.5–34°C). J. W. Lang of Sydney University determined in 1981 that, after the first two weeks of life, the juveniles' temperature falls to around 32°C as normal feeding begins, the body weight being augmented by some 28 per cent during the $2\frac{1}{2}$ months after hatching.

New Guinea crocodiles frequently occur in the same locality as the much larger saltwater crocodile, but because of the disparity in size would not compete for comparable prey. Subadult populations of *Crocodylus porosus* tend to occur in small narrow basins opening off the main streams, and so are separated both from adults of their own species and from the *Crocodylus novaeguineae* population.

Another very similar freshwater crocodile lives further north, in the Philippines, and is regarded by some workers as representing simply a subspecies of the New Guinea crocodile. However, it was first described, on the basis of skulls from Mindoro, as the Mindoro crocodile (*Crocodylus mindorensis*), and the exact status of this form remains essentially unresolved. Its original discoverer was one Joseph B. Steere, who late in the 19th century explored the Catuiran River on Mindoro and succeeded in shooting a specimen of the Mindoro tamarao (*Anoa mindorensis*), a dwarf buffalo previously unknown to science. Steere used flesh from the carcase of this animal as bait for crocodiles and caught a 2.5-m (8-ft) specimen, whose skull was subsequently given to K. P. Schmidt in 1923 when he stopped in Manila on the way back to America from New Guinea. Schmidt was also given three other crocodile skulls, which came from Mindoro, and on this basis he duly described *Crocodylus mindorensis* in 1935, only to find that most other workers regarded it as merely a local variant of the saltwater crocodile.

In fact, the Mindoro crocodile occurs not only on the island from which it takes its common name, but also elsewhere in the Philippines (on Luzon, Mindanao and Busuanga), on Jolo in the Sulu archipelago, and possibly in the Visayan Islands. Its habits are virtually unknown, but it is of modest size, not exceeding 2.5 m (8 ft) in length, and probably lives in freshwater marshes, small lakes, and the tributaries of large rivers in a similar manner to the New Guinea crocodile, constructing a nest in the dry season to receive the eggs.

The third small freshwater crocodile of this region is the Siamese crocodile (*Crocodylus siamensis*), which was first discovered late in the 18th century by French missionaries in Thailand, but also occurs in Kampuchea, south Vietnam, the Malay peninsula (south to the Patani River), Java, Borneo, Celebes, and adjacent small islands (e.g. Bangka). It was described in 1801 by J. G. Schneider from a skull which the missionaries sent back to Europe. Attaining a length of about 3.5 m ($11\frac{1}{2}$ ft), the Siamese crocodile is a smooth-snouted species, but with an elevated bony crest behind each eye that rather resembles the similar feature found in the Cuban crocodile, although considerably smaller in *Crocodylus siamensis*. There are 13–14 teeth in the maxilla, 15 in each mandibular ramus, and the four principal nuchal plates on the back

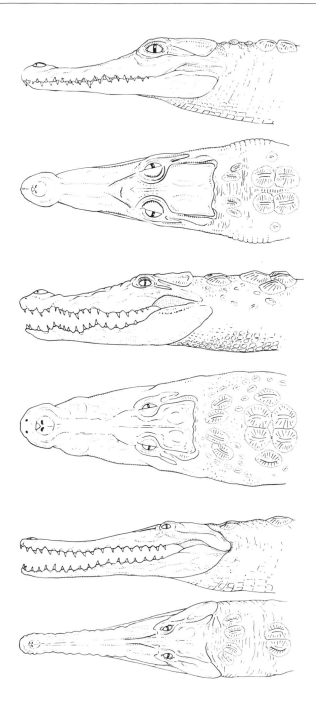

Figure 10   Freshwater crocodiles of south-east Asia and the western Pacific. *Top*, the New Guinea crocodile (*Crocodylus novaeguineae*); *Centre*, the Siamese crocodile (*Crocodylus siamensis*); *Bottom*, Johnston's crocodile (*Crocodylus Johnsoni*)

of the neck are prominently developed (there is an accessory lateral pair). Sexual maturity is reached at 10–12 years.

Occurring principally along rainforest rivers and in adjacent swamps or lagoons, where it feeds mainly on fish, the Siamese crocodile apparently mates in December–March and builds a nest of vegetable debris during April and May. Eggs, laid in clutches of 20–48, are about 75 mm (3 in) long and 50 mm (2 in) in diameter. Hatchlings, measuring approximately 25 cm (10 in), appear in August after an incubation period of about 70 days, vocalising within the eggs when ready to emerge to secure the assistance of the guardian female parent in breaking out of the eggs and leaving the nest. Subadult individuals exhibit four or five dark cross-bars on the body and about ten on the tail, with blackish blotches along the trunk and the anterior third of the tail: these markings are noticeably larger or broader in this species than in the apparently closely related New Guinea and Mindoro crocodiles.

The Siamese crocodile has seemingly been present in southeast Asia for some time, fossil material of Pleistocene age occurring on Java (originally reported as a new species, *Crocodylus ossifragus*, but in reality unquestionable evidence of *Crocodylus siamensis*). The future prospects of the Siamese crocodile in the wild are exceedingly gloomy, however, and in Thailand itself, where it is regarded as edible as well as representing a profitable source of hides, it is virtually extinct in the now dwindling forests that were originally its home, although there are quite substantial breeding stocks in captivity.

Johnston's crocodile

A rather more specialised freshwater crocodile occurs in the southwestern Pacific, where northern Australia is the home of Johnston's crocodile (*Crocodylus johnsoni*), named after Robert A. Johnston, who in the early 1870s collected from Cashmere, on the upper Herbut River, the first specimen of this species to be scientifically studied. When G. Krefft described this form in 1873, it should have had its species name spelt accordingly, but owing to an oversight the Latin name of the species was mis-spelt and the rules of zoological nomenclature should not strictly speaking allow of an amendment. After this confusing start, Johnston's crocodile received little attention from scientists but far too much from hide-hunters, and less than 100 years after its discovery was in some danger of extermination.

It is a small crocodile, large males attaining no more than 2.5 m (8 ft) in length, and occurs only in northern Australia, from the Fitzroy River in the Kimberley region through the Northern Territory to northeast Queensland. The snout is slender, with 14–16 pairs of maxillary teeth (possibly a primitive feature as all other living species of *Crocodylus* have only 13–14 pairs) opposed by 15 pairs of mandibular teeth, and the forehead is flat, but with a low, narrow ridge of convex outline extending forwards to about the mid-point of the muzzle. The largest examples of Johnston's crocodile occur in the McKinlay River, some 130 km (80 miles) southeast of Darwin, where males mature at around 13 or 14 years of age when they are 1.8 m (6 ft) long and grow eventually to 2.50 m (8 ft), while females come into breeding condition at 1.5 m (5 ft) when aged 11 and do not exceed 2.1 m (7 ft). Populations living downstream in the Mckinlay system seem to grow faster, mature at greater overall lengths, and attain a larger size than those upstream, presumably as a result of a better food supply and more favourable habitat, while the Johnston's crocodiles of the Liverpool River, in Arnhem Land, are distinctly on the small side, males not exceeding 1.5 m (5 ft) and females 1.2 m (4 ft). According to a 1982 report by L. E. Taplin of Sydney University, the species possesses lingual salt glands and will tolerate salinities of up to 20‰ in some rivers, notably the Limmen Bight and the Baines, but G. J. W. Webb, S. C. Manolis and G. C. Sack of New South Wales University observed in 1983 that in tidal rivers, such as the Adelaide, *Crocodylus johnsoni* tends to stay upstream of the saltwater crocodile population, moving further and further upriver as the dry season progresses. It would appear that this quite small species is unable to compete with the powerful *Crocodylus porosus*.

Johnston's crocodile is not large enough to represent much of a danger to man, and lives mainly on amphibians, reptiles, birds, small mammals, fish and probably invertebrates. A favourite feeding strategy is to lie in the shallows near the water's edge, snapping sideways at passing prey.

During the dry season (May to October), the Mckinlay breaks up into a series of isolated pools, with communities of Johnston's crocodile occupying the larger, deeper ones, or (in upstream habitats) allegedly taking refuge in burrows. Some 70 per cent of these reptiles return to the pools they used the previous year, and an ability to home in on their chosen domain from nearly 40 km (25 miles) away has been demonstrated. They often travel overland between pools, and the species is evidently very much at home ashore: they not only demonstrate the familiar crocodilian high walk, both at a slow and at a relatively fast pace, but also run (with the body carried lower, so that the hindlimbs are not fully extended, the feet being set down close to the centre line) and gallop—a bounding gait that has been likened to the scamper of a squirrel, with the hindfeet reaching forward ahead of the front feet to strike the ground together and project the animal forward, the main period of no-suspension following the hindleg lift-off and coinciding with extension of the trunk. Galloping may be initiated either from the run or from a static, resting position; it enables this crocodile quickly to surmount obstructions such as logs, rocks or small gullies, and can be amplified if necessary into quite substantial leaps. Although Johnston's crocodiles of all sizes have been seen to gallop, small immature animals do so most frequently.

The nesting season of *Crocodylus johnsoni* begins in the second half of August. Females initially excavate a series of what appear to be trial nests for about two weeks before digging a proper nest, usually in soft sand but occasionally in gravel, clay, or a mixture of sand and humus. The site chosen is usually only a few metres from water, although it may be anything up to 100 m (110 yds) from the lake or river shore, a favourite locality being the sand banks in creek beds. The excavation extends down to a level where the sediment contains about 5 per cent moisture by weight. Laying customarily occurs at night or in the early morning, clutches comprising up to 18 eggs measuring about 66 mm (2½ in) in length, 42 mm (1¾ in) in width and weighing some 68 g (2½ oz). When laying is complete and the nest is covered over, the upper eggs are buried about 20 cm (8 in) from the surface. The older, more massive females seem to nest first, the largest clutches, comprising the biggest eggs, being deposited at the beginning of the breeding season.

Incubation takes 2½–3 months, the internal nest temperature initially being $29 \pm 1.5°C$, rising to as much as 34°C as the embryos approach full term. The hatchlings call from within the nest when they are ready to emerge, and an adult (presumably the female) digs out the eggs, shepherding or carrying the juveniles to the sanctuary of the nearest water, where they will remain together, accompanied by the mother for perhaps a month.

Nest predation by the sand goanna (*Varanus gouldi*) destroys about 55 per cent of nests, while wild pigs account for a further 6 per cent, and a very small number (perhaps 1 per cent) may be accidentally exposed by female crocodiles excavating their own nests adjacent to a pre-existing nest. Early rains at the beginning of the wet season probably flood upwards of 2 per cent of nests, while the rising water table will seep into clutches and drown the embryos as the dry winter months come to an end. The overall mortality is probably around 70 per cent, and 80–90 per cent of hatchlings perish before the end of the ensuing wet season, with birds, large fish and possibly turtles all taking their toll.

West African long-snouted crocodile

Although the reptile fauna of Africa is dominated by the massive and wide-ranging Nile crocodile, the continent is also home to several smaller crocodilians. The West African long-snouted crocodile, or Khinh (*Crocodylus cataphractus*), does not exceed 3 m (9¾ ft) in length and occurs from Senegal to Gabon and the Congo, where it is principally a denizen of rivers, marshes and pools in rainforest areas, although also occurring in more arid savannah country and apparently present in the saltwater lagoons of the Guinea coast and in the Cameroon delta; the extreme easterly limit of its range is reputedly Lake Tanganyika, and in the early 19th century a specimen was obtained from the island of Bioko (Fernando Po), some 30 miles (48 km) off the Cameroon coast. This is a very substantial range, and it seems that in reality two subspecies are present: *Crocodylus cataphractus cataphractus* from Senegal eastwards and south to Angola, and *Crocodylus cataphractus congicus*, occurring only in the Congo region and Zaire.

The snout is extremely slender and devoid of bony ridges, with the nasal bones failing to reach the nostrils. In the maxillary bones there are 13–14 pairs of teeth, opposed by 15–16 pairs in the mandible. The nuchal plates on the back of the neck comprise two pairs that are almost continuous with the six or so rows of scales that make up the dorsal armour of the body: the species name '*cataphractus*', applied to this form by the great pioneer French biologist Baron George Cuvier when he published the first scientific description of it in 1824, means 'clad in armour'.

79

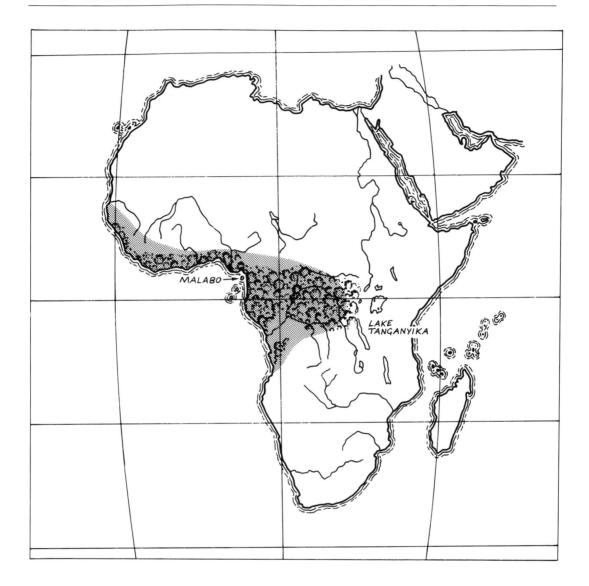

Map 6

The range of the West African long-snouted crocodile (*Crocodylus cataphractus*) corresponds approximately to the African rain forests, although this species has been recorded as far east as Lake Tanganyika. There is also a report of *Crocodylus cataphractus* from the island of Malabo, in the Gulf of Guinea

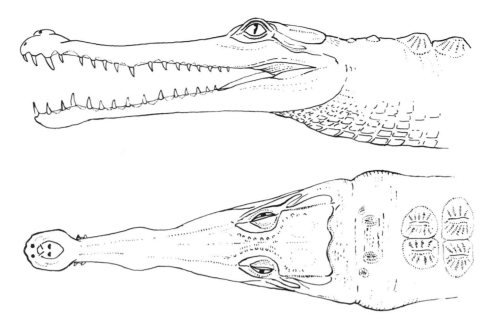

Figure 11   The long-snouted West African crocodile (*Crocodylus cataphractus*)

Adults are of a brownish-yellow ground colour with large black spots, the head being an olive shade spotted with brown (notably along the sides of the lower jaw, which bear four or five dark blotches).

The West African long-snouted crocodile is a rather shy and timid species that appears to live principally on fish, frogs, aquatic reptiles, and waterbirds. W. E. Waitkuwait of Abidjan zoo, Côte d'Ivoire, reported in 1985 that mating begins in February, mound nests of vegetable material being scraped together by the female, using her hindfeet, from March or April onwards at sites a few metres from small rainforest streams on the higher elevations of the banks where there is adequate shady vegetation. The structure is 50–80 cm (20–32 in) high, 1.3–2.2 m (50–90 in) long and 1.2–2 m (40–80 in) wide, 12–30 hard-shelled elliptical eggs being deposited in two layers, the upper ones 25–30 cm (10–12 in) from the top of the nest, the lower tier buried 30–35 cm (12–14 in) down. An incubation temperature of 27.4–34°C is maintained in the egg chamber, with near saturation-point humidity, hatchlings appearing after 90–100 days at the beginning of the rainy season. While river levels are still low, the juveniles float in the shallows or bask on sand banks, but when floods arrive they seek out calm pools and embayments. A few females are still building nests as late as July, but by this time most broods will have hatched and the adults are to be found lying on the banks in a torpid state from which even prodding with a stick will not arouse them (female Nile crocodiles that have gone unfed for a number of weeks while guarding nests are reported to become similarly comatose).

Juvenile individuals of *Crocodylus cataphractus* are relatively short-snouted, the muzzle lengthening proportionately as the animal grows, and are greenish-grey or greenish-yellow in colour, with strong black markings in the form of blotches and cross-bands. They are remarkably agile swimmers, steering themselves dexterously through the water with their legs and feet. The young emit a particularly strong distress cry, described by W. T. Neill as 'a medley of loud squawks, squeaks, honks, and yaps' which, it has been surmised, may have developed because the species is small and possessed of only relatively weak jaws, so that even adults would have a limited capability to see off would-be predators: if the juveniles have an unexpectedly loud distress call, there is perhaps more likelihood that a startled intending assailant will drop its putative victim.

Fossil species

There are thus about a dozen living species of *Crocodylus* (the Mindoro form may be only a subspecies), but although an abundance of fossil remains has been assigned to this genus, its past history is obscure in the extreme. In the early days of biological science, of course, it was not even appreciated that crocodylines and alligatorines belonged not just to separate genera but to separate subfamilies. Much of the fossil material described in the 19th century as appertaining to *Crocodylus* is probably not really referable to this genus at all, but is so fragmentary as to be essentially indeterminate or else has now been lost.

Nevertheless, from the huge volume of fossil specimens identified as *Crocodylus* it is evident that the genus has a very respectable palaeontological pedigree. In the Pleistocene of Madagascar there are remains of large crocodiles that were described as *Crocodylus robustus*. Skulls that are characteristically of very robust proportions (hence the name) have been found, indicating the presence of extremely powerful reptiles on this island a million or so years ago. Occasionally modern crocodile skulls are referred to *Crocodylus robustus*, but these are in reality only unusually well-grown Nile crocodiles of advanced years: the true Madagascan crocodile is now extinct.

Other fossil representatives of *Crocodylus* that have only recently disappeared apparently include *Crocodylus sinhaleyus*, known only from a slender tooth 43 mm ($1\frac{3}{4}$ in) long, with a recurved point, discovered in the Pleistocene of Ceylon, and *Crocodylus nathani*, fragmentary remains of which occur in Queensland, Australia. Fossil crocodile material of Pleistocene age also occurs on the Indonesian island of Celebes, in North America, and on the Indian subcontinent.

Pliocene times found *Crocodylus* proliferating abundantly in southern Asia, where *Crocodylus palaeindicus* and *Crocodylus sivalensis* (a broad-skulled form possibly ancestral to the living mugger) occur in the famous Siwalik fossil beds of northwest India and *Crocodylus greenwoodi* was present in the Jammu hills of Kashmir. Further Pliocene presumed *Crocodylus* remains have been recovered from Australia.

Tracing the line of *Crocodylus* further back still, to Miocene times 25 million years ago, it becomes much more difficult to be sure that fossil crocodile material really should be assigned to *Crocodylus* itself rather than to some other closely related but separate genus. There are, however, extinct species of *Crocodylus* reported from North America, Europe, Africa and southern Asia, and it is quite possible that such a well-adapted genus could have survived unchanged over this substantial span of time. *Crocodylus lloydi*, from the Lower Miocene of Moghara, in Egypt, is regarded by some workers as a likely ancestor of *Crocodylus niloticus*, and has also been reported from fossil deposits in East Africa.

In Egypt, *Crocodylus* has perhaps rather questionably been described from fossil deposits of early Oligocene and late Eocene age, and in North America this genus was extensively described from the Middle Eocene by Edward Drinker Cope and his arch rival, Othniel Charles Marsh, during their pioneer fossil-hunting explorations of the late 19th century. Their Middle Eocene crocodile material came from the Bridger beds, which are exposed in two basins near Fort Bridger, Wyoming: a long way north of any living crocodilian's range in North America, but in Eocene times a warm-temperate zone with palm trees growing in what is now Montana and relatively mild conditions extending as far into the high latitudes as Greenland. The Bridger crocodiles were moderately large and would have had a varied selection of early mammals to prey on: in addition to primitive horses, rhinoceroses and rodents, there were large ungulates (brontotheres, uintatheres) that would have been obvious prospective victims as they came to drink at the streams and lakes where the crocodiles lay in wait. Cope described further species of *Crocodylus* from the Middle Eocene of Utah and the Lower Eocene of New Mexico, but as with the Bridger reptiles it is extremely doubtful if these ancient crocodilians are really referable to the living genus.

A single tooth from the Lower Palaeocene of New Mexico has been attributed to *Crocodylus stavelianus* and another species, *Crocodylus humilis* (referred to this genus by Joseph Leidy as long ago as 1856) is based only on teeth from the Upper Cretaceous of Montana that were of a type subsequently also reported to occur in deposits of similar age in Alberta and Colorado.

On the other side of the Atlantic there were claimed to be species of *Crocodylus* in the Upper Cretaceous of Europe and England, while Sir Richard Owen, the great British palaeontologist of the early 19th century, even described a small fossil crocodilian contained in a Lower Cretaceous slab from Hastings, in Sussex, as *Crocodylus saulii*. This specimen is about 120 million years old, and its assignment to *Crocodylus* must be regarded as erroneous, although understandable in view of the limited knowledge of fossil crocodiles that prevailed in the middle of the 19th century.

African dwarf crocodile

There is one further living genus of crocodylines, an obscure, inoffensive, slow-moving little reptile surviving in the rapidly dwindling rainforests of tropical Africa. *Osteolaemus* does not exceed 2 m (6½ ft) in length and is a markedly primitive form, with strongly developed dermal armour: the nuchal shield comprises two pairs of prominently ridged plates, the anterior ones being very large, while the back is protected by 17–20 bands of scutes each containing six to eight elements, and there are additional isolated bony plates on the lower surface of the body and around the throat. The skull is very short-snouted, with large prominent eyes and only four pairs of anterior upper teeth in the premaxillary bones; there are 12–13 pairs of maxillary teeth, and 14–15 pairs in the lower jaw, with the mandibular symphysis extending back as far as the eighth tooth. A bony septum separates the external nostrils, and the eye has an unusual dark-coloured iris, with a largely osseous upper eyelid.

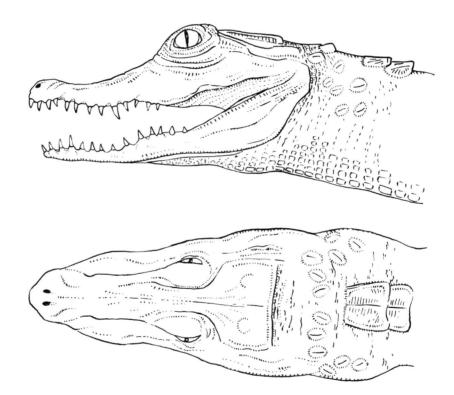

Figure 12   The broad-nosed West African dwarf crocodile (*Osteolaemus tetraspis tetraspis*)

Adults of *Osteolaemus* are a uniform blackish-brown colour above, but parts of the head, tail and back are light brown with black markings. Juveniles are yellowish-brown spotted with black above, black bars occurring on the body and tail, while the ventral armour is black and yellow.

This dwarf genus occurs today as a single species (*Osteolaemus tetraspis*) through West and Central Africa, from Senegal in the west to Zaire in the east (Angola, Benin, Cameroon, Central African Republic, Congo, Gabon, Gambia, Ghana, Guinea, Ivory Coast, Liberia, Nigeria, Senegal, Sierra Leone, Togo, Burkina Faso, Zaire), but its present status in many places is largely unknown. Only in parts of the Central African Republic, Liberia, Nigeria and Senegal are reasonably large populations still believed to exist.

The preferred habitat of *Osteolaemus* seems to be swamps, ponds and small sluggish streams in rainforest areas, with some populations occupying more arid savannah terrain. Major watercourses are avoided, and *Osteolaemus* seems to spend quite a lot of time on land. It does not normally bask in the sun during the heat of the day, and apparently inhabits holes excavated in the banks of streams. The gradual but accelerating retreat of Africa's dense forests, in part a result of climatic change but largely precipitated by human exploitation of natural resources, means that the future of this diminutive crocodilian is decidedly unpromising. The only evidence of the past history of *Osteolaemus* is a subfossil skull discovered in Angola.

The more extensive West African population of this genus comprises the subspecies *Osteolaemus tetraspis tetraspis*, which has a markedly upturned snout and eleven pairs of caudal scales along the top of the tail's anterior third (they then merge to form just a single median crest down the remainder of the tail). The Congo population was at one time believed to represent a separate genus (*Osteoblepharon*), but it is in fact only another subspecies (*Osteolaemus tetraspis osborni*) of even more conservative aspect than the western form: the snout is not upturned, there are 12–14 pairs of anterior caudal scales along the top of the tail immediately behind the pelvis, and the maximum length probably does not exceed 3 ft 9 in (114 cm). One example of this subspecies was reported by C. A. W. Guggisberg to have been found alive in a pit near Lake George, Uganda, the easternmost known occurrence of *Osteolaemus*.

The life history of the African dwarf crocodile is poorly known, but it is apparently a timid, solitary reptile of nocturnal habits and docile temperament. The nest, constructed of vegetation, is some 1.5 m (5 ft) in diameter, and the Ueno zoo, Tokyo, which has succeeded in breeding *Osteolaemus tetraspis tetraspis* in captivity, reported that the ellipsoid eggs measure about 65 by 40 mm (2½ by 1¾ in) and weigh approximately 64 g (2½ oz). Initially a yellowish colour owing to the yolk being visible through the smooth translucent shell, they are laid in clutches of 10–17, and begin to exhibit a narrow white band one day after laying that subsquently expands to give the whole egg a milky-white appearance, even occluding the transparent ends (which are initially pinkish, later becoming dark red). Incubation requires about 115 days, and hatching may take up to a week even after the first crack appears in the shell. Newly emerged hatchlings are 20–30 cm (8–12 in) long, weigh from 42 to just over 50 g (about 1¾ oz), and frequently employ the crocodilian 'gallop' when they wish to move with optimum speed.

Relationships and evolutionary history

The inter-relationships of the living crocodyline species were investigated by L. D. Densmore of Louisiana State University in 1983, using sequencing techniques on 18 different proteins. By combining the results of immunological procedures that compared albumins and transferrins, assessments of the divergence in haemoglobins determined by tryptic peptide 'fingerprints', and genetic distance matrices on blood proteins (coded for by 21 presumed gene loci) that were generated by electrophoretic methods, Densmore determined that the living species of *Crocodylus* are all very closely related and probably originated relatively recently. *Crocodylus acutus*, *Crocodylus rhombifer*, *Crocodylus porosus* and *Crocodylus siamensis* appear to form an allied group, as do *Crocodylus intermedius* and *Crocodylus johnsoni*; *Crocodylus cataphractus* occupies a notably isolated position, and so to a lesser extent does *Crocodylus moreleti*, while *Crocodylus palustris* seemingly has affinities with the New Guinea crocodile (*Crocodylus novaeguineae*). The Nile crocodile (*Crocodylus niloticus*) emerges as a very generalised intermediate species.

Although *Crocodylus* itself cannot certainly be identified further back than the Miocene, and the fossil history of the primitive little *Osteolaemus* is quite unknown, the subfamily Crocodylinae nonetheless traces back into the age of dinosaurs.

At least one rather specialised genus that formerly inhabited Australia seems to have become extinct only comparatively recently: *Pallimnarchus* appears to have been an unusually heavily armoured form, with keeled dorsal scutes and flattened lateral and (possibly) ventral scales, that lived in Queensland during the Pleistocene. A clue to how crocodiles found their way into Australia was unearthed in 1987, when a joint team of scientists from New Zealand and the United States reported that they had found remains of a crocodile among a collection of 40-million-year-old fossils excavated on Seymour Island, in the Antarctic. The southern continents, formerly joined up to form the Gondwanaland supercontinent, were by this time becoming quite well separated and this particular individual was probably part of a surviving, isolated Antarctic population being slowly frozen out of existence, but a southerly migration route from Africa to Australia obviously looks a possibility. Further to the north in the Pacific region, fragmentary fossil remains indicate the presence of crocodiles in the Pleistocene of Japan.

Not until the history of the subfamily is traced back to Miocene times, however, are crocodylines differing significantly from living forms to be found. *Charactosuchus fieldsi*, from the Upper Miocene of Colombia, seems to be an early example of crocodyline adaptation to occupy the ecological niche for a slender-snouted crocodile in South America. The known material is scrappy, consisting primarily of lower-jaw fragments, but even from this tantalisingly sparse evidence it can be deduced that *Charactosuchus* had a long, slim muzzle adapted in all probability for catching fish, with the mandible strengthened by an extensive symphysis extending back to the level of the eleventh lower tooth. A lower-jaw fragment from the Middle Eocene of

7   Nile crocodiles will scavenge carcasses as well as hunting fresh prey

8   Nile crocodile eggs require about 12 weeks' incubation before the young are ready to emerge

9 The largest and most dangerous of all living crocodiles is the saltwater crocodile (*Crocodylus porosus*)

10 The mugger or marsh crocodile (*Crocodylus palustris*) is not usually regarded as dangerous to man

Jamaica in which the symphysis reaches the tenth mandibular tooth may represent an earlier species of this genus (*Charactosuchus kugleri*), and isolated specimens (including long, fluted teeth) from the Pliocene of Florida and the Miocene/Pliocene of South Carolina are also possibly attributable to *Charactosuchus*. Elsewhere in the Miocene world, there is evidence of eusuchian crocodiles living in Japan, and also in South Australia, indicating that the southern fringes of the antipodean continent enjoyed a moist subtropical climate conducive to crocodilian life, which is today restricted to its extreme northern boundary.

Oxysdonsaurus is based on a single striated tooth from the Oligocene of Parana, Argentina, which was described in 1890 and is of little significance beyond demonstrating the probable presence of a crocodyline well to the south of the subfamily's present neotropical range. At least one distinctive genus was, however, present in the New World Eocene, alongside the numerous problematical species of 'Crocodylus' described by the arch rivals Marsh and Cope. *Brachyuranochampsa* is known from two species (*Brachyuranochampsa eversolei* and *Brachyuranochampsa zangerli*), both from Wyoming. This genus had a skull about 40 cm (15¾ in) long and is distinguished by a fifth premaxillary tooth of unusual size, the almost equal development of the fourth and fifth maxillary teeth (the pseudo-canines), and the presence of a V-shaped ridge between the eyes.

Approximately contemporaneous with *Brachyuranochampsa* is *Asiatosuchus*, an Old World crocodyline of considerable geographical range that occurred from China, Mongolia and Kazakhstan westwards to Germany and Spain. This apparently rather generalized early crocodyline first appears in the Palaeocene and survived until the end of the Eocene, a span of perhaps 20 million years, so despite its eventual extinction *Asiatosuchus* must have been a very successful reptile for a substantial period of time.

Orthogenysuchus olseni is one distinct species that has been described from the rich plethora of crocodilian material present in the Eocene strata of Wyoming, this form being based on a skull some 334 mm (13 in) long from the Lower Eocene level. The snout is relatively elongate but nonetheless quite broad, with widely separated eye sockets: it is, in fact, a fairly typical, rather generalised crocodyline type.

Megadontosuchus arduini is an Old World Eocene species of the subfamily, represented by a rather slender-snouted skull found at Verona, Italy, which possessed only four pairs of premaxillary teeth at the front of the upper jaw rather than the five pairs that are usually present in the Crocodylinae, while *Kentisuchus toliapicus*, from the early Eocene of southern England, was another slender-snouted form (possibly closely related to *Megadontosuchus*) whose lower jaw accommodated 20 pairs of teeth and was strengthened by an elongate mandibular symphysis. A presumed crocodyline from the Eocene of China, *Lianghusuchus hengyangensis*, is represented only by upper-jaw fragments and possibly some vertebrae, scutes, and a quadratojugal bone from the jaw articulation.

The Palaeocene, the first geological period that followed the end of the age of reptiles, found the world strangely transformed: after over 160 million years of reptilian domination the scaly giants of the Mesozoic era were gone and their place had been taken by mammals, mostly as yet only small and primitive although with a few precociously large species. Climatically, too, there were changes, with a more seasonal weather pattern replacing the almost universally warm, equable conditions under which the dinosaurs had flourished. Crocodiles nonetheless prospered, although, with only relatively small prey upon which to feed, they were not so large as the giants that had evolved in competition with the now extinct dinosaurs.

One genus, *Leidyosuchus* from North America, actually spans the transition from the age of reptiles (the Mesozoic) to the age of mammals (the Cenozoic), occurring in the Upper Cretaceous of Alberta, Montana and Wyoming, the Palaeocene of Alberta, Saskatchewan, Montana, Colorado, North Dakota and New Mexico, and even surviving as late as the Eocene in Wyoming. Large specimens of *Leidyosuchus* had a rather elongate, triangular-shaped skull about 35 cm (14 in) long. The forelimbs were proportionately rather elongate for a crocodyline, and the dermal armour comprised heavy overlapping scutes. In the lower dentition, the third tooth is nearly as large as the canine-like fourth member of the series, this pair of fangs being accommodated in a broad upper-jaw crocodyline notch at the junction of the premaxillary and maxillary bones.

Two of the Cretaceous species of this genus (*Leidyosuchus canadensis*, *Leidyosuchus gilmorei*) occur in the Oldman formation of the Red Deer River valley, Alberta, which was laid down some 10 million years before the end of the age of reptiles, so *Leidyosuchus* had become a well-established denizen of the marshes and floodplain forests which in those times covered this part of Canada while giant dinosaurs flourished in the region. A long, narrow inland sea effectively bisected North America during the Cretaceous period, extending from what is now the Gulf of Mexico to the northwestern Arctic. Although this tongue of oceanic water was gradually withdrawing, Alberta, Montana, Wyoming and the Dakotas were still on the western shores of a substantial body of water. *Leidyosuchus* continued to hold its own with the last of the dinosaurs in this area during the closing stages of the Cretaceous period, and in Palaeocene times was to be found in North Dakota, associated with an abundant turtle population whose shells ranged in width from 7 to 50 cm (3 to 20 in). Many of these fossil turtle shells show puncture wounds, often with evidence of peripheral healing. It seems likely that *Leidyosuchus* preyed on them, capturing these aquatic chelonians by grasping the rear part of the shell between the sharp anterior dentition, then tossing the victim back for crushing between the posterior teeth. Evidently a considerable number of turtles slipped from the crocodile's jaws during this transference from the front to the back of the mouth, and so succeeded in escaping.

Fragmentary remains of other early Cenozoic crocodylines are known from Patagonia (*Necrosuchus*), Kazakhstan (*Manracosuchus*) and New Mexico (*Navajosuchus* and the curious *Akanthosuchus*, a heavily armoured genus with dermal scutes bearing either a sharp elongate spike or else a broad, crescentic blade-like excrescence). These extinct species from the beginning of the age of mammals were, however, pygmies compared with the gigantic members of the subfamily that had evolved in North America when the great Cretaceous reptiles were at the zenith of their spectacular careers.

With herbivorous dinosaurs 30 or 40 ft (9–12 m) long available as prospective prey, it is not perhaps surprising that, in addition to large flesh-eating dinosaurs (such as *Tyrannosaurus*) waiting to slay them, there were monstrous crocodiles perhaps 15 m (50 ft) in length lurking in the ancient rivers and lakes ready to seize any unwary dinosaurian plant-eater that braved the dangerous waters.

Deinosuchus was first described from the Judith River formation of Montana, a late Cretaceous deposit laid down about 70 million years ago. Published as *Deinosuchus hatcheri* (in honour of the famous American fossil-hunter John Bell Hatcher, who worked as a collector for Marsh), the material initially recovered was fragmentary and consisted only of vertebrae, ribs, a pubic bone from the pelvis, and dermal scutes. It was, however, of extraordinary size, and the discoverer of this crocodilian giant, W. J. Holland, director of the Carnegie Museum in Pittsburgh, appropriately endowed it with a scientific name which means great (or terrible) crocodile.

Subsequently, more remains of *Deinosuchus* were found in the Upper Cretaceous of Texas, this material comprising skull and lower-jaw bones as well as a vertebra, a scapula, and some of this huge creature's armour plates. The Texas animal was named *Deinosuchus riograndensis*, and had a lower jaw 2 m (6½ ft) long. In large modern crocodiles there is a fairly constant ratio of 1 ft (30 cm) total length per 1 in (2.5 cm) of tooth row in the lower jaw. Using this formula, it was possible to work out that *Deinosuchus* measured about 50 ft (15 m) in length. A reptile of such proportions rivalled *Tyrannosaurus* in size and might well have been even bigger, so that the largest known terrestrial carnivore was in fact a crocodile, just as today's largest terrestrial carnivore is the saltwater crocodile. Various isolated teeth, vertebrae, jaw bones and dermal scutes probably attributable to *Deinosuchus* have been reported from Upper Cretaceous rocks in North American localities as scattered as Georgia, Delaware and North Carolina, so giant crocodiles must have been widespread on this continent as the age of reptiles drew to a close.

Although no complete skeleton of *Deinosuchus* has been discovered, the available material demonstrates that this formidable reptile had robustly proportioned teeth, vertebrae that were each 30 cm (12 in) in length, and powerfully constructed limbs, with very heavy protective scales shielding the body and tail. A plaster reconstruction of the skull has been prepared but is largely speculative, based essentially on the skull of a modern crocodile since relatively few skull bones of *Deinosuchus* are known. It does, however, give a remarkable impression of the sheer size attained by this monster, which presumably preyed on the contemporary dinosaurs living in swamps and floodplains along the shores of the Cretaceous inland sea that traversed North America. The duck-billed dinosaurs (hadrosaurs) were once cited as a likely prey for *Deinosuchus* because these large bipedal reptiles with flattened duck-like muzzles and, in many cases, curious skull crests of uncertain function were thought to be semi-aquatic. There is evidence that they may instead have spent most or even all of their time on land, supposed swimming adaptations (webbed forefeet, laterally flattened tails) being either artefacts of fossilisation or misinterpretations of their structural adaptations.

Whatever the reality of the hadrosaurs' way of life, they doubtless came at least occasionally to the water's edge where *Deinosuchus* lay in wait, and probably did provide the giant Cretaceous crocodile with a convenient meal. No doubt other dinosaurs that wandered injudiciously within its reach met a similar fate, and corpses washed down watercourses would presumably have been efficiently scavenged. The sight of a 50-ft *Deinosuchus*, with its teeth fastened in the dead body of a hadrosaur, spinning in the water to tear a limb off the carcase would have been an awe-inspiring sight.

To emphasise the infinitely more temperate climate in which the Cretaceous world basked, a long-snouted crocodyline (*Aigialosuchus*) lived in what is now southern Sweden about 75 million years ago, and even as the Cretaceous period drew to a close there was still a representative of the subfamily to be found in the Transylvanian region (*Allodaposuchus*), although the evidence for its presence comprises only the back of a skull, two vertebrae, a pelvic bone and a femur.

A number of early, bizarrely specialised fossil eusuchians that have no obvious close ancestors or descendants have been assigned to separate families of their own. *Stomatosuchus*, the principal genus of the Stomatosuchidae, comes from the Baharija beds of Egypt, a Lower Cenomanian deposit laid down about 80 million years ago. The skull of this strange reptile was some 2 m (6½ ft) in length, so it must have been a very large crocodile, but one whose habits were wildly different from those of any living form. The muzzle was broad, flat and parallel-sided, with mandibular rami united anteriorly in a notably weak symphysis. All the teeth are missing from the only known skull, but it would seem that in the upper jaw they were small, even-sized and closely set, accommodated in separate alveoli at the front but in a groove posteriorly. The lower jaw may have had no teeth at all, and exhibits a curious external process that possibly supported a sac-like receptacle for holding a catch of fish. Certainly *Stomatosuchus* gives every indication of having been a sluggish creature that spent most of its time in the water: the eye sockets are set close together well to the rear of the skull and are upwardly directed, as befits a lethargic bottom-dweller that spent most of its life lying on a lake floor. Although some post-cranial bones of this genus have been discovered, they are too fragmentary for any deductions to be made concerning the structure of its body, limbs or tail.

Possibly allied to *Stomatosuchus*, and assigned to the same family, are *Chiayusuchus*, based on an incomplete fossil tooth from the Upper Cretaceous of northwest China, and (perhaps a more likely inclusion) *Stromerosuchus*, represented by two poorly preserved mid-caudal vertebrae from the Baharija beds that look as if they came from a crocodile of *Stomatosuchus*-like proportions. The Baharija fauna also included a rather less outlandish crocodile, which has been described as *Aegyptosuchus* on the basis of assorted skull and jaw fragments, with doubtfully associated teeth and vertebrae. This species, usually assigned to its own family, the Aegyptosuchidae, had a skull with a flat, broad roof terminating in elongate posterior corners, the surface of the bone bearing a series of fine grooves rather than the more typical crocodilian sculpture, while the teeth (if they really belong to *Aegyptosuchus*) are markedly recurved.

In northern Argentina, the Upper Cretaceous deposits of Salta province have yielded the remains of a small, slender-snouted crocodile that had procoelous vertebrae and was presumably a eusuchian, although the only known material is too fragmentary for the palatal structure to be discerned. Known as *Dolichochampsa*, this reptile had long, slender, fluted, sharp-pointed teeth which in the front part of the jaws projected laterally. The body and limbs were slenderly proportioned, and the vertebral zygapophysial articular facets were obliquely or sub-horizontally orientated, indicating that swimming was accomplished primarily by lateral undulations of the body, very much as in living crocodilians. Evidently *Dolichochampsa* spent most of its time in the water, where it must have been an agile swimmer and apparently lived mostly on small fish. It has no known close relatives and is best regarded as representing a family of its own, the Dolichochampsidae.

More closely allied to living eusuchians, and indeed usually included in the Crocodylidae, although as a separate subfamily, is a series of enigmatic and poorly known reptiles with remarkable and highly distinctive dentition. Their so-called ziphodont ('saw-edged') teeth are laterally compressed with serrations down both the front and the back edges of the crown so that, when the jaws closed, the tooth rows met in a shearing manner. This type of dentition is characteristic of carnivorous dinosaurs and it seems that these crocodiles may have been primarily terrestrial in their habits: their skulls are deep, with laterally directed orbits (not what would be expected in a primarily water-dwelling reptile), the limbs were relatively long, the toes bore rather hoof-like claws more suitable for movement on land than for swimming, and the tail was rounded in section instead of having flattened sides. It is perhaps significant that this group flourished from the late Cretaceous through the Palaeocene and Eocene periods, the interval in geological time when dinosaurs became extinct and mammals acquired a dominant position among terrestrial vertebrates. In the early post-Mesozoic world there were no large mammalian carnivores, and it is not at all surprising to find that the crocodiles, which alone of the so-called ruling reptiles had survived the great extinctions of the late Cretaceous, immediately evolved a predominantly terrestrial group to fill the vacant ecological niche for a large predator.

Pristichampsus is the most widely reported of these specialised eusuchians that seemingly abandoned the water to hunt on land, and the subfamily is consequently known as the Pristichampsinae. Unfortunately, the remains of *Pristichampsus* are in the main fragmentary or, when more comprehensive, have not been described in adequate detail. However, the principal species, *Pristichampsus rollinati*, measuring about 2 m ($6\frac{1}{2}$ ft) and with a rather long, narrow snout, is claimed to occur at numerous Eocene localities in France, Germany, Italy and Spain, some of these fossil remains having been originally published under different names (e.g. *Weigeltisuchus geiseltalensis*, *Boverisuchus magnifrons*, *Crocodylus bolcensis*).

A second species of this genus, *Pristichampsus vorax*, occurs in the Eocene of North America and seems to have been a rather larger form than its European counterpart, with a slightly wider and shorter snout and 16 pairs of maxillary teeth (instead of the 13 pairs present in *Pristichampsus rollinati*). *Pristichampsus* also allegedly occurs in China, and a tooth from Wyoming may indicate that this curiously specialised eusuchian first appeared as far back as the Upper Cretaceous.

Planocrania is a pristichampsine genus from the Palaeocene of China which is known from relatively well-preserved skull material that displays the involvement of the pterygoid bones in the construction of the secondary palate and confirms the eusuchian affinities of the subfamily. *Planocrania* has a particularly deep, laterally compressed skull, with 11–16 pairs of maxillary teeth and 13–15 dentary teeth, the lower jaw possessing a surprisingly short symphysis for what was presumably an active terrestrial hunter.

The pristichampsines seem not to have persisted very long once large mammalian carnivorous forms had had time to evolve, and they apparently died out in Europe and North America after the Eocene. In Australia, however, the characteristic serrated teeth of these crocodiles have been found in deposits of Pliocene or Pleistocene age, and skull material (described as *Quinkana fortirostrum*) indicating a crocodile about 3 m (9¾ ft) long with a

Figure 13 *Quinkana*, a pristichampsine from the Pleistocene of Queensland, Australia. *Inset*, the serrated ziphodont tooth of a pristichampsine in side view (*left*) to show the backward curvature, and anterior view (*right*), demonstrating the concave inner face

rather short but notably deep muzzle and elongate dental alveoli that presumably accommodated laterally compressed teeth has turned up in strata laid down in eastern Queensland as recently as the late Pleistocene. (The name *Quinkana* is derived from the aboriginal name for a spirit — a Quinkan — that is associated with crocodiles at one of the rock-art sites in the southeast of Queensland's Cape York peninsula.)

Did pristichampsines continue to survive in this remote continent, cut off by sea from the rest of the world since 45 million years ago? Before the arrival of man on the island continent, the fauna of Australia comprised a bizarre selection of marsupials that included giant wombats and enormous kangaroos, but no placental carnivores. With plenty of large prey animals and no competition from advanced mammalian predators, pristichampsine crocodiles might well have prospered in Australia as essentially terrestrial hunters until comparatively recent times, when the huge marsupials became extinct — partly, perhaps, owing to climatic change, but probably largely as a result of over-kill by immigrant human agency. It may be significant that a huge monitor lizard, the 15-ft (4.5-m) *Megalania*, is known to have been prospering in Australia during the Pleistocene. The earliest Cenozoic animal life of the continent is poorly known, but somewhere in this vast and now arid land there may still be undiscovered fossil evidence of pristichampsine crocodiles surviving almost down to the present day.

4.

Alligators and caimans: alternative evolutionary lines

The subfamily Alligatorinae includes not only the genus *Alligator* itself, with two living species (one in North America and one in China), but also the exclusively South American caimans, which today comprise three genera (*Caiman, Melanosuchus* and *Paleosuchus*) that embrace five species and half a dozen or so subspecies. The American and Chinese alligators are the only modern crocodilians that live exclusively outside the tropical zone, ranging as far north as the 40th parallel. South of the equator, the caimans extend the range of crocodilians by a similar extent, occurring down to latitude 40 degrees South, but despite this capacity to tolerate relatively inclement winter temperatures the alligatorines do not seem to have been especially successful in competition with other crocodilians.

At one time alligatorines were quite widespread in Europe, but they had become extinct there by the Pliocene and the subfamily never did establish itself in Africa or Australasia, although a fossil form (*Diplocynodon*) has been reported from North Africa. The western hemisphere has been their main stronghold, and so well entrenched were the caimans in South America that broad-snouted crocodylines, abundant elsewhere in the tropical region, seem to have been unable to penetrate the Amazon basin. It might be supposed that *Alligator* itself would have found its way into South America at some time during the last 30 million years, but this broad-snouted genus, like the similarly proportioned crocodyline species, probably found the indigenous caimans too well established. Evidence from comparative protein analysis suggests that the Alligatorinae separated from the Crocodylinae some time during the late Cretaceous or early in the Cenozoic, with the caimans and the true alligators diverging almost immediately afterwards.

Modern alligatorines are distinguished by having all the lower teeth accommodated in sockets in the upper jaw when the mouth is closed, whereas in the Crocodylinae there is only a notch in the side of the muzzle to receive the enlarged canine-like fourth lower tooth, which is therefore still exposed while the mouth is shut. Sometimes this distinction is not very clear cut, and in some individual alligator skulls the outer wall of the upper-jaw socket for the enlarged lower 'canine' seems to have disappeared.

American alligator

The American alligator (*Alligator mississipiensis*) was first scientifically described by F. M. Daudin, a celebrated 18th/19th-century French naturalist, who formally promulgated its Latin name at a meeting of the French Academy of Science on '26 Frimaire, An X' of the Revolutionary calendar — in reality 17 December 1801. The spelling '*mississipiensis*' follows the then current practice of spelling the name Mississippi, but some modern authors have amended it to accord with today's spelling conventions. This is a large reptile, running to about 6 m (19½ ft) in length, with webbed front toes and about 20 pairs of teeth present in both jaws. Adults are a dark greenish-black above, with yellowish underparts, only four nuchal plates being present to protect the back of the neck, while the widest rows of scutes on the back each comprise eight elements.

The life habits of the American alligator are better known than those of any other species of crocodilian, essentially because this powerful reptile ranges widely across the southeastern United States, on the doorstep of an abundance of scholarly observers. When European colonists first spread across North America, the alligator of this continent occurred across a much more extensive territory than it does today, and in Pleistocene times, half a million or so years ago, it reached as far north as Maryland. After the glaciations of the Pleistocene, the less favourable climate caused the American alligator to withdraw southwards, but European settlers found it still well established from what later became eastern Texas through southern Arkansas, Missouri, Alabama and Georgia to the eastern regions of the Carolinas and even up into the southeastern tip of Virginia, where there was once a boggy wilderness some 10 miles (16 km) wide and 30 miles (48 km) long that extended down into North Carolina above Albemarle Sound and was known appropriately as Dismal Swamp. Since colonial days much of this area has been drained, while the indigenous trees (mostly cedar and cypress) fell to the axes of timber company logging gangs: it is many years since Dismal Swamp last harboured an alligator population. Another marshy alligator-infested area, Great Alligator Dismal Swamp (more recently simply Alligator Swamp) lay further to the south, entirely within North Carolina, and originally extended for 40 miles (64 km) along the Atlantic seaboard with a width of up to 20 miles (32 km).

The eastern shores of the United States reflect in an astonishing way the sea-level changes that have occurred since the Cretaceous period, nearly 70 million years ago. At that time, when dinosaurs still roamed the continent and the ocean extended across the centre of North America to the arctic regions, dividing the land in two, the waves of an embryo Atlantic washed much

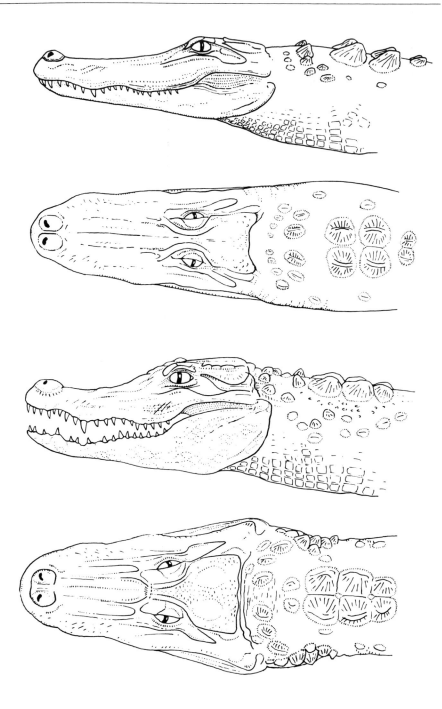

Figure 14 *Top*, the American alligator (*Alligator mississipiensis*); *Bottom*, the Chinese alligator (*Alligator sinensis*)

higher up against the coastline of what is now the Carolinas, Georgia and Florida. The distribution of the American alligator was to be greatly influenced by this marine incursion. After the Cretaceous period, sea levels fell, the interior seaway formerly linking the Gulf of Mexico with the Arctic drained dry, and on the eastern seaboard the Atlantic fell back to leave the former ocean bed exposed as a low-lying coastal plain, with freshwater swamps fronted by rows of dunes. This area persisted until modern times and has become known as the Coastal Plain. Along this marshy tract the American alligator made its home. The old Cretaceous shore is marked by the so-called Fall Line, which runs approxmately through Columbus, Macon and Augusta in Georgia, Columbia and Camden in South Carolina, and thence northwards via Richmond, Washington, Baltimore, Wilmington and Philadelphia to Trenton. Many of these cities grew up at the head of navigation on the local rivers, the Fall Line being marked by waterfalls or rapids, with beyond them the old Cretaceous continental margin, known as the Piedmont Plateau.

The northward range of the American alligator in recent times seems to be demarcated by the 15°F (−9.4°C) isotherm of average annual minimum temperature, and to a slightly lesser extent by the 45°F (7.2°C) isotherm for average January temperature. Up the Mississippi valley, the alligator seems originally to have reached the Arkansas River, some 300 miles (480 km) from the Mississippi delta, but beyond this point the winters become too cold for these reptiles to tolerate; reports of alligators occurring in southwestern Tennessee are of somewhat dubious veracity. A particularly severe cold spell would decimate alligator populations near the northern extreme of the creature's range, and after the very bitter winter of 1779/80 large numbers of dead alligators were reported along the shores of the Big Black River by a Captain Matthew Phelps (recounted in Anthony Haswell's book *Memoirs and Adventures of Captain Matthew Phelps*, published in 1802).

West of the Mississippi the alligator's range was probably limited by aridity almost as much as by winter temperatures. Although reptiles are far better adapted to a terrestrial life than amphibians and have no need to return to water for breeding, modern crocodiles are nonetheless semi-aquatic creatures and they depend on rivers and lakes for their prey and seeking refuge in the water from extremes of temperature — excessive heat or cold. Consequently, any river in which alligators live must flow throughout the year, even if there is a local dry season. The upper courses of rivers that drain into the Mississippi from the west usually run dry in summer, and, since winter temperatures in the interior of Texas can be very low, alligators probably occurred no further west than Del Rio, just over 300 miles (480 km) up the Rio Grande.

There is no well-authenticated record of alligators having extended their range southwards into what is now Mexico, and, although they occurred right down through the Florida Keys to Key West, the 20 miles (32 km) of ocean that intervene between Key West and the Marquesas Keys seem to have been a barrier to any further westward extension, although one or two lizards and snakes commonly found on the Florida mainland did succeed in making the crossing.

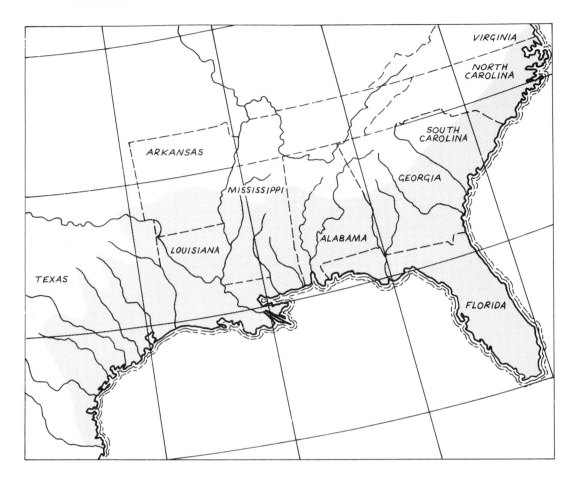

Map 7

The original range of the American alligator (*Alligator mississipiensis*)

During the glacial intervals of the Pleistocene, when temperate climates chilled, ice crept across the continents from the poles, and glaciers spread downwards from high mountain ranges, the southeastern United States would also have experienced a decline in seasonal temperatures. A semi-aquatic reptilian species like the alligator would have been forced back into the only two remaining areas of wetlands at the southern extremity of the continent, the Florida peninsula and the Mississippi delta. W. T. Neill suggested that this did in fact happen to the alligator, and the species was for some time divided into two separate populations without any intercommunication. Presumably, ameliorating conditions subsequently permitted these two disparate groups to rejoin, so that the alligator population was again continuous all along the southeastern border of the United States, but there seems to be a distinction between a Louisiana/Texas population and a

Florida/Georgia/Carolinas population. In the western assemblage, immature animals have light markings of pale yellow hue, while the whitish belly coloration extends high along the sides, neck and head, the lower jaw (and sometimes the upper jaw) exhibiting an especially characteristic white speckling. The eastern population has medium-yellow to deep orange-brown juvenile markings, but these are inconspicuous on the sides of the body, and there is no speckling of the jaws. Neill thought that there could well be grounds for designating two subspecies of *Alligator mississipiensis*, although in adulthood both populations become a similar dark colour (in eastern individuals, this process seemingly proceeds at a faster rate).

The final retreat of the glaciers began about 10,000 years ago, and the resulting mild interglacial may by now have already passed its peak, although human industrial activities could result in some future spurious climatic warming (the controversial 'greenhouse effect'). By the advent of European colonisation, however, the alligator population had probably re-advanced about as far north as temperate winters would permit. Hunting and settlement have since progressively eliminated the alligator from much of its former range, but it nonetheless remains relatively common in southern Louisiana — which still has 4 million acres (1.6 million ha) of alligator habitat, nearly 3 million acres (1.2 million ha) of which is coastal marsh — and in Florida, where it enjoys a substantial measure of protection.

American alligators mate early in the northern spring, as soon as they resume activity after their winter hibernation. Males and females both apparently leave a trail marked by their anal glands at this time, and when a suitor finds a female he will follow his chosen mate for several days, accompanying her from water to land and back to water again until she evinces a readiness to accept his advances, courtship sometimes lasting as long as six weeks. Display activity was reported by Kevin Brewster in 1981, and apparently involves both males and females, although the assertion of territorial priorities by males seems to be a primary factor in the inducement of this behaviour. A common feature is head-slapping, in which the alligator raises its head from the water, arches its tail and lashes it from side to side with increasing vigour, and then slams its chin on the water while at the same time clapping the jaws together. Finally the back is arched and the tail churns the water. Early morning and late afternoon seem to be the most common times for these demonstrations, and the effect (in captive populations at least) is to precipitate the rapid removal of smaller subadults, while at the same time sometimes promoting a ritualistic charge on the part of larger individuals provoked by the display.

When mating is imminent, the members of the alligator pair lie side by side while the male strokes the female's back just forward of the pelvic region with one of his forefeet, accompanying this tactile stimulation with low, soft, fluttering vocalisation. He may also rub his throat across the female's neck, apparently to squeeze out a secretion from his throat glands that serves as an olfactory stimulus to his mate, and the two will circle each other and take turns riding on each other's backs, sometimes submerging to blow bubbles. Occasionally a female will refuse the male's advances with a short, throaty bellow and swim away. Copulation, which probably coincides with ovulation, takes place in shallow water, the female elevating her tail and bending it to one side so that the male can introduce his penis, erected sideways and upwards, into her cloaca. Intromission lasts for from half a minute to around three minutes, and does not require the participants to lie belly to belly as has often been surmised.

The male apparently leaves the female after mating, and early in June she will begin to build a nest for the reception of her eggs. The locality chosen varies according to the nature of the surrounding terrain, but a key requirement seems to be a control of temperature in case the clutch overheats with fatal results to the embryos. A shady spot is therefore desirable, safe from either flooding or excessive drying: dense herbaceous vegetation or a cypress stand are good locations, although alligators do nest successfully at open grassy locations.

At one time, when alligators were common in the southern United States, communal nesting sites were allegedly established, and a survey carried out on Orange Lake, Alachua County, Florida, over a four-year period in 1978–81 showed that the nests were indeed clumped in groups, although, with the general decline in alligator populations, nesting sites are likely to become more isolated.

Working mostly at night, the female scrapes up nesting material with her body and tail from an area with a radius of about 4.75 m (15 ft) around the chosen spot, and then builds it up with her fore- and hind-feet into a heap perhaps 1.25–1.5 m (4–5 ft) across and 5.5–9 m (18–30 ft) high, with the trunk of a convenient tree often providing a useful support. The materials used, which are not, it seems, carried in the animal's mouth, depend on the location: plant materials with the addition of a little soil in a swamp, sand and leaves in a drier location, and freshly uprooted vegetation in marshland. After packing the nest down, the female excavates a hole in the summit of the pile, using one or other of her hindfeet, and then lays in it 30 or more white, oval-shaped eggs about 75 mm (3 in) long and 45 mm (1¾ in), wide, using her back feet to cushion the descent of each egg as it emerges from her vent. Older females apparently lay somewhat larger clutches of up to perhaps 55 eggs.

The top of the nest is then carefully closed, and the female, after crawling across it to re-pack it, begins a lengthy vigil to guard the clutch from predators — perhaps raccoons or black bears, as well as, inevitably, man — lying for many hours at a time with her throat resting on the summit of the nest, possibly to sense the temperature, leaving her post only to lunge open-mouthed and hissing at threatening interlopers, giving token pursuit when they back away. She also temporarily deserts her charges to seek food, and often lies submerged in nearby water still alertly watching the nesting site, ready at a moment's notice to emerge with arched tail, hissing through closed jaws, should an intruder appear. If the interloper persists, the alligator will speedily leave the water at a high walk, inflating its body and hissing or growling open-mouthed before lunging forward with gaping jaws at the offender. A marauding raccoon will be speedily dealt with, but a man commands more cautious behaviour and the alligator may choose to back off, still hissing and probably splashing fiercely in the shallows. When the female returns to the nest, wet and dripping, to resume her recumbent position sprawled partly over the nest, water does of course roll off her scaly flanks on to the nest, but whether this is an intentional effort to cool and dampen the site is unknown. She does not, however, urinate on the nest as is often averred: crocodiles have no urinary bladder.

Development of the eggs seems to proceed at a rate influenced to at least some extent by temperature, but incubation normally takes 60–70 days. Warm conditions, providing the heat is not so excessive as to kill the embryos, will promote quicker hatching than cooler temperatures, and there may be some truth in the belief that the heat generated by the fermentation of rotting vegetable material in the nest helps to offset the cooling effect of night-time temperature fall.

Mark W. J. Ferguson, of Queen's University, Belfast, and Ted Joanen, of the Louisiana Wildlife and Fisheries Commission, demonstrated in 1982 that the sex of hatchling alligators is determined by the internal temperature of the nest during incubation. Heteromorphic sex chromosomes are not present in crocodilians (they lack a reptilian equivalent of the X and Y chromosomes found in man), and when the eggs are laid the embryos are already at a relatively advanced stage of development, so sexual differentiation occurs early in the incubation period, during the second and third weeks. At nest temperatures of less than 30°C, only females are produced, while temperatures of over 34°C result in exclusively male hatchlings, the females being markedly larger and heavier than the males owing to the fact that they carry a much larger abdominal supply of unabsorbed nutrient yolk than the males.

It was found that nests on dry levees had an internal temperature of 34±0.7°C at the periphery and bottom, 35±1°C at the top, and produced 99 per cent male hatchlings; wet-marsh nests had temperatures of 29±1°C and 30±1°C at the same locations and yielded females only; in dry-marsh nests with temperatures of 31±1°C at the periphery and bottom and 34±1°C at the top, females hatched from the periphery and bottom and males from the top. The overall sex ratio of hatchlings proved to be 5:1 in favour of females, marsh nests being more numerous than levee nests, and it would seem that female hatchlings normally remain initially in their marsh habitat while early growth takes place, the corresponding males typically being found in open-water canals.

Females, it will be noted, do not live so long as males, and have a more restricted span of active breeding age. Furthermore, about half the eggs laid by young females are infertile. It is therefore good reproductive strategy to have larger, more numerous female hatchlings, so that the greatest possible number of young females reach breeding maturity at an early age. Were female hatchlings to be as small as their brothers and no more numerous, breeding stocks would be almost totally dominated by older females to the detriment of racial vitality.

Young American alligators emerge from their eggs between late July and early September, the overall hatching success being nearly 60 per cent, with some 16 per cent of nests destroyed by raccoons. The hatchlings can apparently excavate their own way out of the nest if necessary, and some brooding females reputedly seem gradually to lose their protective maternal instinct as the eggs approach full term, simply wandering off back to join the non-breeding alligator population, which includes a number of older females as well as the males.

On the other hand, in September 1978 James A. Kushlan, of the South Florida Research Centre, and Jeffrey C. Simon filmed and photographed a female in the Everglades picking up her eggs one by one when they were due to hatch, rotating her head to the side as she did so, and rolling each egg between her tongue and palate so as gently to crack the shell. After the egg had hatched, she made lateral movements of her head through the water to wash out shell debris, and picked up the juvenile in her gular pouch, in front of the tongue. Rotten eggs, recognised as such by Kushlan and Simon because they were unbanded and discharged an opaque fluid when cracked, were immediately swallowed.

James Kushlan reported in 1973 that the brooding females he observed showed no decline in maternal instinct as the eggs approached full term, and in at least some cases bit open the side of the nest at hatching time. From one nest the female took most of the hatchlings to a nearby pond and canal, where they stayed for several days, but some juveniles remained at the nest site itself and Kushlan removed one of these, squeezing it to elicit a distress call and then setting it down to see if the female came in search of it. The adult quickly left the adjacent water to retrieve her offspring, taking it up in the side of her mouth and then jerking her head to position it in front of her tongue. She then backed into the water with her jaws gaping about 3 cm (1¼ in), finally opening her mouth wide enough for the hatchling to swim out. R. Howard Hunt, of Atlanta Zoological Park, and Myrna E. Watanabe stated in 1982 that females in the Okefenokee swamp vocalise while moving their pods of hatchlings to nursery areas, and would attack (but did not injure) older juveniles which attempted to mix with them.

The embryonic American alligator at the moment of hatching is about 21 cm (8½ in) long, coiled up inside the egg with the head and tail tucked over upon the belly, which is still distended by the remnants of its yolk supply. Using the caruncle on the tip of its snout, the embryo cuts its way through the shell and with or without maternal assistance immediately sets out for the nearest water, possibly in response to the location of the brightest horizon (hence away from the shaded locale of the nest), perhaps also guided in part by a positive response to the presence of humidity. At this stage the juvenile American alligator has plain dullish-white undersurfaces, with greyish-black flanks traversed by up to half-a-dozen irregularly branching whitish bars, black dorsal surfaces that also bear whitish bars, and a black tail ringed by ten or twelve light-toned divisions. There are three indistinct greyish blotches along the side of the lower jaw, and a pale stripe bordered by black extends backwards from the white-coloured eyelid. Within a day or two, the light-hued areas begin to acquire a yellowish colour, save in rare individuals that are vitiligenous (covered in blotches that lack pigmentation), melanistic (abnormally black) or display cinnamon-red dark coloration.

11　Once abundant from Florida through the Caribbean and central America to northern South America, the American crocodile (*Crocodylus acutus*) is now rare throughout most of its range

12　Almost extinct in the wild, the Siamese crocodile (*Crocodylus siamensis*) is fortunately represented by quite substantial captive breeding stocks

13   The slender-snouted Johnston's crocodile (*Crocodylus johnsoni*) of northern Australia is now protected and wild populations have largely recovered their former numbers

For the first few days of its life in the outside world the juvenile can subsist on the remains of its embryonic yolk, but it soon begins to fend for itself, seeking out invertebrate prey or other morsels of food in the bottom sediment by rotating the head so that sense organs along the snout can detect anything edible, which is then seized at the side of the mouth. Young American alligators swim by generating travelling waves along the tail from the pelvic region, the amplitude of which remains constant although the frequency varies with the speed of progression. F. E. Fish determined in 1984 that these waves move back down the tail faster than the animal swims, but alligators have a basically low swimming performance even when small: they are incapable of high speed or rapid acceleration in the water and employ a minimum of effort for prey capture, when possible lunging only at fish or other prey that come within easy range of their jaws, combining lateral undulations of the tail with backward movement of the webbed feet. As the animal grows, there is a progressive decrease in the importance of the feet for locomotion in the water, despite the fact that observations by P. Dodson of the University of Pennsylvania in 1975 showed large alligators to be more dependent on the water than small ones.

Recent hatchlings will happily share any convenient 'gator hole', pond, lake, river or stream with adult alligators, and seem not to suffer much, if at all, from alleged cannibalism on the part of their seniors. Small alligators are, however, vulnerable to a number of predators, notably great blue herons, caracara hawks (in southern Florida), cottonmouth snakes and various large frogs, and if attacked the juvenile alligator will emit a piercing and repetitive distress call that brings any nearby adult on the run to its assistance. The rescuer will not hesitate to press home its charge and bite savagely at the interloper. P. B. Johnson and J. L. Wellington of the Monell Chemical Senses Center, Philadelphia, determined in 1982 that juvenile alligators respond to the cloacal-gland secretions of adults, and also to some extent to the mandibular-gland secretions, but the reason for this is not clear.

Small alligators also grunt, and appear to acquire this habit even before they actually hatch. It takes only a trivial stimulus to promote this reaction, and juveniles will grunt in response to a variety of sounds or disturbances, such as nearby human footfalls, the noise of distant vehicles, and even when surmounting obstacles to their movement or when anticipating food. According to a 1977 report by H. A. Herzog and G. M. Burghardt of the University of Tennessee, the calls of juvenile alligators appear in fact to be graded, from the grunt of mild apprehension to a louder distress cry if definitely threatened and a loud screech if actually seized. Non-distress juvenile grunts in an intermediate frequency range probably serve to determine individual identity and maintain pod cohesion.

Some authorities claim that adults ignore juveniles completely except when the young give a distress call, and others claim that there is a certain amount of juvenile mortality due to cannibalism. The stomachs of some females (notably of those that supposedly have not themselves nested) have been found to contain alligator eggshell, and it appears that these animals may sometimes raid the nests of their own kind, though there is no evidence that a

103

female will eat her own brood, and it is known from James Kushlan's observations that a female alligator will crush and swallow rotten or infertile eggs at the time when her brood is hatching. Cannibalism of adults on subadults (as opposed to juveniles) is widely considered to be a significant factor in the population dynamics of alligators, but a few writers dispute its occurrence, although one fully grown adult has been found with a 45-cm (18-in) juvenile in its stomach, and an analysis of the stomach contents of 350 alligators from lakes in north-central Florida disclosed a number of marking tags that had originally been affixed to juveniles, suggesting that these unfortunate youngsters had been eaten by their peers.

Some offspring possibly remain close to their mother for as long as three years, but at four years of age American alligators are about 1.2 m (4 ft) long and adolescent, wandering about on land (often far from water) as they search for a 'territory' to which they can lay claim and attempting to emulate the adult bellow. Juvenile grunting and distress calls no longer form part of their vocalisation. A length of 2.4–2.7 m (8–9 ft) is achieved after eight years, and the growth rate then begins to slow, with females not normally exceeding 3 m (9¾ ft), although males habitually exceed 3.75 m (12 ft) and may run to nearly 6 m (20 ft): a specimen measuring 17 ft 5 in (5.22 m) was killed at Lake Apopka, Florida, in 1956, and an even larger reptile, with a skull 64 cm (25.2 in) long from snout to occiput, was taken in the Sebastian River, Florida, in 1886.

Young female American alligators achieve reproductive maturity at about five years and at this age probably nest every year if a mate can be found, but older females are likely to breed only at intervals of several years and eventually, in their last 15 or 20 years of life, cease to reproduce altogether, captive specimens rarely living beyond 30 years. Male American alligators probably continue to grow until about their 25th year, but then signs of senility become apparent, although they may survive until approaching 50. Normally there are about 20 pairs of teeth in the upper and lower jaws, which are replaced on a regular basis: a vertical series of replacement teeth is stacked beneath each functional crown, and as the old tooth is shed the new one is revealed, its point having penetrated the pulp cavity of its predecessor. Waves of tooth replacement pass along the jaws, ensuring that old teeth are shed in a systematic manner that leaves no lengthy toothless gaps. Old individuals, however, tend to lose their dentition progressively and eventually become almost destitute of teeth, other indications of senility including cessation of reproductive activity, generally declining vigour, lack of appetite, and some-times the appearance of dorsal lesions that in severe cases even expose the bony scutes of the back. Old or sick individuals also tend to become infested by a green alga that grows on the upper surfaces, limbs and tail, and when very profuse this usually presages death.

Although occasionally seen in brackish estuaries, saltmarshes or even in coastal habitats, the American alligator is primarily a freshwater reptile, often occurring in streams or rivers but apparently preferring the still waters of lagoons or swampy ponds, males showing a distinct preference for open lakes during the spring and summer months. Water temperature is probably the key to its choice of domain, for the creature's optimum body temperature is about 31.5°C (89°F), although alligators will tolerate ambient temperatures substantially lower than this before succumbing to cold. I. L. Brisbin of the Savannah River Ecology Unit, Aiken, South Carolina, reported in 1982 that during an unusually severe winter two male alligators were located in the Par Pond reservoir complex which were so torpid from the cold that calibrated thermistor probes could readily be inserted into their cloacas. One individual, weighing 135 kg (2.7 cwt) and lying 2 m (6½ ft) offshore, survived the winter, but the other, weighing 188 kg (3.7 cwt) and recumbent in the shallows beneath 1.5 cm (¾ in) of ice, succumbed, although whether from cold or from the freezing-over of its breathing hole in the ice is not known. From cloacal-temperature measurements, Brisbin concluded that 4 or 5°C is the lowest temperature which a large alligator can withstand.

Experiments conducted by Edwin H. Colbert of the American Museum of Natural History, C. B. Cowles and C. M. Bogert demonstrated in 1946 that the American alligator's tolerance of excessive heat is strictly limited. Whereas this species will survive temperatures 25° below its optimum temperature, a rise of only 7.5° (to 38°C in the cloaca) is likely to be fatal. Colbert and his colleagues tethered alligators ranging in length from 1.98 m (78 in) to 27.5 cm (11 in) in direct sunlight to determine the physiological reaction of these reptiles to solar heating, with a view to deducing how their extinct relatives, the dinosaurs, would have been affected by changes in Mesozoic temperatures. Small alligators do in fact seem to have a greater tolerance of direct heat from the sun than do large individuals, whose external body regions must have become considerably warmer than 38°C by the time the cloaca reached that temperature (small individuals can radiate away surplus heat more quickly than large ones when placed in the shade owing to their greater relative surface area).

In areas with a marked seasonal water-table fluctuation (e.g. sinkhole country and marshland), the alligator will dig a 'gator hole' — in reality more of a pond — up to 8 m (26 ft) across to a sufficient depth to ensure that it fills with water in the dry season. The animal can then lie in it during the heat of the midsummer days and keep its body temperature down. Some relatively arid areas incorporate a system of sinkhole ponds that form natural refuges for the alligator population, while in shallow, treeless marshes the reptiles will shelter from the midday sun beneath the huge spreading leaves of *Thalia*, an aquatic perennial with stems up to 3 m (9¾ ft) long that grows in extensive colonies. On the other hand, alligators that have made their homes in relatively cold spring-runs, such as those of the Florida or south Georgia limestone country, have a continuous need to warm themselves, even in high summer, and will lie in the shallows around banks or islands to sun their backs. Alligators rarely dive in deep water, their aquatic habitation zone being restricted to the shallows, although a startled reptile will occasionally plunge 6 m (20 ft) or more to a river bed or lake bottom as a means of escape.

E. N. Smith of Texas Tech University determined in 1976 that American alligators, when heated from 15° to 35°C and then cooled back again to 15°C, warmed up faster than they cooled in either air or water, the disparity being greater the larger the individual. The heating and cooling rates in water exceeded those in air, and the heart rate is higher at any given temperature during warming than during cooling. In 1975, while at Baylor University, Texas, Smith had reported that alligators, before engaging in terrestrial basking, lie in the shallows with just their backs exposed, sometimes retreating again to deeper water instead of hauling out. Use is apparently made of conduction heating from the substrate when basking, but the dorsum also heats up rapidly from direct solar radiation. Submerged alligators are evidently able to maintain their body temperature several degrees above the temperature of the water in which they are lying, mature individuals (over 100 kg/1 cwt) probably employing endogenous heat generation. The vascular system seems to play a very important part in heat regulation, with increased blood flow to the skin during warming, and it is noteworthy that there is a higher consumption of oxygen during cooling.

Adult American alligators are primarily predators of other vertebrates, notably such small mammals as the rice rat, the cotton rat, the cotton mouse, the muskrat, the round-tailed water rat, the Norway rat, the marsh rabbit, the swamp rabbit, and the mink, as well as the coypu (introduced by man into the Gulf States from South America), and a number of different birds, among them the pied-billed grebe, the least bittern, the mottled duck, the king rail, the coot, the barred owl, the boat-tailed grackle, the Louisiana heron, the little blue heron, the great white egret, the osprey, the ring-billed gull, the northern pintail, the moorhen, the anhinga, the wood duck, and the cattle egret (at least some of these cited bird species were probably scavenged). Fish that frequently fall victim to alligators include the Florida spotted gar (the long-nosed gar is habitually refused if offered to captive crocodilians and is regarded by the Seminole Indians of the Everglades as poisonous), catfish (other than channel catfish), the gizzard shad and the bowfin, while other regular delicacies in an alligator's diet are amphibians (pig-frogs as both adults and large tadpoles, bull frogs) and a number of reptiles (Florida turtles, yellow-bellied turtles, Florida red-bellied turtles, Florida soft-shelled turtles, banded and broad-banded watersnakes, mud turtles, Gulf saltmarsh snakes, Florida watersnakes, striped swamp snakes, ribbon snakes, and Florida green watersnakes). Very large adult alligators may occasionally take larger mammals, which today means farm livestock, e.g. cattle and their calves, an occasional horse or mule, pigs, and sometimes domestic dogs.

Crayfish and other large invertebrates (snails, giant water bugs) may form a small part of the American alligator's food supply, and this sort of modest-sized prey would obviously be a likely source of nourishment for small juveniles, but claims that the species is a large-scale consumer of insects seems unlikely. The occurrence of insects in substantial quantities in the stomachs of alligators is more likely to be the result of secondary ingestion: spiders, cockroaches, beetles, weevils, flies, moths, ants, aquatic larval forms (dragonfly nymphs etc.), water bugs, back-swimmers and so on have all been reported, but it is probable that these tiny victims had first been eaten by some frog or other small creature that was subsequently devoured by the alligator. The tough chitin of an insect's integument is very resistant to crocodilian digestive juices, and evidence of their presence would persist in the stomach for some time.

Adult male American alligators are large, powerful animals fully capable of dragging a full-grown man into a river, and there is evidence that, when the southeastern United States was first colonised, they were extremely aggressive towards people. René-Robert Cavelier, the Sieur de la Salle, apparently lost his servant, one Dumesnil, in Texas some time in 1685 or 1686 when this unfortunate man was seized by an alligator while attempting to swim across the Colorado, and during the early part of the 19th century it was widely believed across the southeast that negroes were especially vulnerable to the predations of alligators, a number of blacks having been reported taken from river banks and lakeshores. Since it would in those days have been blacks who normally went to draw water or perform similar chores, the relative immunity of whites to attack is not perhaps surprising.

Widespread detestation of alligators led to the wholesale killing of these creatures throughout their range, and by the 19th century the survivors had become extremely wary of man, although children remained at risk, evidently because of their small size: for example, in 1928 a boy was seized and drowned in a pond on a Florida golf course, while his friend, who tried to save him, was severely bitten. Towards the end of the Second World War, concern for the future of the alligator led to protective legislation being passed in various states, and within a few years those populations that were left unmolested by hunters lost their fear of man and began to adopt a threatening attitude towards human interlopers. In 1948 a woman swimming in a large Florida spring-run had both her arms savaged by an alligator which was later killed and found to be a 2.7-m (9-ft) male, and in 1950 a 15-year-old girl found herself seized by the leg when swimming in a creek in southeast Florida, but was fortuitously dragged into her brother's boat.

There were several other cases in the early 1950s of alligators pursuing bathers, and in 1957 a nine-year-old boy vanished in eastern Florida, his mutilated body subsequently being found in a creek. An alligator attack was suspected, and several large specimens discovered in the vicinity were shot, two of them proving to contain allegedly human remains. In 1958 a snorkel-ling swimmer in a central Florida lake was seized by the head and sustained severe lacerations before managing to reach shallow water and safety. The year 1973 brought an actual fatality, when a teenage girl was killed while swimming in a lake, and in 1975 a 3.75-m (12-ft) alligator mauled an experienced wildlife biologist in the Oklawaha River. During 1987 an English visitor to Florida, John Sienesi, had his ankle seized by an alligator while water-skiing on a lake near Daytona Beach; the animal was subsquently caught and killed, and proved to be 2.3 m (7½ ft) long. There is evidence to suggest that American alligators, although normally wary in the wild as a result of persecution, become increasingly hostile to humans in captivity, presumably discovering that in this environment people no longer represent a threat to be feared.

The well-established belief that alligators sweep prey animals on the bank off their feet and into the water with their tails seems to be unproven. No doubt the alligator, in the act of seizing its victim, will thresh about and perhaps give the impression of deliberately using its tail, but a crocodilian's caudal appendage seems to be used almost exclusively as an aid for swimming and to provide a counterweight that helps the animal walk on land.

Like other cold-blooded reptiles living in temperate climes, alligators become inactive during the winter season. They seek a watery refuge from falling temperatures and hibernate (in the broadest sense of the term) for around four months, moving rarely and eating little or nothing. Juveniles are of course small enough to find ready-made protected lairs, but large alligators usually have to make special preparations, althogh some individuals seem to survive without difficulty by simply lying torpid in the still water of large lakes where the water level remains reasonably stable. Many dig out a 'gator hole', making a circular excavation in the peaty bed by pushing the bottom sediment up into a low surrounding parapet. In the Everglades the substratum is shallow and lies on a limestone bed, so 'gator holes' in this region are usually enlarged naturally occurring cavities in the rock. River-dwelling alligators will nose under an overhanging bank to excavate what is loosely described as a den, threshing the body and tail vigorously to drive the snout into the soft soil. In areas where seasonal winter flooding occurs, such as the floodplains of large rivers or slash pine and wiregrass flatwoods with a clayey underpan, W. T. Neill reported that large alligators dig a long horizontal burrow with a small chamber at its farthest extremity, the entrance usually being below the high-water level and not therefore evident until the water table falls in the ensuing dry season. Occasionally an alligator will also dig a hole down into the base of a high bank at an angle of about 45 degrees, sometimes with a horizontal extension.

Both male and female alligators seem to exhibit territoriality to at least some degree. During the springtime mating, these reptiles will occasionally bellow, usually with head and tail arched, apparently to demonstrate to other alligators their whereabouts and indicate that they are in possession of a territory. Bellowing—a series of roars repeated to form a 'segmented' call—is apparently more common after the eggs have been laid, when the sexes have separated, and frequently become a chorus with other alligators answering the initial bellower (before sunrise and in the late morning are common times for this practice). Just before bellowing, male alligators project an infrasonic signal at about 10 Hz through the water which sets up vibrations in the ground or in nearby objects and causes the water to 'dance' around the creature's torso. Females are not known to emit this pre-bellowing signal.

In addition to bellowing, bull alligators seek to exercise their assumed authority over a limited area, or territory, by confronting interlopers with widely gaping jaws, hissing loudly and lunging forward and upward. Although bellowing is accompanied by dilation of the eye's pupil, this may be more an indication of alertness than aggression. American alligators have been seen to bellow or hiss in response to a variety of sounds that are akin to their own vocalisation: the roar of a turbojet aero-engine, plucking on a metal rod, the blowing of a horn, the hammering of a pneumatic drill, the knock of an air compressor, the thump of a jack hammer, or any sound approximating to B flat, two octaves below middle G (57 vibrations/second). E. G. Wever and J. A. Vernon of Princeton University elicited head movement or hissing (but no bellowing) with sounds of up to 341 cycles in research reported during 1957. As subadult alligators grow, they will inevitably seek new territories or habitats more appropriate to their increasing size, and this is likely to bring them into conflict with older animals, although in today's relatively sparse populations this may be much less common than was the case in the alligator's pre-colonial heyday.

Internal parasites of the American alligator include nematodes (in the stomach and small intestine), trematodes, and hemogregarines (in erythrocytes), none of which seem to do any great harm, and pentastomes — a cause of necrosis and haemorrhage in the lungs, where the adults live, nymphs being present in the liver. Leeches (*Placobdella multilineata*) that occur in the mouth and on the upper and lateral body surfaces of alligators are probably vectors for hemogregarines, since when sectioned these leeches were found in 1979 by A. B. Glassman and his colleagues at the University of South Carolina to contain gametocytes and sporozoites, and leech-infested alligators demonstrated significantly higher eosinophil values.

Chinese alligator

Almost on the other side of the world, in eastern Asia, lives the American alligator's closest relative, the Chinese alligator (*Alligator sinensis*). A probable descendant of North American emigrant stock that had crossed into Asia via a land connection in the Behring region, it is only half the size of its powerful New World counterpart, and seems to be a distinctly more primitive alligator, perhaps nearer to the rather conservative caimans than to *Alligator mississipiensis* (although serum protein analysis has demonstrated that *Alligator sinensis* is closely related to its North American cousin at the molecular level).

The snout is very broad and markedly upturned, the dentition numbers 18–19 pairs of teeth in the upper and lower jaws, and the upper eyelid is habitually ossified, as it is in caimans but only infrequently in *Alligator mississipiensis*. There are usually six (occasionally only four), nuchal plates protecting the neck, and the widest rows of scutes on the back comprise six elements; scattered ventral plates are present, but they do not overlap or articulate. The toes of the front feet are not webbed, a feature that tends to confirm the less sophisticated evolutionary level of the Chinese alligator compared with its American relative, the body is stoutly proportioned and the tail rather short. In colour *Alligator sinensis* is greenish-black on its dorsal surfaces, with yellow speckles or streaks on the sides of the head and body, and greyish underparts, juveniles being brightly patterned with yellow and black cross-bands (about five yellow stripes on the body and eight on the tail).

In historical times the Chinese alligator has been restricted to the lower reaches of the Yangtze River where it flows through the provinces of Anhui,

Zhejiang and Jiangsu, flooding annually in summer to turn the bottomlands into marshes, with winding tributaries and deep lakes that make the area an ideal refuge for crocodilians but unsuitable for cultivation and human settlement. Here the Chinese alligator probably preys on the abundant freshwater turtles of the region (which its broad, powerful jaws would be well able to crush), fish, crustaceans, and any available small vertebrates, although with the spread of villages it has also tended to seek out domestic poultry and small dogs in nocturnal foraging expeditions. Nowadays it is active mostly at night, persecution by man having made it shy and wary during the daylight hours, which it spends lying up in the burrows dug for hibernation during the dry winter season (late October to March or April): these excavations are about 30 cm (12 in) in diameter and may extend 3 m (9¾ ft) below the surface, with multiple openings and complex diverticula.

Mating occurs in June and is accompanied by roaring vocalisation, copulation taking place in water. A nest is built from grass and dry leaves in which 10–40 eggs each measuring about 35 by 60 mm (1½ by 2½ in) and weighing on average 44.6 g (1.57 oz) are laid during July and August, with hatchlings emerging after about 70 days' incubation. Newly emerged juveniles are some 21 cm (8½ in) in length, and black in colour with yellow stripes. Sexual maturity is achieved at four or five years, and during growth the skull undergoes a number of proportional changes, including rapid elongation of the muzzle, with broadening and rounding of the snout tip; shortening, widening and flattening of the initially convex table; rounding of the supratemporal fenestrae; diminution in the relative size of the eye sockets; posterior migration of the internal nares; differentiation of the dentition; intensification of sculpture and derived crests; flattening of the occipital surface (which may even become concave); upward warping of both ends of the lower jaw; and a relative increase in the size of the mandibular fenestra. The lifespan can exceed half a century.

Old Chinese records indicate that *Alligator sinensis* sometimes approached 3 m (9¾ ft) in length and was formerly present in the Nine Streams of Jiangxi and along the middle Yangtze River basin as far west as the Yunmeng swamp in Hubei province and the Dongting Hu in Hunan. Fossil material demonstrates its occurrence 6,000 years ago as far north as the Huang Huai plain (36 degrees North), and Middle Pleistocene remains of the Chinese alligator dating back 240,000–280,000 years have been found in Anhwei.

Today the Chinese alligator is not known to exceed 1.5 m (5 ft) in length and it is an endangered species with a restricted range extending from about 30.6 to 31.6 degrees North and 118 to 119.6 degrees East, an area of about 25,000 km² (9650 sq. miles). Formerly it frequented the mudflats of the Yangtze and occupied pools up the ravines cut by its tributaries, living amid the reeds and bamboo of swamps and shorelines, but many of these alligators have now moved from the Jiangnan plain into hill-country pools 100 m or so above sea level on the upper reaches of the rivers Qingyi and Zhanghe, north of the south Anhwei mountains, where they live in terrain covered by thick grasses (*Themeda forskali*, *Imperata arundinacea*, *Setaria viridis*) with numerous small bushes and areas of pine forest. Although probably less

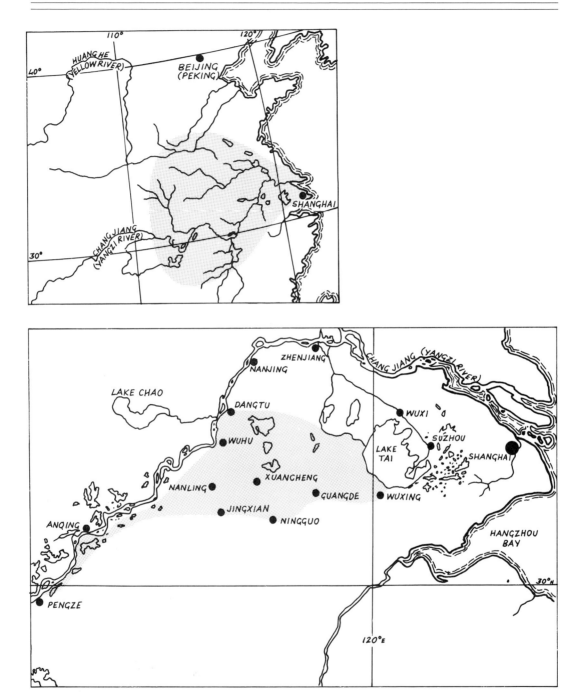

Map 8

The range of the Chinese alligator (*Alligator sinensis*) in historical times (*above*), and the present range of this species (*below*)

111

suitable for alligators than a swamp environment, this area is still only thinly populated and provides an abundance of food for them. Nevertheless, the inexorable advance of agricultural settlement, coupled with widespread persecution by villagers and the use of toxic farm chemicals, means that the prospects of the Chinese alligator in the wild are poor. Severe floods in 1957 drowned many of these alligators in their burrows and the population seems never to have recovered adequately from this setback. As swamps are drained for agriculture and waterways become increasingly polluted, the future of the Chinese alligator must surely be dependent on the preservation of breeding stock in zoos and alligator farms.

Fossil history of alligators

The fossil history of *Alligator* is tantalisingly incomplete. In the Pliocene, central and western North America were acquiring the arid climate typical of the region today, while the east remained relatively well watered. The progenitors of the modern American alligator presumably occupied the southeastern area at this time, but Pliocene beds containing the remains of non-marine vertebrates are few and far between there, and although fragmentary alligator material has been reported it cannot be precisely identified — perhaps *Alligator mississipiensis* itself had already evolved. Further west, in Nevada, there was a separate species, *Alligator mefferdi*, but this form, described on the basis of a well-preserved skull and lower jaw from the Ash Hollow formation, represented the last survivor of an evolutionary line that had persisted in the western portion of the continent since early in the Cenozoic, latterly cut off from the eastern alligator population by dry grasslands spreading outwards in the rain shadow of the rising Rocky mountains. The predecessor of *Alligator mefferdi* was *Alligator thomsoni* from the Middle Miocene of Nebraska, a moderate-sized form possessing a very short, broad skull that suggests affinities with the Chinese alligator. Indeed, it seems likely that *Alligator sinensis* originated from this series of western North American alligators, which probably spread up the Pacific seaboard and across a Miocene-age Behring landbridge into eastern Asia, taking advantage of the mild climate that 20 million years ago extended up the western coast, enabling tropical plants to flourish as far north as Oregon and Washington. The short-skulled, broad-snouted *Alligator luicus* from the Middle Miocene of Shandong province, China, seems to be an intermediate form: the only known remains of this fossil alligator are immature, and there is a strong resemblance to juvenile examples of the living Chinese alligator.

Another Miocene representative of the group, *Alligator mcgrewi* from the Marseland formation (early Miocene) of Nebraska, was remarkable for the great proportionate width of its snout and seems to have been an excessively specialised form, measuring about 2 m (6½ ft), that failed to survive for long: no descendants of this line are known. Over in the east, *Alligator olseni* was the Miocene alligator of the Florida region and differs very little from the living form, attaining much the same size and doubtless being a direct ancestor. The common progenitor of both the eastern and the western branches of North American alligator evolution seems to have been *Alligator prenasalis* from the early Oligocene of South Dakota, but any attempt to trace this line of descent still further back has been unsuccessful.

In the preceding Eocene period there was *Procaimanoidea* with a skull bearing a very distinctive ornamentation and posterior teeth that are blunt, low-crowned and transversely compressed (possibly an adaptation to facilitate the crushing of hard food such as freshwater shellfish). This genus occurs in the Upper Eocene of Utah and the Middle Eocene of Wyoming, and is the best candidate for ancestry of the later North American alligators. Slightly earlier was the curious *Allognathosuchus*, a small or medium-sized form 1.5–3 m (5–9¾ ft) long with a short, broad, blunt-snouted skull, that is present in the Upper Palaeocene and the Lower and Middle Eocene of North America and has additionally been reported from the Lower Eocene of Belgium and the Middle Eocene of Germany (alligators were fairly common in Europe 50 million years ago). *Allognathosuchus* also had blunt, crushing posterior teeth, and again it has been suggested that these may have been for crunching shellfish or perhaps the carapaces of turtles: the evidence is not entirely convincing, however, and the diet of this extinct alligator may not have been very different from that of its present-day cousins. Similarly present on both sides of the Atlantic was *Diplocynodon*, distinguished by the presence of two pairs of upper caniniform teeth: it seems not to have lasted long in North America, occurring there only in the Middle Eocene, but enjoyed some considerable success in Europe, where it ranged from the Middle Eocene to the Middle Pliocene and occurs from Spain to Bulgaria.

In the Lower Eocene of Wyoming and the Upper Palaeocene of Colorado there are remains of *Ceratosuchus*, an alligator with a short, broad snout and curious projections at the rear corners of the skull formed from the squamosal bones, while the Upper Palaeocene of North Dakota has yielded the remains of *Wannaganosuchus*, a small form with a short, pointed rostrum and extensive scutellation. Further back in time still, during the closing stages of the age of dinosaurs, there was an alligator (*Brachychampsa*) in the late Cretaceous of New Mexico, Wyoming and Montana that has been cited as a possible ancestor of *Allognathosuchus*, while the poorly known *Bottosaurus*, represented only by fragmentary fossil material, occurs in the Upper Cretaceous of New Jersey, Colorado, North Carolina and Alberta.

On the Eurasian continent, a very ancient extinct alligator (*Eoalligator*) of moderate size has been found in beds of probable Palaeocene age in Kwangtung, China, and there were alligators (*Sajkanosuchus*) in what is now the Kazak SSR at about the same time, while western Europe supported a varied fauna of rather specialised and sometimes quite large alligators for most of the Cenozoic, *Diplocynodon* being the most widespread. This powerful reptile had an unusually long snout and possessed two pairs of canine-like upper teeth (the fourth and fifth), as well as three pairs of unusually large teeth in the lower jaw (the first, third and fourth). It first appears in the Middle Eocene in both North America and Europe, but quickly died out in the western hemisphere although it may well have originated there, *Prodiplocynodon* from the Upper Cretaceous of Wyoming having been a beast of substantial size with a short, broad triangular-shaped skull nearly 50 cm (20 in) in length. The European representatives of the genus continued to flourish through the Oligocene and Miocene, persisting in Bulgaria as late as the Middle Pliocene, but thereafter deteriorating climatic conditions as the Pleistocene ice age set in brought the European alligator lineage to an end. Several other alligators have been described from Europe, notably *Baryphracta* (a contemporary of *Diplocynodon* in the Middle Eocene of Germany), *Hispanochampsa* from the Lower Oligocene of Spain, with a moderately pointed snout of approximately uniform width, *Eocenosuchus* and *Caimanosuchus* from the Middle Eocene of the famous Geisel valley fossil site in Germany, which had short, triangular skulls suggesting relationship with *Allognathosuchus*, and little *Menatalligator* from the Eocene of France, while at least one species of *Allognathosuchus* itself has been reported from the Middle Eocene of Germany and the Lower Eocene of France.

Although these ancient European alligators normally possess upper-jaw sockets for the lower teeth, in conventional alligatorine fashion, some fossil skulls seemingly have notches instead. *Diplocynodon hantoniensis*, from the Upper Eocene or Lower Oligocene (Headon beds) of Hampshire in southern England is a case in point, this species including material originally described as *Crocodylus hastingsiae* because the maxillary bone is notched instead of socketed.

Caimans

South America has always been the home of the caimans, represented today by *Caiman* itself (a medium-sized genus with two species, the spectacled caiman and the broad-nosed caiman), little *Paleosuchus* (the smooth-fronted caiman, a notably conservative form), and the massive *Melanosuchus* or black caiman, which may reach 4.5 m (14½ ft) in length.

'Caiman' is usually regarded as a Carib Indian word used to describe any crocodile or lizard from the Latin-American region, although there is some evidence that the name is either of African origin (taken to the New World by slaves shipped across the Atlantic) or else was picked up by Portuguese or Spanish adventurers in the East Indies. Zoologists employ the term as a common name for South American alligatorines, which seem to be slightly more primitive than the American and Chinese alligators. For example, in *Alligator* there is a bony septum that longitudinally divides the nasal opening and presumably serves to strengthen the structure of the muzzle. *Caiman* lacks this division, and can also be distinguished by the presence of a greater number of enlarged nuchal plates protecting the back of the neck: eight or more, compared with only four in *Alligator mississipiensis* and four or six in *Alligator sinensis*.

The genus *Caiman* comprises rather small living species of alligatorines, up to around 2.5 m (8 ft) in length, with short, low snouts, eye sockets of approximately circular shape, and rugose upper eyelids bearing small horn-like projections. The upper jaw contains five pairs of premaxillary and 13–18 pairs of maxillary teeth, while the lower jaw has 17–20 teeth each side. The spectacled caiman (*Caiman crocodilus*, sometimes referred to as *Caiman sclerops*) has an astonishingly wide range and is customarily held to comprise up to six subspecies. From southern Mexico this rather narrow-skulled form is present through Central America down into tropical and subtropical South America, its most southerly established occurrence being in the vicinity of Corrientes, near the Paraguay-Argentina border. The 'spectacles' referred to in the common name are bony ridges that surround the eye socket and extend across the top of the muzzle in fanciful similarity to a pair of glasses: their function is possibly to strengthen the skull at areas of maximum stress when the jaws are brought into play to seize and kill prey.

The most northerly subspecies of *Caiman* is *Caiman crocodilus fuscus*, which occurs in southern Mexico (Chiapas and Oaxaca), Guatemala, El Salvador, Nicaragua, the isthmus of Panama, and the northwestern tip of South America (northwest Venezuela, Colombia and Ecuador), with a small artificially introduced population on the Isle of Pines (Cuba). Known as the brown caiman because of the uniformly brown coloration of the subspecies in Mexico and Central America, *Caiman crocodilus fuscus* is a dull olive colour in the Magdalena River of South America, where a population of this subspecies in the Ciénaga Grande which seems to subsist largely on crabs and molluscs has rather blunt-crowned teeth; hatchlings from the Magdalena are marked with black cross-bands that disappear as the creature's coloration darkens with age, although it never attains the rich brown hue of more northerly populations. The brown caiman is rather small, apparently not exceeding 1.5–2 m (5–6 ft) in length, and prefers quiet, open freshwater habitats, although in the mouth of the Magdalena the crab-eating population is found in brackish water, and examples are reported to occur on Gorgona Island, 15 miles (24 km) out in the Pacific off the mouth of the Rio Guapi, having presumably accidentally drifted across the intervening ocean on floating vegetation. Breeding takes place the year round in Colombia, but January to March is the favoured season, 15–30 eggs being deposited in a mound nest where incubation takes 75–80 days.

The first specimen of *Caiman crocodilus fuscus* to be described (in 1868, as *Perosuchus fuscus*, by the celebrated pioneer American palaeontologist Edward Drinker Cope) was notable for the fact that the enlarged fourth lower tooth fitted into an upper-jaw socket on one side of the skull in orthodox alligatorine manner, but was only accommodated in a notch on the other side, a crocodyline feature.

The widest-ranging representative of *Caiman* is *Caiman crocodilus crocodilus*, the common caiman, which occurs east of the Andes from Venezuela, the Guianas and Surinam down through the Amazon basin (Colombia, Ecuador and Brazil), frequenting streams, lakes, swamps and even saltmarsh, but apparently preferring still, open water rather than fast-flowing or shaded aquatic habitats. Its tolerance of salt water is demonstrated by the presence of this caiman on Trinidad, Tobago and other islands off northern South America. In the Venezuelan llanos, a vast low-lying

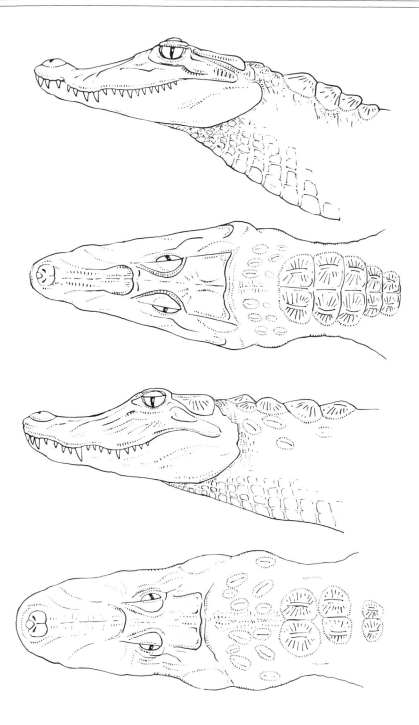

Figure 15 Top, the spectacled caiman (*Caiman crocodilus*); *Bottom*, the broad-nosed caiman (*Caiman latirostris*)

116

savannah region with a markedly seasonal rainfall of 1000–1800 mm (40–70 in) per year and an average temperature of 28°C, the lagoonside populations of these reptiles have a markedly hierarchical structure, based on size, that dominates breeding behaviour. Males are larger than females, and stub-tailed animals that have been injured in fights are common. During the dry season, common caimans avoid overheating by remaining submerged in what water still remains, burrowing into the mud when the terrain becomes really desiccated or seeking a shady refuge in the gallery forest. M. A. Staton and J. R. Dixon of Texas A. & M. University determined in 1975 that at this time of the year the caimans prey largely on armoured catfish (*Hoplosternon*), sometimes taken whole but usually bitten into two or three pieces, the head customarily being severed, as well as eating carrion (especially capybaras, monkeys and armadillos) and indulging in cannibalism on smaller individuals up to 50 cm (20 in) long, but even so deaths caused by malnutrition and disease are common during the dry season. At other times of the year these reptiles will take snails, frogs, small deer and pigs, as well as fish of all sorts which are sometimes herded into the shallows by the bodies and tails of the caimans curving shorewards in the current or are taken in the air as they leap from the water to try and escape the voracious caimans; observers have deduced that common caimans enjoy a 16 per cent successful strike rate when fishing, which compares favourably with the 17 per cent effective kill rate recorded for African lions.

A tail display precedes copulation, which occurs in water and usually occupies about four minutes. At the end of the dry season (from mid-August on) females apparently build a nest largely of vegetable debris and mud, scraped into a pile about 1.2 m (50 in) long, 1 m (40 in) wide and 44 cm (18 in) high, usually in the shade of a thicket or under trees and shrubs, but occasionally in open sunlight. Whitish spherical or elliptical eggs 45–70 mm (1¾–2¾ in) long and 25–40 mm (1–1½ in) wide are laid in clutches of 18–40, 25–30 being the average. If the nests escape the attention of marauding lizards (*Tupinambis*), hatchlings about 15 cm (6 in) long with disproportionately short snouts will emerge after 70–90 days' incubation: they are yellow or yellowish-brown in colour, with half a dozen black cross-bands (frequently discontinuous) on the body and about seven more similar bands on the tail. A dark spot on the posterior region of the lower jaw is virtually the only conspicuous marking on the side of the head. When the clutch reaches full term, the nest is excavated by a parent, reputedly the male, who cracks eggs either in his jaws or with his back feet and tail to release the hatchlings, the female remaining in the water calling for her brood. Grunting is a frequent juvenile habit, and a high-pitched distress cry is emitted by hatchlings if they are endangered: G. A. Romero of Indiana State University reported in 1983 seeing a jabiru stork in the Venezuelan llanos seize a 25-cm (10-in) hatchling that emitted a piercing distress cry, causing its own pod of juveniles and neighbouring pods to swim quickly away echoing the call, while an adult instantly appeared and chased the stork as it attempted to take off, causing it to drop the intended victim (which quickly rejoined its companions). The principal diet of hatchlings seems to be hydrophilid water beetles. Small

117

RIO APAPORIS
CAIMAN

AMAZON

Map 9

Populations of the spectacled caiman (*Caiman crocodilus*), occur as shown:

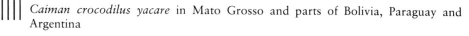 *Caiman crocodilus fuscus* in central America

Caiman crocodilus crocodilus in northern South America

Caiman crocodilus yacare in Mato Grosso and parts of Bolivia, Paraguay and Argentina

The restricted population of *Caiman crocodilus apaporiensis* on the Rio Apaporis

 The broad-nosed caiman (*Caiman latirostris*) occurs in the southeast

14 The American alligator (*Alligator mississipiensis*) is no longer persecuted, and has again become common in some areas

15 The spectacled caiman (*Caiman crocodilus*) ranges from Mexico in the north to Argentina in the south, but the population is divisible into a number of subspecies This example comes from Colombia

16 Despite its fearsome appearance and large size, the gavial (*Gavialis gangeticus*) has only rarely been reported to attack people, and apparently never with predaceous intent

17 The eye of a false gavial (*Tomistoma schlegeli*), which has a yellow-brown iris unique among living crocodiles.

juveniles frequently bask while floating in sunny spots in the flooded forests, and they have been observed lying on the back of the female; individuals up to 60 cm (2 ft) long (about a year old) are still to be seen accompanying their mother.

Adult common caimans are normally olive or yellowish-brown with black cross-bands, but when individuals of this subspecies are chilled the skin colour darkens until the cross-bands are no longer detectable. Melanophores (dark pigment cells in the skin) are presumably responsible for this facility, but its purpose is uncertain, although dark coloration will absorb more heat than reflective lighter hues.

The jacare or southern spectacled caiman (*Caiman crocodilus yacare*) of Mato Grosso is the most southerly of the three major subspecies of *Caiman*, extending southwards down the River Paraguay drainage to Corrientes, and also occurring in southern tributaries of the Amazon in Bolivia and Brazil. Occasional individuals may find themselves marooned on the islands of floating vegetation (water hyacinths and aquatic grasses) that frequently raft down the Paraguay and which may reach Buenos Aires or even Montevideo before disintegrating, depositing the unfortunate caimans well outside their normal range, but it is not conceivable that these castaways ever establish themselves so far south. The jacare may attain 3 m ($9\frac{3}{4}$ ft) in length and has a proportionately rather short snout, its breadth at the level of the first maxillary tooth equalling or exceeding the anterior diameter of the skull table. As in the case of the brown caiman, the jacare occasionally has the enlarged fourth lower tooth accommodated in an upper-jaw notch rather than a socket owing to the breakdown of the lateral wall, this crocodyline trait sometimes appearing on one side of the mouth but not the other. In this subspecies it is also not uncommon to find that the upper-jaw sockets for the lower teeth have perforated right through the top surface of the snout, the premaxillary bones at the end of the nose frequently being penetrated in this way. Distinguishing markings of the jacare include dark black or brown spots on the lower jaw, with one or two similar markings just below the eye.

Jacares may travel considerable distances overland from stream to stream, and seem to seek open-water habitats (lakes, lagoons, marshy savannahs), avoiding salt or brackish environments. Nesting takes place in the rainy season (December to April in Brazil), about 20–40 white, rugose-shelled eggs each measuring approximately 70 by 40 mm ($2\frac{3}{4}$ by $1\frac{1}{2}$ in) and weighing 75–80 g (2.4–2.8 oz) being laid in a mound nest some 1.35 by 1.20 m (53 by 44 in) and 40 cm (16 in) high, constructed of organic material. The female guards the nest to repel potential egg-thieves, which include coatis, the crab-eating fox (*Cerdocyon thous*), tegu lizards (*Tupinambis*) and capuchin monkeys, and when the embryos reach full term after 60-90 days she opens the nest to facilitate the emergence of the hatchlings, which measure about 25 cm (10 in) and weigh 45–55 g (1.6–1.9 oz). Fire ants (*Solenopsis invicta*) will find their way into cracked eggs and kill unhatched embryos as well as attacking newly emerged young, and black hawks (*Buteogallus urubitinga*) also take a substantial toll of very small jacares. The prey of this species includes *Serrasalmus spoilopleura* (a piranha fish) in Corrientes: depletion of jacare stocks has been paralleled by a decline in local game fish, whose larvae are being taken by the unchecked piranha population.

It is possible that at least two other subspecies of *Caiman* are in reality present within what is usually regarded as the range of the jacare: *Caiman crocodilus paraguayensis* has been proposed for the caimans of eastern Paraguay, occurring in the Rio Verde, Rio Monte Lindo, Rio Negro, Rio Confuso and Rio Pilcomayo; and *Caiman crocodilus matogrossiensis* for the caimans of Mato Grosso state, in southern Brazil. In addition, a further subspecies, *Caiman crocodilus medemi*, may be represented by an isolated population of caimans in the Mamore River and the Buena Vista region of eastern Bolivia which are allegedly distinguished principally by their pale brown ground colour and the presence of black spots along the side of the lower jaw.

Another subspecies of *Caiman crocodilus* has been described from a single very restricted region along a 20-km (125-mile) stretch of the upper Rio Apaporis in Colombia, in the northwestern part of the common caiman's range. This caiman has a remarkably slender snout and distinctive coloration comprising blackish spots and vermiculations on a bright yellowish-brown ground. Known appropriately as the Apaporis River caiman, and attaining a length of up to 2 m ($6\frac{1}{2}$ ft), it has been scientifically named *Caiman crocodilus apaporiensis*.

Travellers' tales of doubtful veracity that feature the spectacled caiman are legion, such as the fiction that female jacares will form a protective ring around their hatchlings to fight off cannibalistic males. Despite the frequency with which the species is encountered in zoos and its relative abundance in the wild, however, a great deal still remains to be discovered about its life habits.

In one behavioural experiment, a captive female spectacled caiman was stimulated to display mating behaviour by using a realistic caiman dummy as a 'tease', eliciting responses that included bimodulated grunting and chin-rubbing on the dummy's snout, nuchal region and skull table. Bumping the articular region of the female's jaw with the dummy's snout caused her to evert her lingual (chin) gland while simultaneously making side-to-side movements of the tail, after which she endeavoured to push her snout under the dummy's chin and then sought to crawl forward under the dummy by flattening her body. Normal aggressive behaviour seemed to be inhibited as a result of this stimulation, and the female remained unusually placid for up to a quarter of an hour when subsequently handled.

In 1975 a spectacled caiman in a zoo was observed by Harold A. Herzog of Mars Hill College, North Carolina, opening a nest with her mouth when the eggs were ready to hatch and then using her jaws, hindlegs and tail to crush eggs and release full-term hatchlings, while L. D. Garrick (New York Zoological Society) and R. A. Garrick (New Jersey Medical School) determined in 1978 that the caiman juvenile distress call is given with the mouth either open or closed and yielded a spectrogram consisting of three or four bands between 0.2 and 2.4 kHz. Hatchling *Caiman crocodilus fuscus* were held at the base of the tail at cloacal temperatures ranging from 7° to 36°C and it was found that the lower threshold below which distress calls were not emitted lay at about 9°C, while, although there was no apparent upper temperature threshold for emitting the distress call, vocalisation ceased above 33°C, possibly because it was overriden by gular pulsation. Both the duration of the call and the intercall interval increased as the temperature rose, but the repetition rate was stable between 18° and 33°C and in this temperature range the spectral composition of the calls also remained constant. An extension reflex, which caused the hatchling being held to extend its limbs, lift its head, arch its tail and try to bite the experimenter's hand, was also minimal below 9.9°C. Caiman respiration on land comprises active inspiration and expiration, with full inspiratory breath-holding caused by the glottal sphyncter muscle shutting the glottis. Rhythmic glottal-opening is apparently under the control of the glottal dilator muscle (at the anterior margin of the glottal opening) and the posterior portion of the glottal sphincter muscle. These muscles are responsible for call duration and repetition (which are affected differentially by temperature), but the glottal aperture, which opens moderately at expiration, shapes the spectral composition and is little affected by changing temperature.

The other living species of *Caiman* is the broad-nosed caiman (*Caiman latirostris*), which as its name implies is a notably wide-snouted form, further distinguished by the presence on the muzzle of a longitudinal ridge that exceeds the eye socket in length. Restricted to the eastern part of South America (Argentina, Bolivia, Brazil, Paraguay and Uruguay), outside the Amazon drainage, the broad-nosed caiman ranges from about latitude 5 degrees South down to the Rio de la Plata and incudes two subspecies: *Caiman latirostris latirostris*, up to 2.5 m (8 ft) in length, is present from approximately 6 degrees South to 32 degrees South down the eastern side of Brazil, while the smaller *Caiman latirostris chacoensis*, only 1.8 m (6 ft) long, ranges from 32 degrees South through Entre Rios and Santa Fé northwards to Chaco (hence its name), Formosa and Jujuy.

Rather light-coloured for such a relatively small crocodilian, the broad-nosed caiman has yellowish-green or yellowish-black dorsal surfaces, fading laterally towards the yellow-hued belly. An exceptionally wary species, it favours marshes, swamps, lagoons or small streams with dense aquatic vegetation, including coastal mangroves and other brackish or saline environments. Broad-nosed caimans forage principally at night, feeding largely on snails, crabs and crustaceans, although large individuals will take small vertebrates. Nesting takes place in August–January in Brazil, and rather later (January–March) further south in Uruguay and Argentina. Decaying vegetation is heaped into a mound 1.63 m (65 in) in diameter and 40 cm (16 in) high, built close to convenient water by the female with occasional assistance from the male. Anything from 20 to about 60 eggs are laid, each measuring about 65 by 45 mm ($2\frac{1}{2}$ by $1\frac{3}{4}$ in) and weighing approximately 84 g (2.96 oz). The nest is aggressively defended by the female during the 60–90 days' incubation (egg-predators include the tayra, hawks, and teiid lizards), with both parents sharing the protection of juveniles during their first year of life. In parts of its range the broad-nosed caiman's distribution overlaps that of the jacare, but the two forms do not normally share the same locality.

Fossil remains attributed to *Caiman* occur as far back as the Miocene, when the giant *Caiman neivensis*, nearly 9 m (30 ft) in length, hunted the rivers and swamps of what is now Colombia. This massive reptile probably filled a similar ecological niche to that occupied by the living black caiman, although around twice its size. The skull of *Caiman neivensis* measured over 850 mm (32 in), the muzzle being elongate with steeply sloping sides and a blunt snout. Examples of *Caiman* from the Pliocene were less spectacular but still quite impressive reptiles, *Caiman lutescens* occurring as far south as Parana, Argentina, with a possible precursor in the late Miocene of Colombia. *Proalligator* was another extinct Pliocene alligatorine of southerly distribution which was present in Parana; it had a snout rather wider than that of *Caiman crocodilus* but narrower than in *Caiman latirostris*, the teeth being relatively large and widely spaced, with less size differentiation than in living caimans.

A somewhat enigmatic form is *Brachygnathosuchus*, known only from the front portion of a right lower jaw and some vertebrae that were discovered in the Upper Miocene or Pliocene of Amazonas, Brazil. It seems possible that the jaw bone is pathological — with a large swollen area beneath the socket that in life accommodated the canine-like fourth lower tooth — but this big extinct caiman must nonetheless have been a remarkably broad-snouted genus, with exceptionally prominent anterior teeth and a more abbreviated symphysial region than is customarily found in the present-day representatives of *Caiman*. A probably deformed lower-jaw fragment, found on the Purus River of Brazil, is all that is definitely known of *Purussaurus*, another very short-snouted extinct alligatorine of probable late Miocene age, although a fossil snout from east-central Peru may be assignable to this reptile.

In the South American Oligocene the caiman line of descent has been traced only through the rather aberrant *Balanerodus*, which is represented exclusively by large numbers of isolated teeth that have an almost spherical, acorn-like shape. One of these is a worn crown 35 mm (1½ in) high, so *Balanerodus* must have been a sizeable reptile, but how it lived is obscure: in the brackish or freshwater deposits of the Mugrosa formation these curious teeth occur in association with an abundance of gastropods and molluscs, suggesting a diet of shellfish, but in the Chaparral formation *Balanerodus* teeth are mixed with large quantities of shattered mammal bones, as if this enigmatic alligatorine had been scavenging carcases. It is not known if *Balanerodus* is related to the blunt-toothed *Allognathosuchus* from the early Cenozoic of North America or merely represents a parallel specialisation within the caimanoid stock: it has no known antecedents or descendants, and assignment to the Alligatorinae has been made largely because this subfamily is far more common in South America than the Crocodylinae.

Further back still, *Eocaiman* from the Patagonian Lower Eocene was a relatively common broad-skulled crocodilian that may well have been a direct ancestor of *Caiman* itself and has also been reported from later deposits, of Upper Miocene age, in Colombia.

The oldest known caimanoid is *Notocaiman*, from the Palaeocene of Santa Cruz, Argentina, but it is based only on a robustly proportioned lower-jaw ramus with enlarged 13th and 14th dentary teeth, so its affinities are uncertain. Assignment to either *Caiman* or *Eocaiman* has been suggested.

An unsolved mystery is posed by a huge crocodilian dorsal vertebra found during the latter half of the 19th century in Amazonas, Brazil, but now unfortunately lost. Aptly described as *Dinosuchus terror*, this solitary specimen probably came from deposits of late Miocene age and evidently indicates a crocodilian of terrifying proportions, but no other bones have ever come to light and it may never be known if the Brazilian swamps of 30 million years ago harboured one of the largest crocodilians that ever lived.

The biggest of living caimans is the black caiman (*Melanosuchus niger*), which allegedly may reach 4.5 m (15 ft) in length, although verifiable records suggest that around 4 m (13 ft) is this reptile's maximum measurement. The Amazon basin is the black caiman's territory, from Marajo Island in the mouth of the Amazon westwards across northern Brazil to southern Colombia, eastern Ecuador and northeast Peru, ranging southwards to Guaporé and the northern part of Mato Grosso state. Occasionally it apparently roams northwards up the Essequibo and Rupununi Rivers, thus reaching Guyana, but confusion with the dark-coloured jacare (*Caiman crocodilus yacare*) has led to apparently spurious reports of black caimans in the River Paraguay.

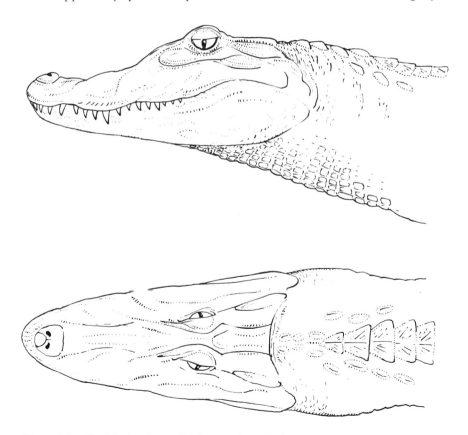

Figure 16   The black caiman (*Melanosuchus niger*)

As its popular names suggests, the coloration of the black caiman is very dark, except for the yellowish underparts, juveniles being a particularly deep black on their dorsal surfaces but exhibiting narrow, broken cross-bands of pale yellow and possessing conspicuous dark stripes and blotches on the light-coloured face and lower jaw. The skull is moderately broad in characteristic alligatorine fashion, but tapers to a rather sharp point, the eye sockets being unusually large while on the palate the vomerine bone is exposed to view (an exceptional feature in a crocodilian skull, more clearly perceived in juvenile black caimans than in adult animals). There are 13 or 14 pairs of maxillary teeth in the upper jaw, preceded by five pairs of premaxillary teeth, with 17 or 18 pairs of lower teeth.

Melanosuchus seems to be primarily a denizen of low-lying grassy savannahs that are subject to periodic inundation, this caiman preferring to lurk in the shallows or around the margins of placid lakes or small ponds, allegedly aestivating partially buried in mud during the dry season. It seems less inclined to venture far afield out of the water than the smaller caimans and preys particularly on capybaras, which it will ambush at the water's edge by charging through the shallows with body high off the ground and head directed straight at the intended victim, which is seized in the front (rather than the side) of the jaws. The indigestible hair of capybara victims is sometimes found in clumps at the water's edge, and local residents claim that it is regurgitated: this has been doubted by some authorities, but *Caiman crocodilus* and *Caiman latirostris* were observed in 1981 by C. O. da C. Diefenbach of the Federal University of Rio Grande do Sul, Brazil, to regurgitate pelletised hair and the opercula of ingested snails that were too large for defaecation (the pyloric opening of the stomach in a 1.15-m (43-in) caiman measures only about 4 mm in diameter), the process taking place after dark and being unaccompanied by any convulsive movement of the flanks or back such as occurs in vomiting.

As befits such an aggressive predator, the black caiman seems to have particularly acute sight and hearing, its night vision being especially keen; indeed, this reptile does virtually all its hunting after dusk and is seldom active in the heat of the day. It will take fish when the opportunity arises, notably towards the end of the dry season in the lower Amazon basin, when ponds and lakes shrink and their fish populations are concentrated into diminishing bodies of water.

Black caiman nests are usually built of vegetable debris and tend to be somewhat larger than those of the American alligator, which is a reptile of comparable size. Clutches normally number 30–60 white, hard-shelled eggs measuring 80–90 mm ($3\frac{1}{4}$–$3\frac{1}{2}$ in) in length, with a diameter of 50–55 mm (2–$2\frac{1}{4}$ in), and are laid in September–November (Bolivia), November–January (Colombia) and October (Ecuador). Incubation takes up to six weeks.

The disappearance of the black caiman from many of its former haunts has resulted in considerable ecological imbalance. Capybaras, breeding unchecked, have proliferated and now destroy village crops. Zooplankton and phytoplankton, including invertebrate larvae, which depended on *Melanosuchus* excrement for nutrients have now declined, so that fish larvae

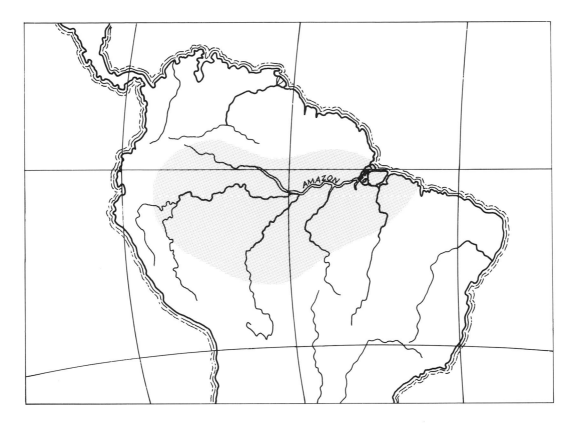

Map 10

The range of the black caiman (*Melanosuchus niger*)

which preyed on these organisms have failed to survive and some fish species seem in consequence to be severely reduced in numbers. Piranhas, on some forms of which black caimans feed, have greatly increased and now threaten cattle crossing flooded grassland.

Almost nothing is known of the black caiman's ancestry, although two incomplete fossil skulls from the Pliocene of Venezuela have been ascribed to *Melanosuchus* as a separate species (*Melanosuchus fisheri*). This seems to have had a more robustly constructed skull than its presumed living descendant, with a deeper, heavier snout, a massively proportioned lower jaw, and only 12 pairs of maxillary teeth.

The smallest and apparently the most primitive of the living caimans is *Paleosuchus*, an enigmatic little genus comprising two species that frequent the tropical rainforests of the Orinoco and Amazon basins. The aptly chosen name *Paleosuchus* does in fact mean 'ancient crocodile', and the appearance of these small caimans certainly supports the belief that they represent survivors of an ancient group that have evolved exclusively in the South

American rainforests after diverging from the rest of the caiman assemblage well before the mid-Cenozoic — 30 or so million years ago — although their fossil history is quite unknown. The skull lacks the bony ridges around the eyes and across the snout that are seen in other caimans, so the species of *Paleosuchus* are known collectively as smooth-fronted caimans, but the head is in fact very strongly ossified, with a bony upper eyelid that completely covers the eye (which has an unusual dark iris) when this is closed. The upper surface of the body is protected by a robust series of bony scutes, and elsewhere the scales are reinforced by osseous platelets to provide *Paleosuchus* with a remarkable dermal armour which contributes substantially to its archaic appearance. F. J. Medem of Colombia's National University published in 1958 a detailed study of the smooth-fronted caiman and concluded that it is a denizen of swift-running streams in tropical forests, frequenting the vicinity of small rapids or waterfalls. The extreme ossification of the skull in adult animals — notably the fully ossified eyelid — and the well-developed dermal armour would provide protection from rocks encountered in fast currents, while the very pointed, posteriorly curved teeth are well adapted for seizing elusive prey in turbulent water. It is a solitary, territorial reptile that inhabits burrows and is generally active only after dark; on land it displays considerable agility, frequently jumping into the water rather than running if disturbed, and when resting in deep water it floats with the body at a relatively steep angle to the surface. The diet is probably more varied than that of any other South American crocodilian, comprising fish, birds, rodents, caimans (including its own species), snakes, frogs, molluscs, crabs and shrimps; in addition, the stomach normally contains a considerable number of small pebbles.

W. T. Neill came to rather different conclusions about *Paleosuchus* from those of Medem. The two species of *Paleosuchus* are Schneider's smooth-fronted caiman (*Paleosuchus trigonatus*), which attains a length of up to 2.25 m (90 in) and occurs in both the Orinoco and the Amazon drainages as far south as latitude 10 degrees, and Cuvier's smooth-fronted caiman (*Paleosuchus palpebrosus*), a smaller reptile measuring only about 1.7 m (67 in) that ranges as far south as latitude 20 degrees and extends further westwards along the Amazon than *Paleosuchus trigonatus*, as well as occurring in Mato Grosso. Neill found that *Paleosuchus palpebrosus*, the more specialised of the two species, with a short, broad, deep skull and blunt, upturned snout, occurred in the still, deeply shaded floodplain ponds. Among floating dead leaves the mottled jaws and reddish-coloured heads of these caimans were difficult to distinguish, and it was claimed that they also carried a growth of filamentous green algae on their bodies which added another dimension of camouflage; captive smooth-fronted caimans which became algae-infested seem, like similarly affected zoo alligators, to be sickly animals in declining health. The species seems to have a remarkable tolerance of cold, Medem reporting in 1971 that a specimen kept without artificial heating at the Institute of National Sciences in Bogota, 2650 m (8700 ft) above sea level, on one occasion escaped and was eventually found thriving on a diet of frogs in a small pool where the night-time temperature was as low as 6°C. On the

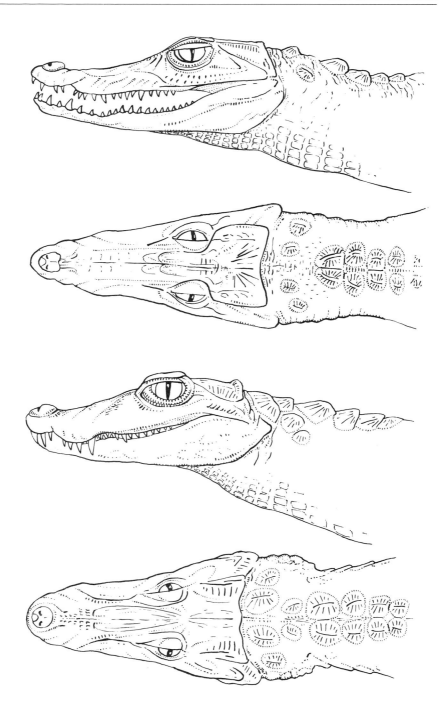

Figure 17 The smooth-fronted caiman. *Top, Paleosuchus palpebrosus*; *Bottom, Paleosuchus trigonatus*

other hand, *Paleosuchus palpebrosus* is also addicted to basking in the sun, sometimes ashore but frequently on rocks and slabs in shallow water, keeping its head erect and gazing alertly upstream.

Cuvier's smooth-fronted caiman builds a nest of rotting and green leaves, grass and twigs, mixed with mud, that measures about 50 cm (20 in) in height and 1.5 m (60 in) in width, the site usually being a shady spot with very limited exposure to direct sunlight. About a dozen whitish eggs, each approximately 60–70 mm by 40 mm (2¾ in by 1¾ in) and weighing 60–70 g (2.1–2.5 oz), are laid in an 'egg chamber' of earth and clay mixed with rotten leaves, similar to that reported to occur in the centre of caimans' nests generally. Eventually the eggs become blackened by a layer of debris and the excrement of ground termites in the course of the 90-day incubation period, during which the internal nest temperature is about 30°C (some 3°C higher than the ambient temperature).

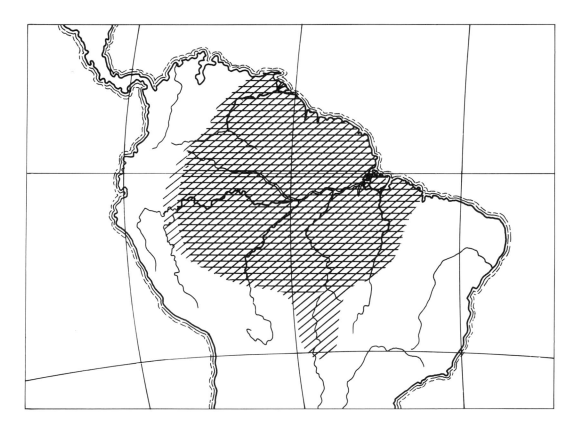

Map 11

The range of Cuvier's smooth-fronted caiman (*Paleosuchus palpebrosus*)

The range of Schneider's smooth-fronted caiman (*Paleosuchus trigonatus*)

Hatching occurs in October–December, the embryos — 22–24 cm (9 in) long at full term — emitting a quacking call from inside the shell when ready to emerge. In the laboratory, it has been found that they make strenuous efforts to break out as soon as an egg is lifted but will otherwise simply puncture the shell with their caruncles and then remain inert for long periods. Most will eventually emerge, but the conclusion must be that the female normally digs out the brood, which probably could not escape unaided from the hard-walled 'egg chamber' of the nest.

The newly emerged young have a yellowish-brown skull table (which does not acquire the adult rusty hue for six or seven months), a light brown lower jaw that eventually becomes pinkish, and black or brown cross-bands on the body and tail. This disruptive coloration is a very effective camouflage, particularly when submerged. Initially the hatchlings are covered in slime, and they do not leave the remains of the nest for a day or two until this dries, after which they enter the water. The female has not been reported to defend the nest or to shepherd the young during their early weeks of life, but this may simply be due to the paucity of observational data on an apparently rather solitary species (claws and scutes of juveniles of both *Paleosuchus* species have been found in the stomachs of adults, suggesting some degree of cannibalism).

Schneider's smooth-fronted caiman is a less specialised form than *Paleosuchus palpebrosus*, with a narrow, elongate snout. Neill believes that it is this species which occurs in fast-flowing streams, the slimmer skull suggesting an adaptation to turbulent waters requiring a streamlined form. On the other hand, *Paleosuchus trigonatus* is also reported to carry an algal infestation, which suggests residence in relatively placid aquatic conditions. Found at altitudes of up to 1300 m (4265 ft) in Venezuela, it has been observed some distance from water and may be a more terrestrial species than *Paleosuchus palpebrosus*, but it is not inclined to bask in direct sunlight and hides in cavities under stream banks by day. The breeding habits of *Paleosuchus trigonatus* are inadequately known.

Paleosuchus possibly finds it difficult to compete with either *Caiman* or *Melanosuchus* and consequently has to seek out environments not dominated by either of the larger caimanoid genera, which would explain its occurrence in fast-flowing streams or deep in the rainforest. Local Indians harpoon these small caimans, but apart from being hunted by man the adults are also known to be killed by anacondas, which may reach 6 m (20 ft) or more in length.

5.

Gavials and false gavials: long-snouted diversification

Although there are narrow-muzzled species of *Crocodylus*, none of these forms has achieved the degree of specialisation found in the gavial and to a lesser extent in the false gavial. These extraordinary crocodilians have developed to an extreme the long slender snouts conventionally considered to be characteristic of fish-eaters and are regarded as harmless to man, although the gavial grows to over 20 ft (6 m) in length and the false gavial to about 16 ft (4.8 m).

The protein-sequencing procedures carried out by L. D. Densmore in 1983 indicate that there is a closer degree of affinity between these two similarly adapted crocodilians than had previously been assumed, although they may perhaps still be regarded as representing two separate subfamilies, albeit relatively closely related ones.

Gavials

The gavial itself (*Gavialis gangeticus*) originally occurred in the river systems of Pakistan, Bangladesh, India, Nepal and possibly Burma and Bhutan, the distribution now comprising a restricted western component in the Indus and a much more extensive eastern population occupying the Mahanadi and Ganges in India and the Brahmaputra in Bangladesh and Assam. Presumably the discontinuity in the gavial's distribution that occurs across northeast India is a relatively recent artefact, the range having previously been unbroken right across the northern part of the Indian subcontinent. Any westward advance beyond Pakistan would have been precluded by the mountains and deserts of Baluchistan and Afghanistan, while the Himalayas constituted an impenetrable northern barrier. To the east, the occurrence of an extinct fossil species in Sumatra that is allegedly referable to *Gavialis* indicates that the genus probably had a much more extensive former range in southeastern Asia than is the case today.

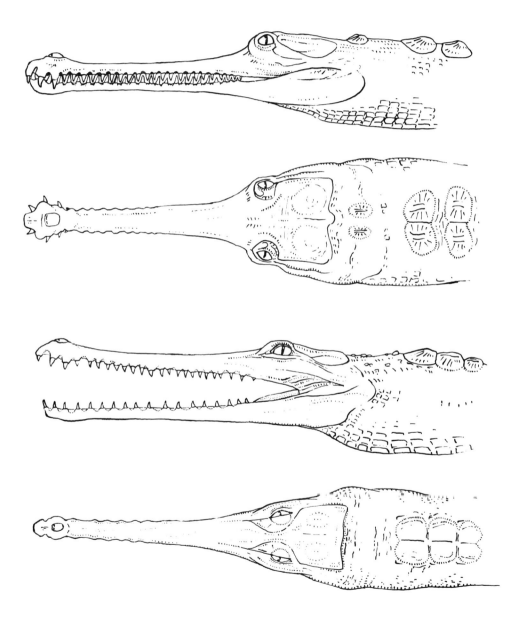

Figure 18 Long-snouted specialisation. *Top*, the gavial (*Gavialis gangeticus*); *Bottom*, the false gavial (*Tomistoma schlegeli*)

131

The name gavial is in fact a corruption of the Hindustani 'gharial'. The animal's astonishingly elongate muzzle is sharply demarcated from the cranial region of the skull, with the maxillary bones expanded dorsally to meet in the mid-line and exclude the nasal bones from contact with the premaxillae at the end of the nose. The teeth, numbering about 100 in all, are slender, elongate and project slightly outward, the upper and lower series interlocking to form a sophisticated mechanism for entrapping and impaling the fish upon which the gavial principally subsists. Contrary to some statements, the eyes of gavials do give a red reflection in the beam from a flashlight, providing the animal is more than 4 m (13 ft) distant if an adult, 1.75 m (4 ft) distant if a yearling about 1 m ($3\frac{1}{4}$ ft) long, and 1 m ($3\frac{1}{4}$ ft) away if a 50-cm (20-inch) hatchling.

The body is slenderly proportioned, with extensively webbed feet and relatively long hindlimbs: features which would be expected in a primarily aquatic fish-eater. The tail, double-crested initially, bears 21–24 single crests along its terminal segment, the first eight of which are black-striped. Ventral armour is absent, as it is in other primarily water-adapted crocodiles, such as the saltwater species, but there are dorsal scutes to protect the back. Adults are various shades of olive, the head and snout being of a darker hue, with numerous indistinct black spots on the body that have been observed to expand or disperse underwater, presumably as the dark pigment of melanophores expands or contracts. The belly is greenish-olive to yellow-white in tone.

Some controversy seems to centre around the large bulbous nasal excrescence which features in 19th-century drawings of the gavial. Early writers suggested that the crocodile of the Ganges had a horn on its head, which the gavial certainly does not, but later claims that the nasal enlargement at the end of the snout is a myth were finally discounted in 1977 when B. G. H. Martin and A. d'A. Bellairs of St Mary's Hospital Medical School, London, fully described this unusual feature, which seems to be restricted to male individuals. It is not, however, universally present in all males, and in one case had developed in a specimen (perhaps sexually aberrant) that possessed ovaries. The excrescence occurs near the tip of the snout and is seated in a depressed area of the premaxillary bones just in front of the external nostrils, which the fleshy protuberance overhangs. In the middle of its posterior face there is a conspicuous lip beneath which a small cavity is enclosed by posterior lobes. In old animals, the excrescence becomes so large that it folds backwards, thus enclosing a hollow area within itself. The function of this curiosity has not been determined, but it seems unlikely to be respiratory as the cavities cannot be closed to the ingress of water, and the structure contains no olfactory-type epithelium that would suggest that it augments the sense of smell. Conceivably it is a secondary sexual feature of males that acts as a resonator, with a stream of exhaled air controlled by the narial muscles modifying a harmonic spectrum of sounds produced by the larynx. A locally made earthenware pot is known in northern India as a 'ghara', and it has been suggested that the resemblance of these vessels to the nasal excrescence of the 'gharial' is the derivation of the creature's common name.

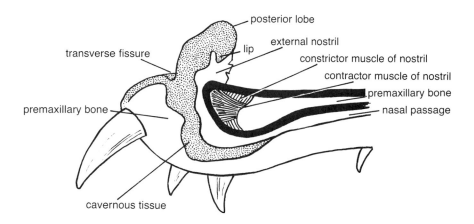

Figure 19 A longitudinal section through the nasal appendage of the gavial, showing the right nasal passage. The excrescence is inclined slightly backwards to overhang the confluent nasal opening, which leads to paired vestibules that bend sharply to join the nasal passages. A transverse fissure runs across the base of the prominence anteriorly, and there is a conspicuous lip in the middle of the posterior face beneath which a small cavity is enclosed by the posterior lobes (after Martin and Bellairs)

Martin and Bellairs also described the presence in adult gavials of enlarged pterygoid bullae. These are bilateral structures comprising a thin-walled expansion of each pterygoid bone that extends forward on either side of the palatine bone and comprises two communicating chambers; the smaller one arises directly from the pterygoid and is separated from a larger egg-shaped anterior chamber by a constriction (or often a partial suture). Only gavial skulls exceeding 60 cm (2 ft) in length exhibit this feature, and like the nasal excrescence it may be restricted to male animals. The structure constitutes a cavity opening into the long tube-like naso-pharyngeal duct and may therefore possess a vocal function, acting as a sound filter.

The largest gavial for which there is an authentic record is a specimen 23 ft (7 m) long killed by Matthew George in the Kosi River of north Bihar in January 1924. Other large specimens include a 21½-ft (6.6-m) individual killed in the Gogra River of Fyzabad, in the United Provinces of India, in August 1920, and a 21-foot (6.4-m) reptile shot in the Cheko River of Jalpaigur in 1934.

Despite its size, the species is normally regarded as harmless to man and feeds primarily on fish, which are brought to the surface after being seized so that they can be either repositioned in the jaws for swallowing whole (head first) or else broken into smaller, more manageable pieces by thrashing movements of the gavial's head, the tail sometimes whipping above the water synchronously. Waterfowl, small mammals, goats and dogs are also apparently sometimes taken, and it has been alleged that gavials feed on human corpses drifting down the Ganges from the burning ghats. The presence of

133

metal armlets, anklets and other human ornaments in the stomachs of gavials led to this reptile being castigated as a man-eater, but these trinkets were more probably ingested from the river bed as gastroliths, having originally been part of the funeral regalia that decorated bodies scheduled for cremation.

A number of attacks on people by gavials have nonetheless been recorded, although without fatal consequences. In 1981, H. R. Bustard and L. A. K. Singh reported an attack on 55-year-old Sankara Behera at the Satkoshia Gorge Sanctuary on the Mahanadi River. On November 14 1979, Behera was washing utensils in the water when his left arm was seized by a gavial of between 3 and 4 m (9¾–13 ft) in length. Either he was pulled or he slipped into the river and lost consciousness, but his son was nearby in a canoe and hauled him to safety by his hair, although not without the gavial taking a further bite at Behera, this time seizing his right thigh. Behera was hospitalised but made a full recovery, his scarred arm and leg bearing testimony to his ordeal. It is noteworthy that Behera's assailant quickly released its jaws after biting and did not apparently prosecute its attack with any serious attempt at predation.

In 1974, a visitor to the village of Naraj, also on the Mahanadi, suffered a nipped ankle but no injury when a female gavial guarding a nest was disturbed, and in the same year a Naraj fisherman who dived into the river to release an entangled net was bitten in the chest area but immediately released. Some 25 years before these occurrences, a fisherman was attacked by a gavial near Talchar, on the Brahmani River, but survived the incident and eventually died in 1979.

A denizen of deep, fast-flowing rivers with high banks, clear water and deep pools, the gavial is not well adapted for fast swimming, the head, with its pronounced facial expansion, being far from streamlined. The narrow snout, however, offers minimal resistance to the water when the reptile snaps sideways at passing schools of fish, and this seems to be the gavial's feeding strategy: to lie passively in wait and make a lightning sideways lunge of the head to seize any fish unwary enough to wander in range of the slender jaws. One captive gavial was reported by W. T. Neill to snap almost exclusively at fishes passing on its right side, largely ignoring those on its left, which suggests a degree of 'handedness' comparable with the right-handedness customary in man. The fish most frequently taken by gavials are catfish (*Clarias*), which are themselves major predators on tilapias — the subject of a substantial commercial fishery, tilapias being a major item in the diet of local native populations. Consequently, the reduction in gavial populations that has occurred since the 1950s has led to burgeoning numbers of catfish, which have in turn decimated the tilapia shoals, thereby depriving villagers of an important food source.

Gavials spend a substantial amount of time basking on sand banks, especially during the winter months. They mate before the spring, with each dominant male gathering three or four females into a breeding group. Courtship ritual includes the emission of loud whistles and hisses by the male, attracting females which respond with softer calls, the two animals also bubbling air through the water. They then move to the shallows where the male mounts his mate, copulation finally occurring, according to observers, on the bottom in deep water.

18   Crocodile farming in Thailand is on a large scale at Samutprakan, near Bangkok

19   Zimbabwe has one of the most flourishing crocodile-farming industries

Nesting begins in March or April, a month after mating, females seeking a location not more than about 10 m (just over 30 ft) from the water. It requires anything up to three hours for a gavial to excavate her nest, using only her hindlegs, after which an average of 40 elliptical eggs measuring about 90 mm by 70 mm (3½ by 2¾ in) are deposited (a clutch of 97 eggs was reported by H. R. Bustard and D. Basu in 1982, 69 of which subsequently hatched in a hatchery incubator). Several preliminary 'trial' nests are usually dug, and great care is taken to choose a spot with just the right substrate balance of sand grain and moisture content so that optimum temperature (32–34°C) and humidity are maintained within the egg chamber. Incubation takes 60–90 days, the female (and possibly also the male) remaining on or adjacent to the nest to protect it from predators such as jackals and monitor lizards: the adults have been seen as far as 1 km (over ½ mile) away from the nest by day, but seem to stay nearer during the hours of darkness, attending more closely as hatching time approaches, apparently to hear the calls of the young as they seek to emerge from the eggs so that the top of the nest can be opened to free them, great care being taken during this process to avoid inadvertently injuring the hatchlings.

Newly emerged gavials measure about 36 cm (14 in), weigh nearly 90 g (3.2 oz) and are of a dark brown colour. They require about 20 minutes to force their heads out of the eggs, but then only a second or two is needed for the diminutive gavial to free itself completely. For a whole brood to hatch, a period of up to ten hours may be required, with the mother systematically shepherding or carrying the active little reptiles to the sanctuary of the nearby water. The umbilicus will dry and drop off the hatchlings in only three to six hours, but each can live on a yolk residue contained in a 30-mm (1¼-in) diameter protuberance for a week or two; a day after emerging, they change colour to a pale hue, becoming a light brown colour. When the monsoon breaks a few weeks after the end of the hatching season, floodwaters pouring down river courses break up the gavial nurseries and many youngsters inevitably perish after being swept away. Combined with an egg mortality of around 40 per cent, this heavy toll means that only perhaps 1 per cent of a season's young will eventually live to become adults.

The origins of *Gavialis* are obscure. A Pleistocene species (*Gavialis bengawanicus*) has been described from the famous *Pithecanthropus* beds of Trinil, Java, that also yielded the remains of Java man, and in the Pliocene of the Siwalik hills there are apparently several representatives of the genus: *Gavialis hysudricus* is an Upper Pliocene species not unlike the modern *Gavialis gangeticus*, and *Gavialis leptodus* is of similar age but with proportionately rather small teeth and a relatively wide, flat muzzle (for a gavial), while the Middle Pliocene deposits have yielded *Gavialis lewisi*, with a slightly upcurved snout and an abruptly concave skull profile just in front of the eye sockets. In the Lower Pliocene Siwaliks there are *Gavialis browni*, possessing a massively constructed skull and very robust dentition, and *Gavialis curvirostris*, with a relatively short, upwardly curved snout and no marked concavity of the skull profile in front of the eyes.

Also present in the Pliocene of the Siwaliks is a gigantic crocodilian that was probably a gavial and attained 15–18 m (50–58½ ft) in length, making it the largest known member of the entire order. *Rhamphosuchus crassidens* is unfortunately known only from tantalisingly fragmentary material. There is a huge snout with the anterior part of the lower jaw, a portion of a mandibular symphysis, a lower tooth, some broken skull and jaw components, vertebrae, two iliac bones from the pelvic girdle, a fibula, and some dermal scutes. With no complete skeleton or even a reasonably comprehensive skull to go on, the status of *Rhamphosuchus* is unclear. The unexpanded premaxillary bones seem to be separated from the nasals by the maxillae, which suggests that it is a gavial, and in front of the nasal opening is a pair of concavities indicating that in life there was a gavial-like nasal excrescence. The evidence points to *Rhamphosuchus* being a giant gavial, although some workers have in the past sought to place it among the false gavials.

The *Gavialis* story continues back through time in the Upper Miocene of Iraq (bone fragments from the Bakhtiari formation) and the Bugti hills of Baluchistan, where a Lower Miocene variant of *Gavialis curvirostris* seems already to have been present and fossil fragments of upper and lower jaws indicate the occurrence of a species with an unusually short, massive snout incorporating expanded premaxillary bones (*Gavialis breviceps*).

Further back than the Miocene, the picture becomes blurred. Some incomplete skull remains from the Upper Oligocene of Coyaima, Colombia, have been described as *Gavialis colombianus* and indicate a relatively advanced level of specialisation, despite the fact that the material is about 25 million years old: there is a sharp transition between the broad cranium and the narrow muzzle, and the snout seems to lack any degree of upward curvature. Whether this material should really be attributed to *Gavialis* is doubtful, and there are grounds for referring it to *Gryposuchus*, which is poorly known but seems to have been a South American representative of the Gavialinae that has been reported from the Pliocene/Pleistocene of Brazil. Other fossil South American gavials include *Rhamphostomopsis* (also possibly referable to *Gryposuchus*), which occurred as far south as Argentina in the Pliocene and may have been present in Colombia in the Upper Miocene, attaining a length of perhaps 7 m (22¾ ft) with an exceptionally elongate snout, and *Hesperogavialis*, a large genus possessing a long, robustly proportioned muzzle that comes from the Upper Miocene of Urumaco, Venezuela. Apart from *Gavialis colombianus*, none of these neotropical forms is adequately known, most of the fossil material comprising little more than fragments of snouts and lower jaws; there are no complete skeletons, or even any entire skulls.

One relatively comprehensive but rather enigmatic skull from the Pliocene of Venezuela that was regarded by its discoverer, W. D. Sill of Yale University, as being the remains of a gavial is of uncertain reference. Described as *Ikanogavialis gameroi*, it measures 1.02 m (just over 3 ft) with a snout that is proportionately even longer than that of *Gavialis gangeticus*. This skull, however, lacks the relatively sharp demarcation between the cranium and the muzzle that is typical of gavials, and furthermore the nasal bones still extend along the top of the nose to reach the premaxillary elements: a feature that should strictly speaking debar this species from association with *Gavialis*, in which the maxillae meet on top of the snout.

If *Gryposuchus*, *Rhamphostomopsis*, *Hesperogavialis* and perhaps *Ikanogavialis* are true gavialines, the question that immediately arises is how did they get to South America in the first place. They seem to be distinctly more primitive than fossil gavials of the Old World, so did they perhaps originate there, and if so could this continent have been the gavial homeland? Or are they a parallel development to the later Asiatic species and their living descendant, the Old World and New World forms having been derived from an unknown common ancestor living no-one knows where?

A clue to the origin of the gavials may have been found in Egypt, where Eocene and Lower Oligocene deposits have yielded the fossil remains of long-snouted crocodilians which in 1982 were ascribed by E. Buffetaut, the eminent French crocodile expert, to a new genus, *Eogavialis* (the 'dawn gavial'). Although undoubtedly gavial-like in their adaptation, these species (*Eogavialis africanus* from the Middle and Upper Eocene, and *Eogavialis gavialoides* from the Upper Eocene and Lower Oligocene) differ in a number of significant features from the living gavial: the edges of the eye sockets are not raised to form a prominent rim; the rostrum-like snout is not sharply demarcated from the rest of the skull; there are fewer teeth; the frontal bones of the skull roof are less wide and less transversely concave; and (most important of all) the nasal bones are still elongate so that they separate the maxillae and make contact anteriorly with the premaxillae.

The retention of long nasal bones like this was originally regarded as a primary means of distinguishing the false gavials (in which this feature is universal) from the true gavials (which were supposed to have short nasal bones that do not reach the premaxillae). Since the basic crocodilian skull pattern incorporates long nasal bones, it must be presumed that in ancestral gavials these elements were also still elongate. Whether these putative forebears of the modern gavial should be assigned to the subfamily Gavalinae is largely a matter for a zoologist's individual opinion: some might favour a vertical subdivision of crocodilians, seeking to trace the gavialine stem back to its roots and including ancient ancestral forms that display only incipiently gavial-like traits, while others may prefer what is in effect a horizontal classification that cuts off the subfamily from the rest of the crocodylids only when its gavialine characteristics are fully developed.

The presence of *Eogavialis* in Egypt suggests that the gavials may have originated there and spread from this area westwards across a then much narrower South Atlantic region to South America (where they remained relatively primitive and ultimately died out), and eastwards into southern Asia, acquiring on the way specialisations such as the reduced nasal bones.

False gavials

Both the species of *Eogavialis* were originally described as extinct representatives of *Tomistoma*, the false gavial, because of their long nasal bones. The living species, *Tomistoma schlegeli*, attains a length of about 5.5 m

(18 feet) — there is a skull in the British Museum of Natural History measuring 84 cm (2 ft 9½ in) along the dorsal line — and occurs in the lakes, swamps and freshwater rivers of Borneo (e.g. the Baram, Sadong and Kapuas Rivers), Sumatra (notably the Musi, Blindaban, Singilino and Inderapura Rivers), the Malay peninsula, and southern Thailand.

The skull of *Tomistoma* tapers progressively to form a long slender rostrum (there is no sharp demarcation between the snout and the facial region as in *Gavialis*), and the maxillae, each containing 20–21 teeth, are separated by the long nasals, which nonetheless fail to reach the external nostrils. The second premaxillary tooth is usually lost before maturity is reached, so the anterior upper dentition customarily comprises only four pairs of teeth, and the lower dentition numbers 18–20 pairs of teeth which are received into pits between the maxillary dentition when the jaws close. The mandibular symphysis extends posteriorly as far as the 14th or 15th lower-jaw teeth: much further back than in long-snouted crocodylines, but not so far as in the gavial.

Nuchal and dorsal plates form a continuous series protecting the back of the false gavial, with four longitudinal rows of scutes made up of 22 transverse bands. The toes of the forefeet are webbed at their bases, the outer digits of the hindfoot being even more extensively united by skin as an aid to swimming. In colour, adult false gavials are olive above, with dark spots or blotches, notably along the sides of the lower jaw. Juveniles have blackish dorsal cross-bands, dark spots along the lower flanks, and irregular black bands around the tail. The eyes of false gavials have a distinctively yellow-brown iris, pigmentation which no other living crocodilian possesses.

The habits of *Tomistoma* are poorly known, but it is believed to feed mainly on fish, although the natives of Borneo used crab-eating macaques (*Macaca fascicularis*) as bait to catch false gavials, and B. M. F. Galdikas and C. P. Yeager reported in 1984 seeing a false gavial seize a young crab-eating macaque from a river bank in the Tanjung Puting reserve in Kalimantan Tengah and disappear beneath the water with its victim. Evidently this crocodile is a more catholic feeder than has been generally assumed.

Female false gavials attain sexual maturity at about 4½–6 years when around 3 m (9¾ ft) in length. Breeding takes place in the dry season, and a mound nest about 60 cm (2 ft) high composed of vegetable matter (mostly dead leaves) is constructed in the shade of trees adjacent to a river or lake. The clutches of 20–60 large elliptical eggs, each about 70 by 100 mm (3 by 4 in), require 2½–3 months for incubation at nest temperatures of 28° to 33°C. Parental assistance to release hatchlings has not been reported, and mortality among newly emerged false gavials is believed to be high as they make their way quickly to the nearest water and seek to fend for themselves in streams and lakes. In captivity, this species digs burrows where it can take refuge, a practice that presumably occurs also in wild populations.

Fossil remains of long-snouted eusuchian crocodiles have been found from practically every level of the Cenozoic and many of them have been referred to *Tomistoma*. Much of the material is fragmentary, and many of these assignments to a living genus must be regarded as highly questionable,

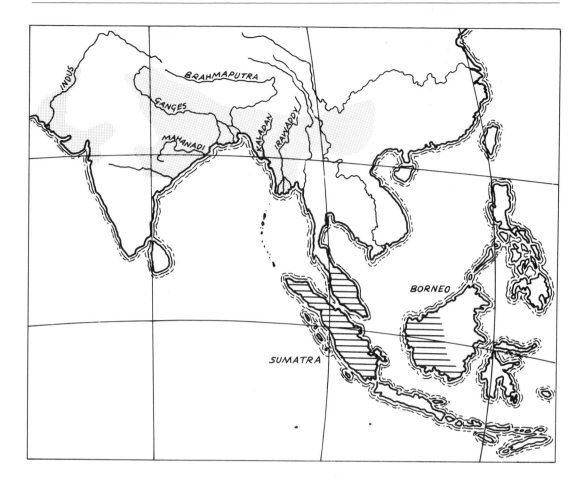

Map 12

The gavial (*Gavialis gangeticus*) occurs in two separate populations: a western one (mainly in the River Indus) and an eastern one, occupying the Mahanadi, Ganges, Brahmaputra, Kaladan and Irawaddy drainages

False gavials (*Tomistoma schlegeli*) are present in the Malay Peninsula, Sumatra and the western half of Borneo

especially those based on petrified bones from formations preceding the Miocene.

Tomistoma has been reported from the Upper Villafranchian of Taiwan (*Tomistoma taiwanicus*) and the late Pliocene or early Pleistocene of central Honshu, Japan (a skull 1.04 m/nearly 3½ ft long, described as *Tomistoma machikanense*, which has an enlarged seventh maxillary tooth and may represent a distinct genus, *Toyotamaphimeia*). Those occurrences suggest that false gavials were far more widespread in the past than they are today, the present distribution probably being the result of progressive withdrawal from higher northern latitudes as the climate has deteriorated.

In the much milder conditions that prevailed during the Miocene, false gavials twice the size of the living species lived on Malta (*Tomistoma champsoides*) and the genus was also present on the neighbouring island of Gozo (*Tomistoma gaudense*), as well as on Sardinia (*Tomistoma calaritanus*, also reported from northern Italy and the Iberian peninsula), in Egypt and Libya (*Tomistoma dawsoni*), and in Portugal (*Tomistoma lusitanica*), while an isolated tooth found in southern Poland may indicate false gavials in a region of Europe now far too cold for any but the smallest reptiles.

During the early Oligocene, there was a long-snouted crocodile in Egypt that was originally described as *Tomistoma tenuirostre* but which may in fact be an early representative of *Gavialis*, two Middle Eocene species from the same area (*Tomistoma cairense, Tomistoma kerunense*) also being regarded by some authorities as early gavials. Elsewhere in Eocene times, *Tomistoma* is alleged to have been present in India (*Tomistoma tandoni*), China (*Tomistoma petrolica*), and possibly Europe (fragmentary fossil remains from Spain and France). A rather ill-defined species of the genus (*Tomistoma macrorhynchus*) has been reported from the Palaeocene of France, and seems also to have occurred in the Upper Cretaceous of northwest Europe, but the known remains comprise only incomplete skull and lower-jaw material together with isolated vertebrae, limb bones and dermal scutes, making a positive determination very difficult.

Undoubted fossil remains of the subfamily do occur before the end of the age of dinosaurs, although they are not attributable to *Tomistoma* itself. On the eastern seaboard of North America, in New Jersey, Delaware and Maryland, there are relatively abundant (although fragmentary) bones of *Thoracosaurus*, an extinct false gavial with spatulate premaxillary bones at the end of its snout and about 24 teeth on either side of each jaw. This genus, from which the false gavial subfamily normally takes its name (the Thoracosaurinae, although some workers prefer to call them the Tomistominae after the living form) seems to have persisted through the Palaeocene before finally becoming extinct in the early part of the Eocene period. *Thoracosaurus* includes the forms described as *Holops* by Cope (in 1869) and *Sphenosaurus* by the eminent French-born naturalist Louis Agassiz (in 1849).

In Eocene times, some 50 million years ago, the mild climate that prevailed to high northern latitudes enabled false gavials to prosper in Europe. *Dollosuchus* was a rather broad-headed form discovered in the Middle Eocene of Brabant, Belgium, which has also been reported from rocks of similar age across the English Channel in Bracklesham, Sussex; it seems to have had a closely related forerunner in the Lower Eocene of northern France called *Eosuchus*, which possessed a proportionately somewhat longer and narrower skull. Further afield at this time, there was allegedly a false gavial in China, but the known remains of *Tienosuchus* comprise only a tooth, a dorsal vertebra, a mid-caudal vertebra, and three dermal scutes, which is scanty evidence upon which to base an identification.

In the Miocene, there occurs on both sides of the North Atlantic a rather enigmatic genus, *Gavialosuchus*, that is generally regarded as a false gavial very close to (and perhaps identical with) *Tomistoma*, although there are dissenting voices which claim it to be a primitive gavial. *Gavialosuchus* does, however, have long nasal bones that are in contact with the premaxillary elements at the end of the snout, which suggests that it is indeed a thoracosaurine, although one that differs from the extant species in having a lower, broader, more robust skull with fewer teeth in the maxilla and mandible, five pairs of premaxillary teeth, a larger, wider skull table, and an abrupt expansion of the snout where the first maxillary tooth is implanted. *Gavialosuchus eggenburgensis*, with a skull 73 cm (29 in) long and 15 pairs of maxillary teeth, occurs in the Miocene of Austria, France and also possibly Yugoslavia, while *Gavialosuchus americanus* — a huge reptile attaining 14 m (45 ft) in length, but with only 14 pairs of maxillary teeth — is present in the Upper Miocene and Lower Pliocene of Florida. Quite a number of specimens of *Gavialosuchus americanus* have been discovered, many of them in pebble phosphate deposits, which led to the suggestion that this species frequented the neighbourhood of offshore guano islands and fed chiefly on large fish. In Europe, however, *Gavialosuchus* remains occur in fluviatile deposits, indicating a river-bank habitat.

The North African Pliocene and Pleistocene fauna included *Euthecodon*, a very specialised long-snouted crocodile which, although customarily included among the false gavials, may not be a true thoracosaurine. Its bones have been found in Egypt, Libya and Ethiopia, but, although a skull 67 cm ($2\frac{1}{4}$ ft) long is known, most of the other material is fragmentary and there are no complete skeletons. *Euthecodon* had greatly elongate premaxillary bones and a prominent crest on the lacrimal bone, just in front of the eye. Along the dental row, the rims of the teeth alveoli were elevated to more than 1 cm ($\frac{1}{2}$ in), with deeply rounded notches between adjacent sockets and an unusually conspicuous gap between the last premaxillary tooth and the first of the maxillary teeth. In the lower jaw there were 24–27 pairs of teeth, which would have fitted into the notches between the upper teeth when the jaws were closed. An earlier occurrence of a *Euthecodon*-like crocodilian is indicated by a lower-jaw fragment and isolated elongate teeth from the Miocene of Kenya: probably these strange forms had a long history in Africa that is still unknown.

There is one alleged fossil false gavial reported from South America. *Leptorrhamphus* is known only from a broken snout discovered in the Pliocene of Argentina during the late 19th-century, and its true identity is questionable. There is no other record of thoracosaurines in the neotropical region, and it may be that this species was a recently arrived immigrant from the north.

The history of the gavials and the false gavials is thus very incompletely known. It evidently traces back at least to the early part of the Upper Cretaceous, since rocks of this age in Inner Mongolia have yielded the right-hand side of a long, slender crocodilian muzzle that has been described as *Eotomistoma* ('dawn tomistoma'), with the species name *multidentata* because the upper jaw must have held at least 48 striated, sharply pointed teeth each side, while minute palatal teeth seem to have been present on the ectopterygoid and maxillary bones.

Eotomistoma is regarded as the oldest known false gavial. Since it is much older than the first known true gavials, it is tempting to suggest that the gavials are derivatives of the false gavial stock. Perhaps the gavials did arise from thoracosaurines in Africa in Oligocene times, as has been suggested. Perhaps they did spread westwards to South America and eastwards into Asia. But the history of the false gavials themselves is obscure in the extreme, and no coherent pattern of evolution or distribution can be derived from the available fossil material, save the speculation that they were once far more widespread but have now been forced to retreat to a relatively small area of southeast Asia, driven there by the vicissitudes of climate and possibly also by competition from other crocodiles, notably the gavials and the slender-snouted crocodyline species. Although intensive hunting by man has drastically reduced the numbers of false gavials that still survive in the wild, the restricted geographical range of *Tomistoma schlegeli* was determined by factors operating before primitive man acquired the capability seriously to deplete crocodile populations.

For most of the age of mammals, South America was cut off from the rest of the world by severance of the land connection with North America at the isthmus of Panama. On this vast isolated continent there evolved an extraordinary menagerie of animals like nothing present on any other land area. Among these bizarre forms was a long-snouted eusuchian crocodile of such strange appearance that it is usually assigned to a separate family of its own. Known as *Mourasuchus*, it had a wide, flattened muzzle curving upwards anteriorly and stiffened by a broad longitudinal median ridge formed from the nasal bones. The external nostrils were partially surrounded by raised, swollen bony rims extending around their posterior edges, and the lower jaw was long and slender, with a short, unfused symphysis between the two rami and only a very small retroarticular process for attachment of the muscles that helped to open the mouth. The cranial region of the skull was, in contrast to the depressed snout, short and relatively deep, the eye sockets having high, rugose bony rims and an essentially upward orientation. There were about 40 pairs of conical, moderately fluted teeth with pointed crowns in each jaw, including five pairs in the premaxillae. Superficially, *Mourasuchus*, which first appears in the Upper Miocene, rather resembles the enigmatic *Stomatosuchus* from the Upper Cretaceous of Egypt, but these two crocodilian oddities are separated by some 70 million years in time as well as by the width of the South Atlantic Ocean, and it seems probable that they represent parallel developments to exploit a similar environment. In addition to its long flat muzzle, elevated external nostrils, high cranium and raised eye-socket rims, the skull of *Mourasuchus* lacked the heavy sculpture so typical of crocodiles in general, and was of light construction with generally weak sutures: all features suggesting predominantly aquatic habits. Probably *Mourasuchus* was a passive denizen of deep pools, floating with jaws agape to ingest small fish, arthropods or plankton; alternatively (or perhaps additionally), the duck-like snout may have been employed for grubbing in the mud as caimans are sometimes observed to do. The presence of a sac-like

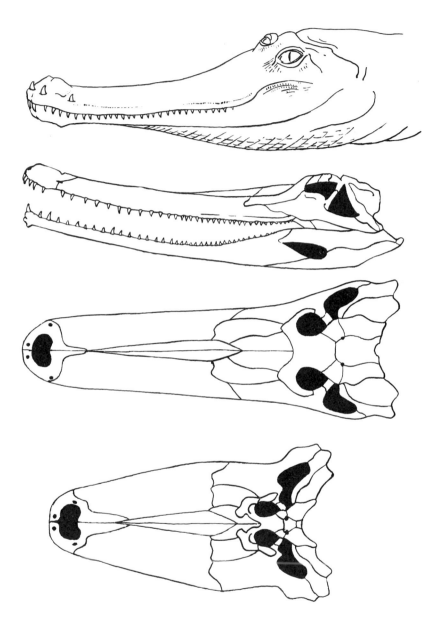

Figure 20 Nettosuchids. *1*, life reconstruction of *Mourasuchus atopus*, from the late Cenozoic of Brazil; *2 and 3*, skull of *Mourasuchus atopus*; *4*, skull of *Mourasuchus amazonensis*

143

receptacle beneath the jaw to store food strained from the water or sediment by the numerous small teeth seems likely.

It appears probable that this strange crocodile is related to the alligator group, having possibly evolved in South America from a caiman of Miocene or earlier age. Particularly noteworthy is the fact that when *Mourasuchus* closed its mouth some of the teeth in the front of the lower jaw perforated to the upper surface of the snout through specially deep sockets; this also occurs quite frequently among caimans, thus tending to support alligatorine kinship.

The oldest known species of *Mourasuchus* was in fact initially described (in 1965) as *Nettosuchus atopus*, on the basis of a partial skeleton from the Upper Miocene of Huila, Colombia. It was soon realised that it in fact belonged to the same genus as *Mourasuchus amazonensis*, the name given only a year previously to a skull and lower jaw of believed Pliocene age found in Brazil. Compared with this later species, *Mourasuchus atopus* has a proportionately rather longer snout with more nearly parallel sides. A third species, *Mourasuchus arendsi*, comes from the Urumaco formation of Venezuela (an Upper Miocene deposit) and is distinguished by having four pairs of sockets perforating the upper surface of the premaxillae to receive lower-jaw teeth, rather than the two pairs which did so in the other species, and (as in *Mourasuchus amazonensis*) a muzzle with less parallel sides. Although *Mourasuchus* is the name by which this interesting genus is now known to science, a subfamily based on the invalid name *Nettosuchus* had already been established for its reception before the superfluousness of that designation was realised, so the collective Nettosuchinae remains in use for this purpose.

6.

Crocodiles of the past

Although crocodiles of the modern eusuchian type were present during the latter part of the Mesozoic age of reptiles, the dominant crocodiles of the dinosaurs' world constitute a less advanced group known as the Mesosuchia.

Outwardly most of these ancient crocodilians would have looked very little different from their living descendants, but anatomically they display a number of characteristics that clearly demonstrate a less sophisticated level of evolution. The most important of these distinctions is to be found in the secondary palate, that most important of crocodilian features, the development of which is probably largely responsible for their successful exploitation of aquatic environments for some 200 million years. The mesosuchians did indeed have a secondary palate, but it was basically constructed only from the premaxillae, maxillae and palatine bones; the pterygoid elements, which form an integral part of the secondary palate in eusuchians, either play no part in it at all in mesosuchians or at best make only an incipient contribution. In life, the mesosuchian secondary palate was probably extended posteriorly by soft tissue that is not preserved in fossil skulls, so that functionally it reached just as far back as that of modern crocodiles, but a bone-floored secondary palate is obviously a more satisfactory structure than one relying partially only on flesh and cartilage.

The other skeletal distinctions of the Mesosuchia are rather less conspicuous but nonetheless significant. The vertebrae, for example, were almost universally platycoelous, that is the two ends of each centrum were slightly concave, which would have given a weaker articulation than the ball-and-socket procoelous type found in eusuchians, while the cervical vertebrae lack the ventral keels typical of modern crocodiles. Especially primitive mesosuchians also have a post-orbital bar behind the eye socket that has still not become recessed below the skull surface as it is in modern crocodiles, and some members of the group lacked a bony eustachian tube connecting the ear cavity to the throat (ossification of this tube has occurred in all eusuchians).

The members of the suborder Mesosuchia were the typical crocodiles of the Jurassic period (which opened 200 million years ago), continued to prosper through the Cretaceous (from 135 million to 65 million years ago), and even persisted into the Cenozoic (the age of mammals). Perhaps the most primitive mesosuchians, though not the oldest known, are the little atoposaurids, whose remains occur principally in the Upper Jurassic, although with some indication that they also survived into the Lower Cretaceous. In appearance they must have looked rather like juvenile modern crocodiles, as the scientific names bestowed upon them suggest. None was more than 40 cm (16 in) in length, and they had broad heads with proportionately large eyes and a short pointed snout. Their limbs were unusually long and slender for crocodiles, and a paired row of flattened dorsal scutes protected their backs. Some atoposaurid specimens undoubtedly are juvenile fossils, but many are obviously fully mature despite their diminutive size. The roof of the mouth is of characteristic mesosuchian type, with the secondary palate formed by the premaxillae, maxillae and palatines, and it seems likely that these tiny crocodilians are sufficiently generalised to be very close to the central stem of the entire order, representing the basic mesosuchian stock from which the Eusuchia eventually emerged. Their absence from formations preceding the Upper Jurassic is presumably due to the fact that early Jurassic history is recorded almost entirely by sediments laid down in the shallow seas which had invaded most of the continents at that time. Atoposaurids were probably fairly active little reptiles that spent a good deal of time on land: they must have existed during the opening phases of the Jurassic, but presumably frequented forest habitats or relatively dry areas through which streams and rivers wended their way to the incursive seas, so that fossil remains recording the initial history of the family have not been preserved.

The Upper Jurassic of Europe has yielded the remains of several atoposaurids. *Alligatorellus*, about 30 mm (12 in) long, from France and southern Germany had a remarkably long tail incorporating at least 30 vertebrae and is considered to have been probably an agile, essentially terrestrial little predator. Its misleading name should not be taken to imply any close relationship with alligators, since no such affinity exists, any more than it does between alligators and *Alligatorium*, the largest known atoposaurid at 40 cm (16 in) from nose to tail, which occurs in the Upper Jurassic of France, Germany and Spain and had unusually long, robustly proportioned hindlimbs. *Atoposaurus* itself, from which the family takes its name, is also from Europe (the Upper Jurassic of France and Germany) and had no fewer than 50 caudal vertebrae in its elongate tail, while *Hoplosuchus*, 20 cm (8 in) long, with the tail completely encased by dermal armour, is the sole North American representative of the group, occurring in the Morrison formation of Utah — an Upper Jurassic horizon that has yielded a rich fauna of dinosaurs with which this little crocodile was obviously a contemporary.

Karatausuchus comes from the Upper Jurassic of Kazakhstan, the long-tailed skeleton measuring 19 cm ($7\frac{1}{2}$ in) on which this genus is established being allegedly immature; there is a steeply sloping forehead region and the

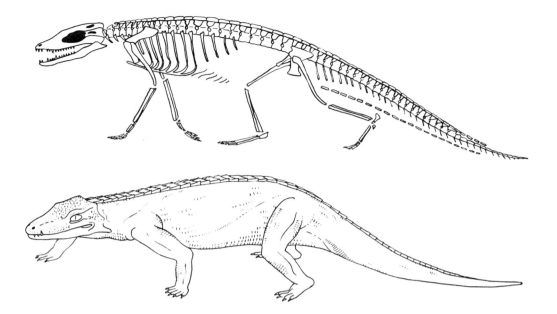

Figure 21 Skeleton (after Wellnhofer) and life reconstruction of *Alligatorellus*, from the Upper Jurassic of western Europe

eyes are exceptionally large, even for an atoposaurid. Further east still, in Shantung, China, the family was represented by *Shantungosuchus*, based on a skeleton of Upper Jurassic age with an estimated length of 33 cm (13½ in). Of special interest is *Theriosuchus*, from the Purbeck beds of Swanage, in southern England. This formation is usually regarded as being of Upper Jurassic age, but has sometimes been assigned to the Lower Cretaceous. *Theriosuchus* was no bigger than any other members of the family (some particularly diminutive fossil specimens may indeed be the remains of juveniles), but there was apparently some tendency in this genus for the pterygoids to contribute towards the structure of the secondary palate — perhaps an initiation of the structure seen in eusuchian crocodiles. Furthermore, a vertebra (probably from the base of the tail) found associated with remains of *Theriosuchus* seems to be of the procoelous type, which also suggests transition to the eusuchian level of evolution. There are small isolated teeth and vertebrae in the Lower Cretaceous Wealden beds of southern England that may be attributable to *Theriosuchus*, indicating that this seemingly very progressive atoposaurid possibly survived somewhat longer than the rest of its family.

Important though the atoposaurids are, because they seem to be possible eusuchian ancestors, they must have played only a modest role in the reptile faunas of the Mesozoic. Other mesosuchians, of much more impressive mien, were apparently far more numerous.

Teleosaurs

Along the shores and estuaries of the extensive early Jurassic seas there was an abundance of superficially gavial-like crocodilians with the long slender snouts usually attributed to fish-eaters. They were the teleosaurs, whose fossil remains were at first assumed to represent extinct ancestors of the living Indian gavial. In fact, the teleosaurs have a typically mesosuchian palatal structure and were not antecedents of *Gavialis*, despite the fact that their nasal bones were short and excluded from contact with the premaxillae by the maxillary elements, which met along the top of the muzzle: a construction that is characteristic of eusuchian gavials but in teleosaurs represents merely a parallel evolutionary adaptation to a similar piscivorous way of life.

All along the edge of their jaws the teleosaurs had numerous pointed teeth (as many as 200 in some species) that must have constituted a remarkably efficient fish trap, while there was an extensive mandibular symphysis (where the two halves of the lower jaw were joined at the front of the muzzle) to provide the elongate structure with adequate strength. The hindlegs of teleosaurs were about twice as long as the forelimbs, which was presumably an adaptation for swimming, and extensive dermal armour protected the body: a paired row of large overlapping plates dorsally, articulated with each other by means of peg-and-socket joints, and a ventral cuirass of irregularly arranged but closely interlocked scutes to shield the belly. The teleosaurs were evidently specialised water-dwellers, possibly preferring calm, sheltered environments in the intertidal or supratidal zones, but also no doubt venturing out into the shallow Jurassic seas on hunting forays and perhaps ascending the lower reaches of rivers to colonise lakes and swamps. Their feet may possibly have been webbed, but the teleosaurs were obviously quite capable of leaving the water, and oviparity seems to be confirmed by the presence of reputed fossil teleosaur eggs in the Lower Jurassic of England. A presumed tolerance to sea water suggests that these reptiles must have had some means of adjusting the salt balance of their bodies to cope with saline conditions, but from fossil remains it is impossible to determine whether they possessed salt glands comparable with those of the living saltwater crocodile.

In the Lower Jurassic, the family is abundantly represented in Europe by *Pelagosaurus* and *Platysuchus*. The more conservative of these two genera was *Pelagosaurus*, a rather small, slimly proportioned reptile some 1.75 m ($5\frac{3}{4}$ ft) long with a narrow, elongate, progressively tapering skull. The snout is less attenuated than in later members of the family and there is no sharply defined demarcation in the facial region between the cranium and the muzzle. Along the edges of the jaws some 30 pairs of slender, finely grooved teeth were implanted almost vertically in well-spaced alveoli to provide a typically piscivorous dentition. *Pelagosaurus* was apparently quite common in the Liassic sea that covered substantial areas of Europe in Lower Jurassic times, remains occurring in southern Germany, France and England.

Platysuchus was a larger, more specialised genus than *Pelagosaurus*, attaining nearly 3 m ($9\frac{3}{4}$ ft) in length, which is represented by a skeleton from the Lias of Holzmaden, in Württemberg. The head of this teleosaur was relatively small, and the tail rather short (comprising only about 38 vertebrae), while the trunk was protected by a series of very wide, deeply pitted dermal scutes that extend back along about three-quarters of the tail. Evidently *Platysuchus* was a powerfully built, well-protected species that must have been a formidable marine predator of 200 million years ago.

Throughout the Jurassic period, the commonest and most widespread teleosaur was *Steneosaurus*, which measured up to 4 m (13 ft) and had an elongate snout (varying somewhat in relative length between the numerous species) of more or less rounded cross-section anteriorly but becoming flattened nearer the facial region, where the cranium flared out abruptly to provide a sharp transition between the muzzle and the rest of the skull. The eye sockets were directed predominantly upwards, and the teeth slanted outwards from their sockets, while the relatively long tail incorporated 40 or more caudal vertebrae.

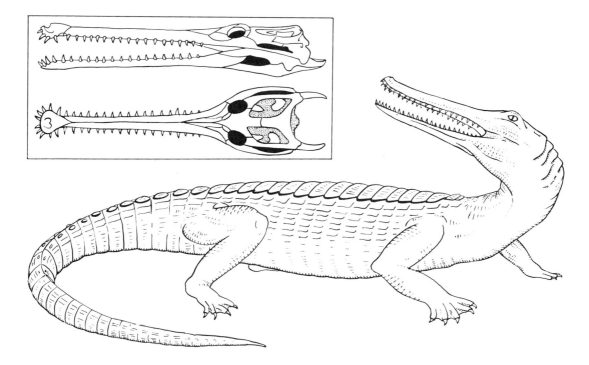

Figure 22   *Steneosaurus* from the Jurassic, with (*inset*) the skull

The shallow sea which covered most of western Europe during the Jurassic period extended from the Iberian peninsula into Asia, with its northern shoreline running across the English midlands. This was the now dwindling Tethys, which had formerly separated Africa from Eurasia. Today all that remains of it is the Mediterranean, the Black Sea and the Caspian Sea, but in Jurassic times its much more extensive waters were the established domain of

Steneosaurus, which may well have ventured far out from Tethyan shores: two vertebrae from the Upper Jurassic of Switzerland were found with fossil remains of organisms normally occurring in water some 200 m (750 ft) deep, and evince osteological features indicative of a deep-water swimmer.

Steneosaurus was already numerous in the Lias (Lower Jurassic), some particularly fine complete skeletons having been recovered from the famous fossil quarries of Württemberg, where rocks of this age are abundantly represented. Liassic *Steneosaurus* skeletons also occur in England, and a solitary vertebra from Mendoza province, Argentina, apparently indicates the presence of this genus in South America during those times. By the Middle Jurassic, *Steneosaurus* was abundant in the western Tethys and could also be found in the waters covering what is now Madagascar, suggesting the presence of a Jurassic seaway connecting the Tethys with southern Africa and providing an oceanic link with the west coast of South America.

The fortunes of *Steneosaurus* continued to flourish in the Upper Jurassic, although the extraordinary abundance of species that have been described from English and French rocks of this age may reflect variations in relative skeletal proportions that occurred during growth to maturity rather than the presence of an exceptional number of different species, and possibly also demonstrates *Steneosaurus* was in any case a reptile which exhibited a great deal of structural variation among individual members of the same species. Indeed, little *Aeolodon*, with a skull not much more than 16 cm (6½ in) in length, which has been reported from the late Jurassic of Germany and France, is probably based only on small examples of *Steneosaurus*.

Contemporaneous with *Steneosaurus* in the European Jurassic was *Teleosaurus* itself, which was obviously very closely related to *Steneosaurus* and in the opinion of some scientists cannot legitimately be separated from it. However, the species of *Teleosaurus*, which measure up to about 2.5 m (8 ft) in length, seem to be slightly more specialised than those of *Steneosaurus*, having exceptionally long, slender, markedly flattened snouts that are consid-

The fossil skull of a teleosaur, *Steneosaurus bollensis*, from the Lower Jurassic of Holzmaden, Wurttemberg.

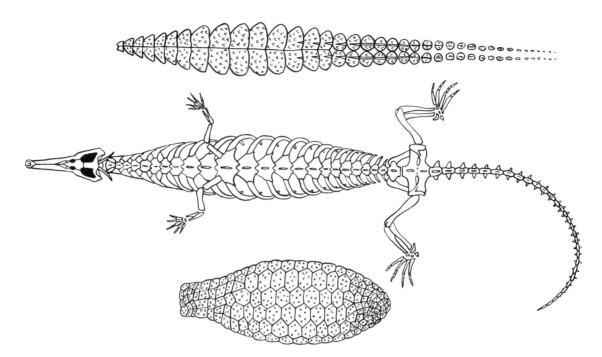

Figure 23 Skeleton of *Steneosaurus*, with (*above*) the dorsal armour and (*below*) the ventral cuirasse which protected the belly

erably expanded at their tips, the premaxillary bones being extremely short. The edges of the jaws in *Teleosaurus* were crenulated, with about 200 pointed, recurved teeth projecting partly outwards from their sockets. The orbits seem to have been orientated essentially upwards, and the skull table, covering the brain case, was considerably wider than it was long.

In the Middle Jurassic, *Steneosaurus* and *Teleosaurus* were joined in the European epicontinental sea by the massive *Machimosaurus*, a teleosaur some 9.5 m (31 ft) long with a relatively short-snouted skull which nonetheless measured 1.5 m (5 ft). The jaws contained stoutly constructed conical teeth bearing a characteristic series of fine longitudinal canals, and the vertebrae articulate by means of zygapophysial facets which indicate that *Machimosaurus* was probably an open-sea dweller, swimming by lateral undulations of the tail and using the limbs only for steering and balancing in the water. At the back of the skull there was a pair of prominent basioccipital tubera (as there are in the living gavial), which it has been suggested may indicate the presence of a powerful ventral neck musculature that possibly endowed *Machimosaurus* with considerable diving capabilities.

The close of the Jurassic period, 140 million years ago, also meant virtually the end of the teleosaurs. Only a few vertebrae and teeth of very questionable identity allegedly indicate their presence in the early Cretaceous, and thereafter no trace of them has been found. They seem to have been a group whose ancestral home was the western Tethys, and profound changes took place there at the close of Jurassic time. For many millions of years this long-established ancient sea had separated the northern and southern continents, its tropical waters teeming with life, its waves lapping gently on the shores of prehistoric continents. Yet even the apparent immutability of the venerable Tethys was subject to inexorable forces of change constantly at work everywhere in the world. At the beginning of the Cretaceous, the formerly dry, semi-arid climate became warm and seasonally wet, while the sea retreated from the land, leaving the future site of London located on an extensive island at the edge of a swampy wilderness extending across southern England to France, with a series of lagoons and salt lakes. A huge river originating somewhere to the northwest, beyond the present shores of Ireland, drained through this region into a vast Wealden delta and finally reached the shores of the shrinking Tethys somewhere in central France.

Not only had the Tethyan environment undergone a substantial revolution in the early Cretaceous, but the old races of Jurassic fishes (holosteans) upon which the teleosaurs presumably preyed were also vanishing, to be replaced by new stocks that were the precursors of today's prolific bony fishes (the teleosts). Deprived of their traditional prey and faced with a radical upheaval in their formerly secure and equable Tethyan realm, the teleosaurs seem to have declined abruptly at the end of the Jurassic and quickly vanished altogether in the Cretaceous period.

Pholidosaurs

They were succeeded by the somewhat similarly adapted but rather less specialised pholidosaurs, a family of slender-snouted mesosuchians with nasal bones extending forward to meet the premaxillae at the end of the nose and with much smaller supratemporal fenestrae for accommodating the jaw musculature than the teleosaurs possessed. They had an extensive series of dermal scutes to protect the neck, body and tail that very much resembled the armour developed by teleosaurs, with similar peg-and-socket articulations between the dorsal plates. They seem, however, to have been denizens of fresh water rather than marine-dwellers, although the remains of one pholidosaur (*Teleorhinus*) occur in sediment laid down by the shallow sea that encroached across much of North America during the Cretaceous.

One of the earliest pholidosaurs was *Anglosuchus*, from the early Upper Jurassic of Oxfordshire in England, other Jurassic representatives of the family including *Crocodilaemus* from France, *Peipehsuchus* from China, and two species of *Pholidosaurus* itself from southern England. By Lower Cretaceous time there was a huge species, *Sarcosuchus imperator*, in northern Africa that attained an estimated length of 11 m ($35\frac{3}{4}$ ft), as well as rather more modestly proportioned species in Portugal and in the Wealden delta that covered northwest Europe (*Suchosaurus*, *Pholidosaurus*), and *Teleorhinus* in the Benton Sea that had submerged Montana and Wyoming (the slender *Teleorhinus browni* and the more powerfully built *Teleorhinus robustus* seem to have lived contemporaneously in this body of water). In

South America during Lower Cretaceous times there was in Brazil what has been termed a 'Gondwana Wealden', a southern area of shallow lacustrine deposition that probably resembled the Wealden swampland on the other side of an Atlantic Ocean which was just beginning to widen between the eastern and western hemispheres. In this part of the now fragmenting Gondwanaland, pholidosaurids were represented by *Sarcosuchus harti*, apparently demonstrating close faunal links between the Old World and the New until quite late in the Mesozoic era; *Meridiosaurus*, from the Lower Cretaceous of Uruguay, may also be a pholidosaurid, but the only known material is a very incomplete fossil snout.

Teleorhinus apparently survived into the Upper Cretaceous of North America, a massive form (*Teleorhinus mesabiensis*) with the tip of its snout turned markedly downward occurring in the Coleraine formation of Minnesota, which was transitional between open shallow sea facies to the west and estuarine deposits to the east. An upper-jaw fragment from Bavaria possibly indicates the presence of *Teleorhinus* in the eastern hemisphere during Upper Cretaceous time, and some teeth from São Paulo, Brazil, may indicate a late surviving species of *Pholidosaurus* in South America.

Dyrosaurs

The pholidosaurids failed to bridge the Mesozoic-Cenozoic gap, but long-snouted mesosuchian evolution continued briefly beyond the age of dinosaurs when the dyrosaurs, which had first appeared in the late Cretaceous, underwent a major diversification. These reptiles have left their bones principally (although not exclusively) in marine deposits, and seemingly enjoyed their greatest success in the southern continents — the former Gondwanaland, now rapidly becoming disrupted by rifting between the tectonic plates. The earliest dyrosaurs are represented by teeth, jaw fragments and vertebrae in the late Cretaceous of North and South America (*Hyposaurus*) and North Africa, together with a well-preserved skull from the Upper Cretaceous of Nigeria (*Sokotosuchus*) that bears a deeply sculptured surface, exhibits a nasal constriction at the junction of the premaxillae and maxillae, and has proportionately large, conical teeth of circular cross-section numbering four in the premaxilla and 13–14 in the maxilla.

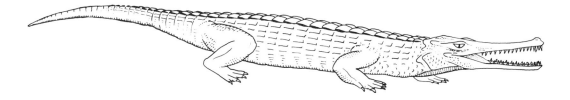

Figure 24 *Dyrosaurus*, from the early Cenozoic of northern Africa

During Palaeocene times dyrosaurs apparently persisted in South America (a vertebra, one or two teeth and a couple of dermal scutes from northern Lake Titicaca, Bolivia), but North Africa became their principal centre of evolution after the end of the Mesozoic era. In the late Cretaceous, this area had been inundated by an extensive shallow sea. In these now retreating tropical waters that nonetheless still submerged much of northern Africa in the early Cenozoic, dyrosaurs were evidently common, their remains occurring from Senegal in the west to Saudi Arabia in the east, and from Tunisia in the north to Angola in the south. Fossil bones of *Dyrosaurus* itself are exceedingly abundant in the phosphate deposits of Tunisia, which were laid down during Palaeocene times. This genus, with a skull some 2 m ($6\frac{1}{2}$ ft) in length, had an exceptionally long and slender muzzle, even for a dyrosaur, and its pointed teeth indicate fish-eating habits. *Rhabdosaurus*, with rather widely spaced teeth, was another dyrosaurian genus present in the Tunisian phosphates, along with *Phosphatosaurus*, a much more massive member of the family measuring about 9 m (nearly 30 ft) which has a long but robustly proportioned snout ending in an enlarged premaxillary region, a strong deep lower jaw, and stoutly constructed dentition, the posterior teeth being blunt-crowned for crushing hard-shelled prey—possibly marine turtles. *Atlantosuchus*, from the Lower Palaeocene of Morocco, had an exceptionally extensive mandibular symphysis that reached as far back as the 17th pair of lower teeth, and *Hyposaurus*, the New World late Cretaceous dyrosaur, has been reported additionally in the Palaeocene of West Africa, together with *Rhabdognathus* (distinguished by the presence of 23–24 pairs of maxillary teeth and a mandibular symphysis extending back to the 16th pair of lower teeth). In the Middle Eocene of Mali there was *Tilemsisuchus*, with a rather less elongate snout than was customary in the more specialised members of the family and large, close-set teeth of circular cross-section. One specimen of *Tilemsisuchus*, a lower jaw, bears two sets of oblique grooves on its surface that were apparently inflicted by the teeth of another member of the same species; the wounds caused by this internecine combat of over 40 million years ago had evidently healed satisfactorily.

During the Eocene dyrosaurs abounded in these waters, ranging as far south as Nigeria and as far eastwards as the Sudan, but with the seas continuing to retreat from the emerging land their days in the region were numbered. Further to the east, there were dyrosaurs in what is now the Indian subcontinent during Upper Palaeocene and Middle Eocene times, and as late as the Upper Eocene there is evidence (teeth, scutes and a large vertebra) of a dyrosaur surviving in Burma, but by this time the family was in steep decline and had already died out in its earlier North African centre of evolution.

Goniopholids

The typical crocodiles of the age of dinosaurs were the goniopholids, a less specialised group than the teleosaurs or dyrosaurs, which had retained a greater dependence on the land than their gavial-like relatives. In general appearance, the Goniopholididae must have looked very like the familiar broad-snouted crocodylines of the present day, although their less extensive secondary palates clearly identify them anatomically as mesosuchians. A characteristic feature is a depressed facial area just in front of each eye socket, and the distinctive dorsal armour, comprising two or more rows of scutes that usually interlock by means of peg-and-socket articulations, is complemented by a well-developed ventral shield.

Goniopholids seem to have been predominantly northern forms, alleged records of their occurrence in the southern supercontinent of Gondwanaland being largely unverified. The typical genus is *Goniopholis* itself, which had a skull up to 70 cm (nearly 2½ ft) in length and some 23 pairs of stoutly proportioned, slightly recurved teeth ranging along the upper and lower jaws. Present in the Upper Jurassic of both Europe and North America, *Goniopholis* subsequently survived only into the early part of the Cretaceous in the Old World but persisted into Upper Cretaceous times in the United States. It seems to have ranged eastwards as far as Thailand during the late Jurassic heyday of the Mesosuchia, but reports of *Goniopholis* from the Brazilian Cretaceous are based on such fragmentary material as to be of very doubtful validity.

Figure 25 Goniopholis, the typical crocodilian of North America and Eurasia in the Jurassic and Cretaceous

Contemporaneous with *Goniopholis* in the Upper Jurassic of North America was *Eutretauranosuchus*, a rather long-skulled genus with about 24 pairs of small, striated, slightly compressed teeth in both the upper and the lower jaws. As in North American goniopholids generally, the mandible exhibits an external fenestra to accommodate the contracting jaw musculature, a feature that does not occur in European representatives of the family. On the eastern side of the embryonic Atlantic Ocean at this time there were some small goniopholids in the Upper Jurassic of southern England (*Oweniasuchus, Petrosuchus*), but they are represented only by very fragmentary fossil remains. Further east still, in what is now eastern Asia, there was a much larger member of the group (*Sunosuchus*) which seems to have been a long-snouted freshwater form: *Sunosuchus miaoi*, with a skull about 40 cm (16 in) long, is from China and may in fact be of Lower Cretaceous age, while *Sunosuchus thailandicus* was an even larger and more massive species, with about 30 pairs of teeth in the lower jaw, from northeast Thailand that is possibly early Jurassic in date rather than Upper Jurassic. Unlike the European goniopholids, *Sunosuchus* agrees with North American forms in possessing an external mandibular fenestra.

In Lower Cretaceous times the family was still present in southern England, the little slender-snouted *Vectisuchus* being a denizen of the great Wealden delta that covered the area at this time, and in the Upper Cretaceous of Portugal there are late-surviving examples of *Oweniasuchus*, although the material upon which *Oweniasuchus lusitanicus* and *Oweniasuchus pulchelus* are based comprises only jaw fragments and isolated teeth. Goniopholids were still represented in the earlier part of the North American Upper Cretaceous (*Coelosuchus, Dakotasuchus, Pinacosuchus, Pliogonodon, Polydectes*), but none of these forms is adequately known and they were presumably a rare and dwindling band in this area, finally vanishing well before the end of the period.

In Asia the family clung on until towards the close of Cretaceous time, *Kansajsuchus*, with a broad-snouted skull about 50 cm (20 in) long and protective scutes along the back bearing characteristic median crests and tubercles, being present in Tadzhikistan and Uzbekistan, while in Mongolia there was *Shamosuchus*, a short-snouted genus (probably including several species described under the name *Paralligator*) that had facial ridges on the frontal and lacrimal bones, with dentition comprising four premaxillary and 13 or 14 maxillary teeth. *Shamosuchus* seems to have been fairly common in the late Cretaceous of Mongolia, which in those times was not the arid desert area it is today, but a deltaic region fed by a huge river, with ponds, lakes and lush vegetation. Even here, however, the goniopholids failed to survive into the last stages of the Cretaceous, when huge tyrannosaurid dinosaurs stalked their prey where the sands of the Gobi now stretch from horizon to horizon, and two supposed South American goniopholids of Upper Cretaceous age, *Microsuchus* and *Symptosuchus*, are poorly documented and of uncertain provenance. In the opinion of some scientists, however, modern eusuchian crocodiles may be of goniopholid ancestry rather than atoposaurid origin, in which case the descendants of these ancient crocodiles are still with us today.

Small land crocodiles

Two families of rather small, short-nosed crocodiles that seem to have been essentially terrestrial forms occur in Cretaceous rocks on opposite sides of the South Atlantic but nonetheless appear to be closely related and probably shared a remote but unknown common ancestor. Their simultaneous presence in South America and North Africa provide strong evidence for a land connection between the two continents still persisting some 110 million years ago, although it must have been severed by the steadily widening proto-Atlantic ocean very shortly afterwards. The Notosuchidae had conspicuously large eye sockets and a reduced tooth count, *Notosuchus* itself (from Argentina) having only seven maxillary and ten dentary teeth, the premaxilla containing three small incisiforms and an enlarged canine-like element that has no counterpart in the lower jaw, while *Araripesuchus* (from Brazil and North Africa) has four small conical premaxillary teeth, eleven maxillary teeth (including enlarged anterior caniniforms) and about 16 pairs of lower teeth. *Uruguaysuchus* comes, as its name suggests, from Uruguay, and was just over 1 m ($3\frac{1}{4}$ ft) long. It had a well-differentiated dentition with the second maxillary tooth enlarged and most of the maxillary and mandibular teeth exhibiting the sort of laterally compressed crowns normally associated with predatory terrestrial carnivores rather than aquatic fish-eaters; one species of *Uruguaysuchus* is distinguished by the presence of 13 pairs of maxillary teeth, a second member of the genus (possibly a more specialised form) possessing only nine pairs. *Brasileosaurus*, based only upon a femur about 11.5 cm ($4\frac{1}{2}$ in) long and a humerus from São Paulo, Brazil, may be a junior synonym of *Uruguaysuchus*.

The Libycosuchidae includes only a single species, *Libycosuchus brevirostris*, from the Baharija beds of Egypt. The short, high skull, about 18 cm (7 in) long, of this quite diminutive crocodilian hinged with a lower jaw whose two constituent halves diverged widely behind an abbreviate but unusually massive symphysis, the muscles for opening and closing the mandible having apparently been exceptionally strong. The teeth were of markedly differentiated type and set very close together.

There may be some grounds for including these two families (the Notosuchidae and the Libycosuchidae) in a separate infraorder, the Notosuchia, and it is possible that among these rather poorly known but apparently essential terrestrial forms there are to be found the South American ancestors of a much larger group of land-living crocodiles that enjoyed a very successful career during the earlier part of the age of mammals: the relatively large and powerful sebecosuchians.

Miscellaneous mesosuchians

Throughout the Jurassic and Cretaceous periods, fully mesosuchian crocodiles were evidently a major feature in the reptile faunas of a world which for the most part enjoyed warm, equable, tropical or subtropical conditions far into the high latitudes. This span of geological time represents an interval of over 130 million years, a very considerable slice of evolutionary history during which there must have been a multitude of different crocodilians taking advantage of opportunities to exploit widely varied ecological conditions. Many of the major groups that prospered in what must have seemed like a timeless, unchanging succession of endless centuries are well represented in the fossil record: the teleosaurs, the goniopholids and the pholidosaurs, for example. There must, however, have been many mesosuchian types that chose to dwell in areas or circumstances that were inimical to the preservation of their fossil remains. Some have certainly vanished without leaving any trace at all in the geological record; others are represented by isolated (sometimes unique) specimens and have no obvious close relations.

There is, for example, *Trematochampsa*, from the Upper Cretaceous of Niger, in northern Africa and Madagascar, which was relatively small (up to 3 m/9$\frac{3}{4}$ ft in length) with a deep, narrow but relatively short-snouted skull. This genus, a surprisingly primitive crocodilian for a mesosuchian occurring so close to the end of the Mesozoic, has serrated anterior teeth and blunt-crowned posterior dentition.

By contrast, *Bernissartia* from the Lower Cretaceous of Belgium is a very progressive mesosuchian. Only about 1 m (3$\frac{1}{4}$ ft) in length, *Bernissartia* had the vertical bar of bone behind the eye socket displaced inwards below the level of the skull surface in a manner typical of modern crocodiles. The dorsal armour comprised four longitudinal series of dermal scutes, those of the median rows bearing two antero-posteriorly orientated ridges which become progressively more prominent further back in the sequence, and those of the lateral rows only a single ridge. Two complete skeletons of *Bernissartia* were found at the famous coal mine near Bernissart which yielded the remains of innumerable iguanodonts, massive plant-eating dinosaurs that walked primarily upon their hindlegs. Teeth that may be referable to *Bernissartia* occur in the Lower Cretaceous of southern England, and a juvenile specimen only 30 cm (12 in) long was found in rocks of similar age in Spain.

Artzosuchus is a rather obscure mesosuchian from Mongolia, and *Sphagesaurus* is even less understood, the only known material being several isolated laterally compressed teeth from the Upper Cretaceous of Brazil that have short crowns coated with coarsely pebbled enamel exhibiting prominent, irregularly spaced longitudinal ridges. The roots are exceptionally long for a crocodilian, and there is a prominent ridge running down the posterior edge of the crown that bears on its crest a series of small tubercles. *Sphagesaurus* teeth are not the sort of dentition normally associated with crocodiles, and there must be some doubt as to their true affinities.

Two major groups of strongly contrasted crocodilians that had not achieved the eusuchian level of palatal evolution (with the pterygoid bones fully incorporated in the secondary palate) had become so highly specialised for totally disparate habitats that they are customarily assigned to entirely separate suborders: the Thalattosuchia, which were wholly aquatic and lived in the open sea, probably never venturing on land at all, and the Sebecosuchia, which seem to have spent most of their time out of the water altogether.

Sea crocodiles

The thalattosuchians, or sea crocodiles, were contemporaneous with the teleosaurs from the Middle Jurassic to the Lower Cretaceous and flourished in the same shallow Tethyan seas that covered much of Europe at this time. They had become totally adapted to life in the ocean, with their limbs transformed into paddles (the hind ones relatively long and slender, possibly to provide swimming thrust, the front ones short, broad manoeuvring appendages) and the end of the spine diverted downwards to support the bottom lobe of a vertical tail fin: beautifully preserved specimens of thalattosuchians from Germany show a fossil impression of the fin's fleshy upper lobe. As would be expected in fully aquatic forms, these crocodiles had lost all vestiges of dermal armour.

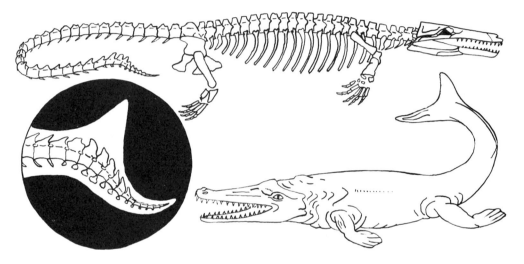

Figure 26 Skeleton and life reconstruction of the sea crocodile *Metriorhynchus* with (*inset*) the tail skeleton and caudal fin of the related *Geosaurus*

The thalattosuchian skull was smoothly streamlined to facilitate passage through the water, with no well-defined demarcation between the muzzle and the facial region such as the teleosaurs possessed. The frequently pitted or grooved prefrontal bones were considerably enlarged and overhung the forwardly and outwardly directed orbits, presumably providing a measure of protection to the eyes (which incorporated rings of sclerotic plates), these bones together with the frontals and nasals being considerably lightened by the presence within them of spongey bone and large cavities. The secondary palate was of a conservative mesosuchian type, with the internal nares opening from the palatal bones rather than the more posteriorly located pterygoids, and the dentition comprised numerous conical teeth which were often of a compressed pattern.

Whether animals as fully committed to an aquatic existence as the thalattosuchians were still capable of venturing out of the water at all is a matter of conjecture. If they were unable to haul themselves ashore after the manner of living marine turtles to lay eggs, then they must perforce have brought forth their young alive, in ovo-viviparous fashion, perhaps ascending river courses to do so in the relative security of fresh waters. The contemporary ichthyosaurs were also reptiles that had become fully aquatic, with legs converted into paddles, a vertical tail fin and, in their case, a fleshy dorsal fin as well; there is evidence that ichthyosaurs certainly were ovo-viviparous, fossilised skeletons of embryos having been found within the body cavity of presumed females or even emerging from the birth canal, death having overtaken both the mother and the newborn at the same instant.

A typical rather generalised thalattosuchian is *Metriorhynchus*, which was common in the earlier Upper Jurassic Tethyan sea. A relatively long-snouted form, its remains are quite abundant in rocks laid down on former shorelines of this Mediterranean precursor, notably in northern France (Normandy) and across the southern midlands of England (Oxfordshire). *Metriorhynchus* had also managed to spread to the southern hemisphere along seaways opening out between the old continents of Gondwanaland and flourished as far afield as the western coast of South America. Indeed, remains of thalattosuchians occur in Chilian deposits as old as the Lower Jurassic, although the material is too fragmentary for reference to any particular genus or species. Evidently the origins of the thalattosuchians must lie well back in the early Jurassic: perhaps their ancestry is to be found among the oldest of the Liassic teleosaurs, such as *Pelagosaurus*, which some workers do in fact regard as a primitive thalattosuchian. The Middle Jurassic *Teleidosaurus*, from France, was also at one time customarily classified among the teleosaurs, but seems in reality to be a rather short-snouted thalattosuchian of early date that is apparently at a somewhat primitive stage of specialisation for its fully aquatic life style. The presence of thalattosuchians in Chile right at the beginning of the Jurassic suggests that their main centre of evolution may not necessarily have been the Tethys, despite their subsequent abundance in its warm tropical waters.

Metriorhynchus survived in western Europe until towards the close of Jurassic time, but by then other, more specialised thalattosuchians (possibly direct descendants of *Metriorhynchus*) had made their appearance. *Dakosaurus*, some 4 m (13 ft) in length, represents a short-snouted line of thalattosuchian development that seems to have prospered through the European Upper Jurassic, *Cricosaurus* apparently being another representative of this group. By contrast, *Geosaurus*, although relatively small (only 2.5 m/8 ft long) had a narrow, elongate snout and seems to represent a distinct evolutionary advance over *Metriorhynchus*, occurring in the upper levels of the European late Jurassic and possessing shorter, broader and more specialised paddles. *Geosaurus* had also lost most of the bone ornamentation seen in *Metriorhynchus* skulls, while the caudal vertebrae at the bend that diverted the spine downwards into the lower tail-fin lobe had developed massive, forwardly directed neural spines and enlarged chevron bones which strengthened the structure and virtually eliminated any movement save in the lateral plane. *Geosaurus* may have persisted briefly into the Lower Cretaceous of western Europe and was also present in the Upper Jurassic of Argentina, along with *Purranisaurus* (a less advanced, *Metriorhynchus*-like form). *Neustosaurus*, *Capelliniosuchus* and *Enaliosuchus* are poorly known thalattosuchians from the European early Cretaceous, but the group does not appear to have survived any later than this. One reason for their extinction may have been the withdrawal of the shallow Tethys Sea from much of Europe, with similar epicontinental seas likewise retreating elsewhere in the world. The rise of teleost fishes could also have deprived the thalattosuchians of their holostean prey, and it is perhaps significant that in both England and Argentina the bones of *Metriorhynchus* occur with those of a holostean fish (*Hypsocormus*) upon which it may have preyed and which became extinct at the end of the Jurassic. Further evidence of how *Metriorhynchus* lived came to light when a skull bone from another holostean fish closely related to *Hypsocormus*, the huge *Leedsichthys*, was discovered with a *Metriorhynchus* tooth embedded in it. *Leedsichthys* was perhaps double the size of a large *Metriorhynchus*, so these extinct sea crocodiles were evidently voracious predators game to tackle prospective prey far larger than themselves. In this case the attack was apparently unsuccessful, as new bone had formed around the embedded tooth as the wound healed. D. M. Martill of Chicago's Field Museum found some specimens of *Metriorhynchus* in the Oxford Clay of England that included some of the fossilised stomach contents. These discoveries were described in 1986 and demonstrate that *Metriorhynchus* did not live exclusively on fish. There were hooklets from cephalopod arms, part of the guard from a belemnite (an extinct relative of the living cuttlefish), and two hollow elongate bones possibly from an unfortunate pterosaur — in all likelihood snatched as it swooped low above the surface hawking for fish. Also present was a rounded quartz pebble that may have been a gastrolith.

Invading the land

Entirely different from the fully aquatic thalattosuchians were the sebecosuchians, which apparently spent most of their time on land. First appearing in the late Cretaceous, this group of crocodiles (usually made the subject of a separate suborder) possessed high, narrow skulls with a deep facial region and the eye sockets orientated more or less laterally. The post-orbital bar was recessed below the surface of the skull, but the very wide internal nares were situated at the end of a comparatively short secondary palate of mesosuchian type that did not extend to the pterygoid bones. The lower jaw was deep and narrow, and the dentition had become numerically reduced: only 13 or 14 pairs of teeth in each jaw, with four pairs of premaxillary dentition. These teeth were a very distinctive feature of sebecosuchians, their laterally compressed configuration with serrated edges being the ziphodont pattern found also in carnivorous dinosaurs and the pristichampsine eusuchians. The post-cranial skeleton of sebecosuchians is unfortunately not well known, but the vertebrae are apparently platycoelous (the centra are of a relatively conservative type with slightly concave ends)

161

and dermal armour seems not to have been extensively developed.

Manifestly these were land-living crocodiles, their eyes being designed to look sideways, rather than to a greater or lesser extent upwards as in aquatic forms. The remarkable ziphodont teeth are very difficult to distinguish from those of theropod dinosaurs and pristichampsine crocodiles, and the occurrence of isolated presumed sebecosuchian teeth has in the past created considerable confusion. The sebecosuchians apparently arose in South America late in the Cretaceous and succeeded in surviving the mass extinctions that marked the end of the Mesozoic era. During the late 19th century, their compressed, serrated teeth were found by a pioneer Argentinian palaeontologist, Florentino Ameghino, in association with the remains of Cenozoic mammals. Sebecosuchian crocodiles were still unknown to science at this time, and Ameghino jumped to the conclusion that the teeth must be dinosaurian, which meant that in South America these reptiles had survived beyond the end of the Cretaceous. The persistence of dinosaurs into the Cenozoic would have been a revolutionary discovery, but eventually it became apparent that Ameghino was mistaken, although his error was understandable in view of the limited information then available. The compressed, serrated teeth were crocodilian, of sebecosuchian origin.

Another problem is posed by the presence of ziphodont teeth in the early Cenozoic of Europe, Asia, North Africa and North America, and the late Cenozoic of the Australian region. Some of these undoubtedly belong to pristichampsines, but where dentition occurs without associated skull material it is almost impossible to be sure if the teeth are from those eusuchians or from late-surviving sebecosuchians. Ziphodont teeth of Pliocene age from New Guinea and Australia have been identified as sebecosuchian, and it is quite conceivable that the group might have persisted in this isolated zoological backwater until a very late date, having spread to the area from a South American homeland before the southern supercontinent of Gondwanaland finally broke asunder. On the other hand, pristichampsine eusuchians were certainly present in Australia during the Pleistocene: were they recent arrivals from the north that temporarily displaced the sebecosuchian survivors as major terrestrial predators until themselves exterminated after the arrival of man, or did two similarly adapted, competing crocodilian groups persist more or less side by side in Australia throughout most of the Cenozoic? Certainly Australia lacked any placental mammalian carnivores in prehistoric times, which would have left an ecological niche available for crocodilian exploitation, but whether sebecosuchians and pristichampsines could have co-existed there for very long must be rather doubtful.

The oldest and most primitive sebecosuchians belong to the family Baurusuchidae, which first appears in the Upper Cretaceous of South America. Short-snouted forms of quite modest dimensions, with the dentition limited to a relatively small number of large teeth in the anterior part of the jaws, they include *Baurusuchus* itself (an early genus, from the late Cretaceous of Brazil, with two pairs of large canine-like teeth in the front of the maxillary bone), and *Cynodontosuchus* (of similar age, from Patagonia, with only a single upper 'canine' and a matching tooth in the lower jaw). Often assigned to the Baurusuchidae, but not certainly members of the family, are two crocodiles from the European Eocene with ziphodont teeth (*Bergisuchus* from the famous fossil quarry at Messel in West Germany, and *Iberosuchus* from Portugal), but these two genera may represent a separate parallel development from *Trematochampsa*, the small mesosuchian that was present in northern Africa and Madagascar during the late Cretaceous. There is also an alleged sebecosuchian in the Eocene of the United States, fragmentary remains of a small crocodilian that include serrated, laterally compressed teeth having been identified as *Limnosaurus* by O. C. Marsh in 1872, but the material is poorly documented and cannot be accepted as unequivocal evidence of a North American sebecosuchian.

Whether or not these outlying forms were true sebecosuchians, the most progressive members of the group unquestionably flourished in South America, where there were no large placental mammalian carnivores for most of the Cenozoic, just as was the case in Australia. In their absence, powerful terrestrial crocodilians filled the vacant ecological niche for a predator capable of hunting down the extraordinary fauna of bizarre herbivorous mammals, often of substantial size, that had evolved in this isolated continent.

Peirosaurus was a notably broad-snouted genus from the Upper Cretaceous of Brazil and possibly Argentina that probably merits assignment to its own special family (the Peirosauridae), and by Eocene times *Sebecus* itself (named after the Egyptian crocodile god, Sebek) was present in Patagonia. The oldest species of *Sebecus* (*Sebecus icaeorhinus*) had a skull about 45 cm (18 in) in length that was not only deep and laterally compressed but also relatively long-snouted, although the characteristic ziphodont teeth numbered only 14 pairs in the upper jaw (with four in each premaxilla) and 13 pairs in the mandible. There was a notch at the junction of the premaxilla and maxilla to receive the enlarged fourth lower tooth, and the jaw articulation was of an unusual double configuration, with the quadratojugal and surangular forming a subsidiary joint alongside the conventional quadrate/articular hinge.

By Miocene time *Sebecus* had nearly doubled in size and become an even more powerfully proportioned reptilian predator. *Sebecus huilensis* occurs in Colombia and possibly eastern Peru, and had teeth that were substantially longer, slimmer, more laterally compressed and more recurved than its Eocene forerunner. Despite its formidable bulk, however, time was running out for *Sebecus*. Some time during the Pliocene a land link became re-established between North and South America, allowing a southward influx of modern mammalian species. The archaic indigenous fauna of South America quickly succumbed to this invasion, and sebecosuchian crocodiles suffered extinction, presumably unable to compete with newly arrived specialised mammalian carnivores and finding the immigrant herbivores a less vulnerable prey than the rapidly dwindling South American plant-eaters.

Closely related to *Sebecus* and assigned to the same family (the Sebecidae) were the Lower Eocene *Ayllusuchus* and the Oligocene *Ilchunaia*, both from

163

Argentina, so it is apparent that South America really was the heartland of sebecosuchian evolution; reports of this assemblage from elsewhere in the world have not been adequately substantiated. There is even a claim for a Chinese sebecosuchian: *Wanosuchus* was a small short-snouted crocodilian, probably of Palaeocene age, that is represented only by half of a lower jaw about 15 cm (6 in) in length found in Anhui province which has the typically sebecosuchian 'double articulation' (quadrate/articular, quadratojugal/surangular) and contains 13 ziphodont teeth. At the beginning of the Cenozoic, China was effectively at the other end of the world from South America so far as animal migration was concerned, the only viable routes being either via North America, Europe and Asia or via Africa, assuming that the Atlantic had not yet widened sufficiently to cut off completely the eastern and western hemispheres. If *Wanosuchus* really is a sebecosuchian, its presence so far from the group's presumed centre of origin in South America is difficult to explain, but on the other hand a piece of broken jaw is not a very comprehensive basis for identification.

The oldest crocodiles

Modern crocodiles, the Eusuchia, are evidently descended from the mesosuchians, with the thalattosuchians and sebecosuchians as sterile side branches, but the question which then arises is where did the mesosuchians come from. Ultimately they must have sprung from the primitive archosaur stock (the thecodonts) early in the Triassic period, some 225 million years ago, but what filled the hiatus between then and the first mesosuchians of the Lower Jurassic?

In the 200-million-year-old Upper Triassic rocks of Arizona, there are the remains of a small reptile only 1 m or so ($3\frac{1}{4}$ ft) in length that is without doubt a very early crocodile. Initially named *Archaeosuchus* ('ancient crocodile') but subsequently re-identified as *Protosuchus* ('first crocodile') because it was discovered that the designation *Archaeosuchus* had already been employed (for an extinct mammal-like reptile), this little creature had a relatively short skull with only an incipiently crocodilian snout, the dentition including about four premaxillary and 13 maxillary teeth, with an intervening diastema (a gap in the tooth row), opposed by approximately 17 mandibular teeth, one of which was enlarged and canine-like. The vertebrae had amphicoelous centra (concave at both ends), and there were five toes on each front foot and four toes on the hind (the fifth toe of the back foot is represented only by a vestigial metatarsal bone). Along the back, a row of large rectangular dorsal scutes was present on either side of the spine, with small rectangular plates protecting the belly and the ventral surface of the tail.

There are grounds for believing that *Protosuchus* was in fact already beginning to acquire specialisations for an essentially terrestrial way of life that would debar this archaic genus from the direct ancestry of subsequent crocodilians. Its eyes were orientated laterally rather than upwards, for instance, and some of the limb bones — notably the humerus, the femur, and the proximal carpal elements (radiale and ulnare) — were becoming elongate, while the calcaneum (or heel bone) had a prominent tuber for the attachment of flexor muscles (this feature occurs quite frequently in the pseudosuchian stock from which later archosaurs are descended, but is rare in dinosaurs and absent in all post-Triassic crocodilians).

Close relatives of *Protosuchus*, referable to a common family (the Protosuchidae) occur in the Upper Triassic of South Africa (*Baroqueosuchus, Lesothosuchus*) and Argentina (*Hemiprotosuchus*); there is also a second protosuchid in the Upper Triassic of Arizona (*Eopneumatosuchus*), and another example of the group has been found in Massachusetts (*Stegomosuchus*).

Some scientists believe that the terrestrial specialisations of *Protosuchus* and other very early crocodilians indicate a cursorial stage in the evolution of the group, with subsequent regression to a less energetic life style. The rather long hindlimbs of crocodiles and an ankle-joint construction that suggests initiation of the dinosaurian ankle-joint structure (which enabled many dinosaurs to run on their hindlegs) perhaps remain as lingering legacies of an initial rather more ambitious stage in crocodilian evolution. A. D. Walker of Newcastle-upon-Tyne University in England even suggested in 1970 that one small fossil reptile usually regarded as a bipedal dinosaur (little *Hallopus*, from the Upper Jurassic of Colorado) was in reality a late-surviving cursorial crocodile. Certainly *Lesothosuchus* has unusually long limbs and may have been a cursorial form: a crocodile adapted for running may seem strange in the light of subsequent crocodilian evolution, which led to predominantly semi-aquatic forms more at home in the water than on land, but in Triassic days there were wide-open opportunities for archosaurian reptiles to exploit practically every available ecological niche. From the turmoil of inter-species conflict, the dinosaurs eventually emerged as the dominant predators on land, while the crocodiles retreated to the water, where they seem to have supplanted a group of extraordinarily crocodile-like thecodonts (the phytosaurs) that had their external nostrils shifted back in the skull to an elevated position only just in front of the eyes. The phytosaurs are typically Upper Triassic forms and therefore too late in time (and much too specialised in their own way) to have been actual crocodile ancestors, but it was their ecological niche that the crocodiles ultimately annexed and exploited with such success for the next 200 million years. Whether the crocodiles actually displaced the phytosaurs, or simply moved into the Triassic lakes and rivers when the phytosaurs became extinct for some other reason, it is impossible to say.

The Protosuchidae are associated in the suborder Protosuchia with a second family, the Sphenosuchidae, whose members are distinguishable only with difficulty from some of the contemporary pseudosuchian thecodonts. *Pedeticosaurus* (with a rather low skull, and limbs and feet that might conceivably be those of a biped) and *Sphenosuchus* (notable for its pneumaticised skull and functionally three-toed hindfeet) are from the Upper Triassic of South Africa, while *Platyognathus* (a flat-skulled species with a terminally expanded snout) is from rocks of similar age in southwest China.

A broad-skulled, short-snouted crocodile (*Edentosuchus*) from the Lower

Cretaceous of Wuerho, China, was initially interpreted as a late-surviving protosuchian, but it is hard to envisage a markedly primitive Triassic group managing to survive through the Jurassic in competition with mesosuchian crocodiles except perhaps in total geographical isolation, and China does not appear to have been cut off from the rest of the world during the Mesozoic. Subsequent re-assessment of *Edentosuchus* suggests that it is in fact a mesosuchian, although a somewhat specalised one, with a reduced dentition differentiated into anterior incisor-like teeth, caniniforms, and cheek teeth.

A second suborder of Upper Triassic crocodilians seems to have comprised less ambitious forms quite happy to remain skulking in the early Mesozoic lakes and streams. The Archaeosuchia had relatively long snouts, eye sockets orientated essentially upwards, the post-orbital bar already depressed below the surface of the skull, and primitive amphicoelous vertebrae. The secondary palate, however, was only at an early stage of development: the pterygoids were not involved in it, and nor were the palatines. Only a single family, the Notochampsidae, is assigned to this group, with three constituent genera. Two of these are from southern Africa: *Notochampsa* (which includes *Erythrochampsa*), known only from fragmentary material which represents two species; and *Orthosuchus*, about 66 cm (26 in) long, with a flattened, slender-snouted skull measuring 90 mm (3½ in). *Microchampsa* comes from Yunnan, China, but the two published specimens comprise just articulated series of vertebrae with a few associated ribs, foot bones, and dermal scutes.

None of these late Triassic genera is an obvious ancestor for the mesosuchians of later Mesozoic days, so the line of crocodilian descent remains obscure. There can be no doubt, however, that crocodiles are today the sole surviving archosaurs—the only 'ruling reptiles' still living, over 200 million years since they first emerged from some unknown ancestor among the Triassic thecodents.

Extinction

This remarkable feat of survival makes crocodiles a significant factor in attempts to determine what caused the 'great dying' at the end of the Cretaceous period, when whole major groups of animals seem to have abruptly become extinct. The most conspicuous casualties were the great reptiles: not just the dinosaurs, but also flying reptiles (pterosaurs) and the mighty 'sea dragons' of the Mesozoic oceans—the ichthyosaurs, plesiosaurs and mosasaurs. Other formerly flourishing forms to disappear at this time included ammonites (cephalopod shellfish related to nautiloids) and rudist bivalves, which looked more like corals than like molluscs.

Conventional wisdom declared that the dominant life forms of the Mesozoic era became extinct at the end of the Cretaceous period over an interval of time that was brief in geological terms but nonetheless probably ran to several million years. One or two groups of Mesozoic reptiles—stegosaurian dinosaurs, for example, and the ichthyosaurs—were in fact already in steep decline early in the Cretaceous and disappeared long before the end of the period, but the fossil record undoubtedly indicates that the end of the Mesozoic was marked by extensive extinctions. Climatic change was frequently cited as the probable cause, perhaps triggered by the redistribution of land masses following the break-up of the two Mesozoic supercontinents (Laurasia and Gondwanaland). Such a major geographical revolution would have disrupted long-established weather patterns and perhaps ushered in a more seasonal climate than the almost universally equable warmth which typified the age of reptiles, as well as cutting off intercontinental animal migration routes.

The discovery of a thin layer of rare metals such as iridium and osmium at precisely the dividing line between Mesozoic time and the succeeding Cenozoic era suggested to some scientists that the late Cretaceous extinctions took place in just a few years (perhaps less than a hundred) and were caused by some cataclysmic occurrence of extra-terrestrial origin. It was claimed that the iridium and osmium originated in an asteroid, giant meteorite or comet that had collided with the Earth, perhaps exploding on impact to raise a huge cloud of dust that would have completely blotted out the sun for up to five years, or generated torrents of lethal acid rain. Few plants would have survived, and all animals exceeding 75 lb (34 kg) in weight must inevitably have died.

Once the idea that the late Cretaceous extinctions could have been almost instantaneous had acquired a degree of scientific credibility, other theories were put forward. The explosion of an unstable giant star — a supernova — in the neighbourhood of the solar system was one. Another was disruption of the Earth's magnetic field during one of the periodic reversals of the planet's polarity that have occurred at intervals throughout geological time, permitting deadly cosmic rays to reach the surface.

A major stumbling block to all these proposals of sudden ecological catastrophe at the end of the Cretaceous has been the remarkable durability of the crocodiles, for these reptiles had no apparent difficulty in surviving the transition from Mesozoic to Cenozoic time. Quite large genera, such as *Leidyosuchus*, occur on both sides of the dividing line, and some Palaeocene forms, such as the dyrosaur *Phosphatosaurus*, were huge creatures up to 9 m (about 30 ft) in length. Not only did some of the ancient mesosuchian stock and early representatives of its eusuchian successors successfully survive the great dying, but even the curious terrestrial sebecids made the transition to Palaeocene time and continued to flourish until relatively late in the Cenozoic.

It could perhaps be argued that only small crocodiles (weighing less than 75 lb/34 kg) survived the late Cretaceous extinctions to give rise to the post-Mesozoic stocks. But then why did small dinosaurs not survive as well? Not all the dinosaurs were giants. Some were no larger than a chicken, even when adult. The extraordinary persistence of crocodiles remains a serious objection to the acceptance of cataclysmic theories allegedly accounting for the extinction of their dinosaurian relatives and other Cretaceous life forms. The crocodiles have become a living key to the unsolved mystery of mass extinctions in the geological past.

7.

The case for conservation

Crocodiles first appeared at the same time as the earliest dinosaurs. More than holding their own in a world of Mesozoic reptilian giants, they long outlasted their archosaurian relatives, surviving the cataclysmic extinctions at the end of the Cretaceous period and continuing to flourish throughout the age of mammals.

Even the ice ages of the Pleistocene had little adverse effect on them, except to reduce somewhat their geographical range as higher latitudes became too cold. Less than 200 years ago, crocodiles were as numerous and as flourishing in the tropical zone as they had ever been. Today their numbers have been decimated by hunting and habitat destruction, and everywhere they are a beleagured race, clinging precariously to the last vestiges of their former wilderness homelands.

Nile crocodiles, which once teemed in uncounted thousands along the watercourses of Africa, had disappeared from the Nile delta by 1700 and two centuries later were rare anywhere below Aswan. Morelet's crocodile was so abundant in Belize early in the 20th century that K. P. Schmidt, from Chicago's Field Museum, reported hundreds of these reptiles readily visible at any time from the causeway that linked Belize City to the adjacent high ground. A British zoologist, Ivan T. Sanderson, visited Belize in the 1930s and found that Morelet's crocodile was common in roadside ditches, taking virtually no notice of passing traffic, and as late as the 1940s these reptiles were often to be seen beneath the Haulover bridge that carries the country's busiest road from the city to the airport. By the end of the 1960s, none was left in these situations and the locations of surviving colonies in Belize, Guatemala and Mexico were difficult to ascertain because the local people tend to try and keep such information secret: to poor Indians, the profit from even a small number of crocodile hides is an invaluable source of revenue, and organised parties of hide-hunters, who would speedily wipe out such remaining groups, or conservationists intent on stamping out hunting altogether, would be exceedingly unwelcome.

Before European colonisation, the American alligator abounded throughout the coastal plain of the southeastern United States, but its subsequent decline was abrupt. By the middle of the 20th century, indiscriminate hunting and habitat destruction had almost eliminated it from Texas, Arkansas, Oklahoma, northern Louisiana, most of Mississippi and Alabama, the clay hill country of the Florida Panhandle, the upper coastal plain of Georgia and the Carolinas, and all areas north of Albemarle Sound.

For every living species of crocodile, this melancholy story has been repeated. In New Guinea, populations of both the saltwater crocodile and the New Guinea freshwater crocodile have been decimated and in some areas totally wiped out along the Fly and Sepik Rivers, where they were once common. The Siamese crocodile is now almost unknown in the wild and substantial breeding stocks exist only in captivity, while the Chinese alligator formerly infested the Yangtze and was greatly feared by local people but has declined rapidly throughout its already limited range. The mugger had become rare everywhere in India by the early 1970s and was extinct in Burma, while the American crocodile population of southern Florida had been reduced to an estimated 500 individuals in 1973, over half of them in the Everglades National Park, where more than 80 per cent of active nesting sites were located.

Johnston's crocodile was still being intensively hunted for its skin until the 1970s, although protected in Western Australia since 1962 and in Northern Territory from 1964, and a 1973 survey of 5000 km (3100 miles) of waterways in India and Bangladesh revealed only six gavials in this part of the reptile's former range, whereas 40 years previously these rivers had been described as 'teeming with crocodilians'. From South America, it was reported by Federico Medem in 1976 that at most 300 Orinoco crocodiles remained in the Colombian Orinoco plains, formerly one of the principal strongholds of *Crocodylus intermedius*.

Native tribes have habitually killed crocodiles with spears, harpoons or other primitive weapons for meat or for skins, but only to satisfy their own needs. Nets were often used for the initial capture, while baited lines to which pronged hooks had been attached served to secure crocodilians in many parts of the world. In Guyana, the Indians used a four-pronged device with the spring-loaded points wedged apart by blocks of wood, baited with agouti intestines wound around the prongs to hold them together· when swallowed by a crocodilian, the prongs sprang open in the creature's stomach. In Malaya and Sarawak, a crescentic piece of wood with sharpened ends, baited with fish, served a similar purpose, and in the Congo two crossed pieces of wood were used to catch crocodiles. Such methods were inevitably inefficient and time-consuming: the number of crocodiles taken was small, and not a scrap of usable hide or eatable meat was wasted. There is some additional demand for crocodile products to be used as personal jewellery by native tribes, teeth or claws for example often being attributed with magic or protective qualities. In China it was at one time believed that the contents of the Chinese alligator's

169

gall bladder helped women in childbirth, would disperse boils or skin eruptions, and was an efficacious remedy for the bite of a mad dog, while in the Sudan the tribeswomen anointed themselves with pomades and ointments made from compounded crocodilian musk glands (sometimes complete glands were worn like beads, in a necklace). Even in mediaeval Europe, whores tried to beautify themselves by applying powdered crocodile dung.

Unrestricted killing was a consequence of the availability of firearms, and the appearance of an international trade in crocodile skins. The creatures were not only abundant and relatively easy to kill with a rifle, they were also widely detested and could be dangerous, so professional crocodile-hunters generally found themselves welcomed by native communities. There was a substantial profit to be made, and destroying crocodiles was regarded only as the elimination of vermin. Passengers on vessels proceeding down the Mississippi, the Nile or other large, crocodilian-infested rivers would idly take pot-shots at alligators or crocodiles lying on the bank, wantonly killing or injuring them.

Only the skin of the belly and flanks is normally saleable, as this lacks the rough, scaly armour which protects a crocodile's back. Some species, notably the caimans, have very broad dorsal armour and bony platelets in the ventral scales, which makes their hides less valuable than those of, for example, the saltwater crocodile, which has very little dermal armour and is furthermore an exceedingly large reptile. Crocodile skins are traditionally employed for a wide range of expensive luxury goods, such as suitcases, shoes and handbags, later applications including watch straps, fancy belts, and (in the 1980s) Filofax bindings. Fashionable and possessed of a rarity value, they constitute an immensely profitable trading commodity. The consequences for crocodile populations have been catastrophic. In the early 1970s, there was a worldwide trade of 100,000 skins a year from the saltwater crocodile alone, while the relatively small state of Tchad annually exported 15,000 Nile crocodile skins through three licensed dealers (of the country's estimated population of 700,000 crocodiles in the 1940s, only about 10 per cent remained three decades later), and Gabon was exporting about 20,000 hides a year.

With recruitment to stocks estimated at only 2 or 3 per cent per annum, such wholesale exploitation meant that crocodile populations crashed. Rivers and lakes formerly full of crocodiles now lacked any at all. Their disappearance meant, of course, that some of the natives who had been earning a little money on the side supplying hide dealers with skins (usually at derisory rates of remuneration) were now without this useful perk. More important still, the stocks of small fish (e.g. tilapias) which in many parts of the world form a staple part of the local diet now also began to decline. The reason was easy to discover. Crocodiles had been an integral link in the ecology of tropical lakes and rivers, preying on the catfish which themselves eat tilapias and other small fish. With no crocodiles to act as a control, the catfish multiplied unchecked and ate all the available smaller fish. Riverside communities thus lost one of their major sources of food, as well as their lucrative trade in crocodile skins.

Obviously it makes good economic sense to conserve crocodile stocks at a level which would enable them to fulfil their ecological role and also to support a steady but modest skin trade. The other major factor in the decline of the world's crocodiles, however, is habitat destruction. Conservation measures have no chance of success if the animals' habitat has been destroyed by agricultural and urban development, with swamp drainage, waterway pollution and the construction of dams and harbours. Conversely, if habitat still exists, crocodiles have proved to be remarkably efficient at recolonising an area, given a chance to do so by protective legislation.

Habitat destruction is particularly rapid and irreversible in societies that have developed an affluent, consumer-orientated economy with high living standards which generate a demand for luxurious, attractively located housing and sophisticated recreational facilities such as yacht marinas and safe bathing beaches. The United States is an obvious example of this head-on conflict between the needs of wildlife and the aspirations of a moneyed working population constantly seeking to enhance its living standards. In Florida and Louisiana, alligators and crocodiles had no place in the real-estate boom that took off during the mid-20th century as Americans sought living space, recreation or retirement in the sun-soaked south. In the 1970s, development of just six south Florida counties resulted in the destruction of 23 per cent of the area's alligator habitat. Elsewhere in the world the story is similar: crocodiles and people do not readily mix. Increasingly, wild crocodile populations are in danger of being killed out either for their hides or because encroaching urban and agricultural communities will not sanction their continued presence.

Crocodile-farming

So-called alligator farms have existed in the United States since late in the 19th century, but many are really only tourist attractions, drawing most or all of their revenue from admission charges to visitors. Some of these enterprises, however, do hold adult alligators for breeding purposes and can legitimately call themselves farms, while others are in effect rearing stations, where eggs or juveniles either taken from the wild or obtained from captive stocks are reared for hides, sometimes under the umbrella of an official trading permit that specifies returning a percentage of juveniles to the wild, the stipulated figure depending on the number of eggs originally collected.

Crocodile-farming could be a practical proposition, maintaining breeding stocks of crocodilian species and financing itself from the sale of skins. For some species, the proportion of eggs in the wild producing hatchlings which ultimately grow to adulthood may be as low as 2 or 3 per cent, owing to nest predation, flooding, and juvenile mortality. Under protected artificial conditions it should not be difficult to improve substantially on this survival rate. Unfortunately, it is proving less simple than it looks at first sight, and many crocodile farms started in America and elsewhere have quickly gone out of business.

171

Crocodilian eggs are not like hens' eggs, only bigger. They require special treatment if successful hatching percentages are to be obtained. The membranes are very thick compared with those of a hen's egg, and the shell consists of 40 per cent calcium, 42.6 per cent carbon dioxide, 2.82 per cent magnesium and 0.37 per cent phosphorus (compared with, respectively, 38.7 per cent, 42.9 per cent, 0.59 per cent and 0.13 per cent in the domestic fowl). Crocodilian egg shells are therefore richer in calcium than the shells of birds' eggs, although the developing embryo derives only about $2\frac{1}{2}$ times as much calcium from the shell as it does from the egg contents, compared with five times as much in birds.

Within 24 hours of laying the embryos become attached to the shell membrane on the upper surface of the yolk, and if the orientation of eggs is subsequently changed by turning them over the embryos will die. University of New South Wales scientists G. J. W. Webb and S. C. Manolis, working with other researchers, determined in 1987 that at first a crocodilian egg contains albumin, yolk, and the small aggregation of embryonic tissue. As development proceeds, water is withdrawn from the albumin and accumulates beneath the embryo, above the yolk. Shrinkage occurs first in the albumin immediately above the embryo enabling the vitelline membrane (surrounding the yolk sac) and the embryo to become adherent to the shell membrane. Subsequently the albumin below the yolk is eliminated, allowing the vitelline membrane to attach itself to the shell in a band around the middle of the egg, visible externally as an opacity. Finally, even the albumin at the poles of the egg disappears, leaving the shell completely opaque.

Optimum temperature and humidity conditions have to be ascertained for incubating the eggs of each crocodilian species and rigidly monitored during development. Eggs of the Chinese alligator, for example, have to be maintained at 30–33°C and 88 per cent relative humidity, with hatchlings kept in a temperature of 30°C until they reach a weight of 40 g (1.3 oz). The eggs of American alligators require a temperature of 28–30°C and up to 100 per cent relative humidity, and must also be surrounded by nesting material that permits the growth of the nest bacteria normally found in wild nests: these generate acidic metabolic by-products which M. J. W. Ferguson of Queen's University, Belfast, discovered in 1981 attack the outer densely calcified layer of the shell, causing progressive crystal dissolution with the production of concentrically stepped erosion craters. This increases the porosity of the shell (no air space develops in an alligator egg, conventional pores occurring only in the centre of the shell) and at the same time reduces its strength so that the shell cracks away from the underlying membranes after 60 days or so and the juveniles emerge five days later. Without this bacterial presence to progressively weaken the shell, the young may find it difficult or impossible to break out and could asphyxiate.

Eggs from farm-reared alligators were in 1983 determined by V. Lance of Tulane University, New Orleans, and two colleagues, to have lower fertility and hatchability than eggs collected from wild alligators, apparently owing in part to an excess of fish in the parents' diet. Captive females were found to exhibit higher plasma selenium levels and lower vitamin E levels than wild alligators. It was suggested that, since wild alligators eat substantial quantities of coypu (allegedly up to 70 per cent of their total food intake in some localities), adding coypu meat to the diet of captive animals should improve the quality of eggs they produced. This revised regime certainly boosted vitamin E levels and lowered the plasma selenium count, but the eggs of the captive females still did not match wild eggs in quality.

Congenital defects in hatchlings are quite common, and in the wild severely affected individuals do not survive for long. A malformed, indented rib cage affected nearly 3 per cent of newly emerged New Guinea freshwater crocodiles in a survey conducted by J. Jerome Montague of Crocodile Farms (NT) Pty Ltd in the Northern Territory of Australia, while other defects noted included hunchbacks, misaligned jaws, and an absence of claws. L. A. K. Singh and H. R. Bustard reported in 1982 that gavials suffer from bent necks, absence of one or both eyes, corneal defects or a malfunctioning pupil that fails to close properly in the light, squints, bent tails, hunchbacks, crossed jaws, absence of the palatal valve, incorrect umbilical construction, a bulged belly, and an upturned tail tip. Some of these malformations (e.g. bent necks, upturned tail tips) are self-correcting, but animals with bent tails could not swim properly and kept to shallow water, and some of the other defects were obviously incompatible with survival.

It is believed that congenital defects of one kind or another do occur quite regularly in hatchlings of wild populations, and are to at least some extent attributable to such causes as desiccation of the nest or too high (or too low) an incubation temperature. There is also a suspicion that a 'blindness gene' is present in the gavial populations of the Kali, Narayani, Gandaki and Karnali Rivers of Nepal, since eggs taken from these locations always yield a significant number of hatchlings with eye defects.

If artificial incubation is to be undertaken, it is evidently vitally important to ensure that eggs are as healthy as possible if derived from captive parents and, whatever their source, are given the most natural possible incubation conditions.

Successful rearing really starts even before any eggs are transferred to a hatchery. If eggs from captive animals are to be incubated, attention must be paid to the stocking density of adult holding pens, ensuring a proper diet for breeding females, providing nesting materials, and avoiding any unnecessary disturbance of mating pairs and brooding females. Adult breeding stock requires a substantial area of land for the creatures to haul themselves out, with secluded spots shaded from direct sunlight. Fresh water must be kept circulating through breeding ponds to avoid a build-up of algae and pathogenic bacteria, but frequent drainage of these large tanks for cleaning and/or treatment of water to clear algae has not been found necessary.

At the Samut Prakan crocodile farm in Thailand, there are separate feeding ponds, about 8 m (26 ft) square and 50 cm (20 in) deep, in which fish is supplied daily: these always need to be cleaned out every 24 hours, with the removal of left-over food to avoid contamination. This establishment provides nesting stalls measuring 4 m by 4 m (13 ft by 13 ft), each with a 60 cm by 60 cm (2 ft by 2 ft) entrance, around the outer edge of the land area surrounding the breeding ponds, nesting materials (dried grass) being placed in each stall. After the eggs have been laid, the female is denied access to her stall and the incubation of the eggs is carefully monitored by farm staff, who add extra grass if the nest temperature falls below 95°F (35°C) or take grass away if it exceeds 98°F (36.6°C). Hatching rates of 40–60 per cent are achieved at Samut Prakan with saltwater crocodiles and Siamese crocodiles. Subsequently juveniles are raised in concrete nursery tanks, 30 × 50 × 40 cm (12 × 19¾ × 15¾ in), each accommodating up to 15 hatchlings. As the animals grow, they are moved to progressively larger tanks — 1.25 m (4 ft) square, 2 m (6½ ft) square, 3.6 m (11¾ ft) square — with removable intervening partitions to make still bigger pens. A mortality of up to 30 per cent during the first year of life is experienced at Samut Prakan (these fatalities may be taxidermised for the tourist souvenir market), losses of only 5 per cent per year being experienced with older crocodiles.

In Africa, Anthony Pooley has successfully reared Nile crocodiles on a substantial scale from eggs obtained in the wild. At the time of collection the eggs are carefully marked to show the upper surface as they lay in the original nest, and they are then transported in well-padded corrugated cardboard containers to a hatchery for reburial in rows of specially excavated artificial nests. Sand is added to or removed from the top of nests to maintain the temperature at 28–34°C, and watering may be necessary to ensure optimum humidity. After hatching, juveniles are transferred to rearing pens, which in Africa need to be 60 cm (2 ft) deep to prevent the water from becoming too hot under the tropical sun; copper sulphate will help to control algae, but daily draining and cleaning is necessary. In areas with a relatively low winter temperature, earth rearing ponds are advisable, as the juveniles can dig their own burrows in which to take refuge from the cold. Confining fences, however, should go down deeply enough to prevent the inmates from burrowing their way out altogether, and since young crocodiles can climb with agility it is better to roof the entire enclosure with wire netting (which will also keep out marauding predators). The main disadvantage of earth pools is that they cannot be cleaned on a daily basis: the only practical procedure is to drain them completely every two months or so and then leave them to bake in the sun as a means of purification. The stock, of course, have meanwhile to be accommodated in alternative ponds, so if earth pools are in use the farm is obliged always to have a substantial surplus of rearing pens.

Very young crocodiles are notoriously difficult to keep in a flourishing condition, requiring careful attention to diet and accommodation. Recommended stocking densities vary from a suggested 400 individuals in a 12 by 12 m (40 by 40 ft) enclosure to a more generous 100 youngsters in a 15 by 15 m (50 by 50 ft) pond with a depth of 50 cm (20 in). Pooley prefers low stocking rates of 25 juveniles per rearing pen, as this reduces competition and fighting at feeding time, limits the spread of disease, and enables the well-being of each individual crocodile to be properly monitored. Pens should be about 8 m (26 ft) apart to minimise transference of pathogens from one pen to another (by flies, air currents, or on the clothes and footwear of attendants).

A less sophisticated system of crocodile-farming has been successfully implemented in Papua New Guinea, with the involvement of the local population, who have thus been encouraged to become supporters of crocodile conservation instead of actively prosecuting the wholesale destruction of these creatures. Both *Crocodylus porosus* and *Crocodylus novaeguineae* are still relatively abundant in the interior swamps of this country, so it was scarcely practical to try and persuade the natives to build village crocodile farms when crocodile populations existed on the doorstep. On the other hand, indiscriminate hunting of New Guinea's crocodiles was by the 1960s beginning to make serious and potentially disastrous inroads into the stock.

Initially the export of crocodile skins with a belly width exceeding 50 cm (20 in) was banned, so that breeding adults would be protected. At the same time the natives of Papua New Guinea were encouraged to take very young crocodiles (which suffer a substantial mortality in the wild during their first year of life) for farm rearing, and a number of 'demonstration ranches' were established by the government to serve as models for proposed village ranches which it was anticipated would hold about 100 crocodiles in simple pens constructed from readily available local materials. By the late 1970s about 200 village ranches were in existence, holding a total of 8,000 or so crocodiles, but these local sites tended to flood in the wet season or to run out of water in the dry months of the year, and it proved unexpectedly difficult to ensure a regular food supply for the captives.

Meanwhile two large commercial crocodile farms had been established, one at Port Moresby, the other at Lae, and it was therefore decided that these operations should be encouraged to act as rearing centres for young crocodiles caught by villagers, with the former demonstration ranches functioning as intermediate holding points from which captive animals were airlifted by the commercial undertakings in batches of 300–400, the 50–90 cm (20–35 in) crocodiles being packed in specially made cardboard tubes and boxes. The government controlled the price villagers were paid for juvenile crocodiles, ensuring that it was high enough to make bringing in live animals more profitable than simply selling skins. Some medium-sized private ranches were also established in Papua New Guinea, sited near abattoirs and fish plants that could provide a regular supply of offal for the crocodiles, and these undertakings sold their surplus stock to the large commercial ranches at Lae and Port Moresby.

This official government scheme, which has United Nations Food and Agricultural Organisation assistance, means that villagers can earn a legitimate living from their local crocodiles, effectively 'farming' them without having to destroy forest and swampland habitats as they would if they were engaged in more conventional livestock husbandry. In their first year, young crocodiles have a food conversion rate of 50 per cent (i.e., for every 2 lb/kg of food they consume, they put on 1 lb/kg of weight, only about a fifth the amount of food required by domestic animals for a similar weight gain), so these animals represent a very efficient means of exploiting the natural resources of Papua New Guinea's wilderness areas. By the time a crocodile is three years old, its food conversion rate is only about 30 per cent, and at this age the animals are slaughtered by severing the spinal cord behind the skull, yielding a belly skin up to 2.25 m (7½ ft) long and 25–50 cm (10–20 in) wide that was worth about 150 US dollars in the early 1980s. The feet and the dorsal armour are of no value and must be thrown away, but the meat will be fed to other crocodiles or sold to tourist hotels, where guests find crocodile steaks a palatable novelty!

All crocodile skins exported from Papua New Guinea are shipped by licensed companies whose cargoes are checked and tagged by government inspectors. In 1983, 37 per cent went to France, 62 per cent to Japan and the small balance to Singapore, the number of farm skins sold that year being 1,605, with wild-caught skins totalling 16,941. Strict Papua New Guinea licensing laws restrict hunting or trading in crocodiles, and it was anticipated that the proportion of ranch-raised skins in the annual sales figures would show a steady rise. About three-quarters of ranch stocks are freshwater crocodiles, the rest being of the saltwater species.

Papua New Guinea probably still supports a population of ½ million wild crocodiles, producing perhaps ¾ million eggs a year, so the scheme has plenty of potential, although it has been criticised on the grounds that it encourages the continuance of an international trade in crocodile skins, thus providing an incentive for poaching activities elsewhere in the world. The solution must be to secure international co-operation in regulating this trade so that only legally acquired hides eventually reach the manufacturers of fashionable goods in Europe and Japan. Attempts on the part of the Indonesian authorities to promote similar crocodile-breeding schemes in Irian Jaya have not been particularly successful: the saltwater crocodile is now greatly depleted in western New Guinea and only the freshwater species occurs there in sufficient numbers to support a farming enterprise.

By the 1980s, there was an estimated world trade of over 1 million crocodile skins a year. At least 700,000 of these are derived from *Caiman crocodilus* (the real figure is probably considerably more), while some 80,000 skins are attributable to the major crocodilian species; the balance comprises hides from crocodilians not highly regarded by the tannery trade, and illicit smuggled skins for which there are of course no official statistics. In addition, there is a tourist market for stuffed juvenile crocodiles, and in Florida visitors buy live baby 'alligators' (now usually spectacled caimans) to take home; these unfortunate juveniles have a short life expectancy, and once their novelty value fades they are frequently either just dumped in a convenient pond to die in the next northern winter or else flushed down the toilet (rumours that survivors from the bathroom exit route were subsequently breeding in the sewers beneath New York are pure fiction!).

Only some 12,000 skins a year are produced on crocodile farms worldwide and the trade is still developing only gradually. Hides from wild *Caiman crocodilus* are cheap, while production costs of an American alligator on a farm were estimated at about 110 US dollars, with a slaughter value of around 300 US dollars, and in Australia a 6-ft (1.83 m) crocodile with a skin worth 180 Australian dollars probably cost 55 Australian dollars to raise. Between 1980 and 1984 the Samut Prakan farm in Thailand was obliged to reduce its slaughter rate from 1,500 animals a year to only a few hundred as prices for unprocessed hides tumbled from 250 US dollars to 90 US dollars: a market as unstable as this makes the establishment of viable commercial breeding operations a particularly hazardous undertaking.

Australia, for example, had four farms in the Northern Territory in 1983 (one established as far back as 1973) and one in Queensland, with licences being granted only to suitably experienced prospective operators. China could boast only a single farm of any size breeding Chinese alligators (the Anhui Xuancheng farm), and in Cuba there is the large establishment at Laguna de Tesoro with 1,000 adult crocodiles (80 per cent *Crocodylus rhombifer*, 5 per cent *Crocodylus acutus* and the rest hybrids) together with a small unit at Tasajera.

A crocodile breeding and management project was initiated in India in 1975, with some 2,000 eggs a year being collected from the wild for incubation at rehabilitation stations (specially selected sanctuaries or national parks) which by 1983 numbered 34. Madagascar has at least one major crocodile farm, which accommodated 450 Nile crocodiles in 1983, and in Mexico seven government-department-backed centres are endeavouring to breed *Crocodylus moreleti* (which has a highly esteemed hide, lacking osteoderms, that makes a top-class leather) and *Crocodylus acutus*. There have been crocodile farms in South Africa since 1968, under the auspices of the South African Crocodile Farmers' Association, with total stocks of some 2,200 Nile crocodiles in 1983, while Zimbabwe in 1984 had nearly 28,000 Nile crocodiles in six ranches (16,000 rearing stock, 11,466 hatchlings, 52 mature males, 186 mature females). Crocodile-farming in Zimbabwe began in 1965 and is now overseen by the Crocodile Farmers' Association of Zimbabwe, the industry still being based largely on the collection of eggs from the wild (10,908 in 1983, of which 91.3 per cent hatched).

Taiwan has about 35 farms producing 2,000 or so hatchlings a year, the total stock comprising about 8,000 *Caiman crocodilus* (this is the only country breeding this species, which is raised for meat, on a large scale), 300 gavials and 300 saltwater crocodiles. Operations in Thailand centre on the massive Samut Prakan facility, where over 10,500 crocodiles were held in 1984 (mostly *Crocodylus siamensis*, but with some saltwater crocodiles and hybrids between the two species); this farm sells 60 per cent of its hides locally, the rest going principally to France and Japan, while the meat is sold for human consumption (it is regarded locally as a remedy for asthma) and the teeth find uses in Thai medicine.

Most of the technical problems involved in breeding and rearing crocodiles in captivity have now been solved, but the future of these enterprises must surely lie with large, efficiently run and properly equipped plants. A situation such as that which pertains in Singapore, with large numbers of small-time 'backyard' crocodile-rearers keeping half a dozen or so of these reptiles behind shops and houses or on small conventional farms under very poor husbandry conditions, is not likely to be maintained in the face of competition from large-scale units. Farmed skins are in fact often of a higher and more uniform quality than hides derived from wild crocodiles, so the business potential is considerable.

Management in the wild and in captivity

Maintenance of the original wild stock in its natural habitat is nonetheless still exceedingly important, partly because most farming enterprises continue to rely on eggs collected from the wild (under official supervision in Zimbabwe, the United States and Australia), but also to provide periodic genetic re-enhancement of captive-breeding stock.

The handling of small crocodiles obviously poses no major problems, but adult individuals of species that grow to a large size are another matter. Even animals only 2–2.5 m (7–8 ft) in length are a considerable handful if attempts are made simply to net them, and securing the jaws with rope is an urgent priority once a reptile of this size or larger has been caught. G. J. W. Webb and H. Messel of Sydney University reported in 1977 that they found three-ply 21-gauge fish netting suitable for hand-netting crocodiles up to 1.5 m (5 ft) long, and employed set nets of 25-cm (10-in) stretched mesh with a 40-kg (88-lb) breaking strain to block creeks and surround basking crocodiles of relatively large size. Smaller mesh (6–10 cm/2½–4 in) with a 10-kg (22-lb) breaking strain can also be used: it will snare small fish, and crocodiles then entangle their teeth in the net while trying to steal the fish, usually ending up with their jaws securely bound by the mesh becoming wrapped around their snouts. Webb and Messel sometimes used a harpoon made from a brass rod with the straightened ends of two no. 10 shark hooks attached to it, this device being attached to a 3–5 m ($9\frac{3}{4}$–$15\frac{1}{4}$ ft) pole. Crocodiles were harpooned either in the neck or in the tail, the flattened portion of the hooks preventing deep penetration, so that the superficial wounds need no medication. For animals over 2.5 m (8 ft) long, two harpoons were recommended.

Small crocodiles hiding in vegetation can be extracted with 'Pilstom' tongs, taking care not to catch hold of a limb, as a struggling reptile can result in injury to the leg. A successful rope trap to catch crocodiles ashore (thus ensuring that they cannot drown) can be constructed of 20-mm ($\frac{3}{4}$-in) circumference synthetic rope sewn into a net of 25-cm (10-in) stretched mesh, each crossover being bound with heavy cord. A good size for such a trap is about 5.5 m (18 ft) long and 1 m ($3\frac{1}{4}$ ft) wide across the mouth, which should face the river.

Tranquillisation or the use of muscle relaxants to permit capture or relocation of crocodiles is frequently practised, as well as being used for moving or trans-shipping zoo animals and administering veterinary treatment. Essential criteria for the use of these drugs include the need for a short induction period, availability of an antidote, compatibility with other drugs, absence of adverse reaction at intramuscular injection sites, and a small volume of injectant to achieve required dosage rates. Additionally, drugs should be inexpensive, and safe for human operatives to handle.

The reaction of different species of crocodiles to the same drug may vary, and there are very few data available on this aspect of drug administration. Dose rates are normally computed on the basis of body weight, which is often difficult to estimate, especially in the case of wild crocodiles, although tables that give the probable weight for estimated total lengths are available. Favoured sites for intramuscular injection are the base of the tail, the biceps femoris muscle of the upper hindleg, and the intraperitoneal route, while if a projectile is employed the aiming site is the flank or the base of the tail. Intravenous injection is not a well-established procedure, and the intracardiac route is considered to be potentially dangerous to the subject.

Muscle relaxants should not be used for surgical procedures on humanitarian grounds, but are invaluable for translocating crocodiles. Gallamine triethiodide, a synthetic drug which is similar to curare in its action, has proved particularly good, a safe dosage being 0.64–4.0 mg/kg of body weight (2 mg/kg for animals of less than 10 kg, 1 mg/kg up to 200-kg body weight, 0.5 mg/kg up to 500 kg). Immobilisation takes 8–30 minutes, recovery times varying from 45 minutes to 15 hours, using neostigmine methyl sulphate as an antidote at dosages of 0.03 to 0.07 mg/kg. Crocodiles on which gallamine triethiodide has been used normally resume feeding within about four days (translocation by simple restraint has sometimes led to crocodiles refusing food for up to 18 months).

Succinylcholine chloride has also been used successfully on crocodiles as a muscle relaxant, but there seems to be a wide range of individual tolerance to this drug. Delivered intramuscularly at rates of 3–9 mg/kg, it induces muscle relaxation in about four minutes, with spontaneous recovery requiring seven to nine hours (there is no antidote available). According to A. M. Klide and L. V. Klein of the University of Pennsylvania in 1973, resumption of normal feeding habits takes up to two weeks.

Although d-Tubocurarine has been used on crocodiles intramuscularly or intraperitoneally at rates of 12–18 mg for a 90–180 kg adult, its effects are not sufficiently well documented to justify its regular use on these reptiles, and nicotine alkaloid is not recommended for crocodiles (it fails to work satisfactorily and has hazardous after-effects).

Scoline (suxamethonium chloride BP) was used intramuscularly by H. Messel and D. R. Stephens of Sydney University to immobilise saltwater crocodiles and Johnston's crocodiles in the Northern Territory of Australia for the purpose of affixing radiotelemetry devices. They reported in 1980 that the action of the drug was sometimes blocked if the animal remained on land, but became operative in 7–12 minutes if its body was immersed; conversely, Scoline did not work if the animal's head was held below the water, taking effect in five minutes after the reptile was brought ashore (although sometimes only partially). Dosage rates were just over 1 mg/kg for a 5-kg Johnston's crocodile, and about 0.5 mg/kg for a 20–35 kg animal of this species, with saltwater crocodiles needing up to ten times this dosage.

When using muscle relaxants for translocation, it is important to keep the subject warm, with noise reduced to a minimum and an eye bandage applied to minimise stress. Large animals should be carried on a rigid stretcher to obviate internal injury from the unsupported weight of their bodies.

For general anaesthesia, etorphine hydrochloride at 0.4 mg/kg for large individuals induces immobility in about 25 minutes subcutaneously (more quickly intraperitoneally) and will be effective for up to three hours. It is, however, an expensive drug, and uneconomic for field usage or translocation. Pentobarbitol sodium injected at 7–28 mg/kg produces anaesthesia in 10–45 minutes, but the onset of ataxia and immobilisation is unpredictable, pentamethylenetetrazol must be administered to prevent respiratory failure, and the effects take up to five days to wear off. Other injectable anaesthetic drugs that have been used on crocodiles include phencyclidine (11–22 mg/kg, but requiring a long induction period and an extended recovery), ketamine (44–50 mg/kg) and tiletamine (2.2–4.4 mg/kg).

Inhalation anaesthesia has been employed on manually restrained crocodiles with their jaws taped shut, using a bag over the nostrils. Tracheal intubation and the use of a rebreathing veterinary anaesthetic apparatus stabilises narcosis under halothane, 3:1 nitrous oxide/oxygen or chloroform. Generally speaking, inhalation anaesthesia is best regarded only as a supplementary method of immobilisation for crocodiles following the use of etorphine or pentobarbitol: it is difficult to administer and suitable life-support systems are not readily available, but for major surgery, e.g. limb amputations, it is inevitably the procedure of choice.

Hypothermia is a viable technique for subduing crocodiles, particularly for translocation in zoos, but it is not very practical for large individuals and should be employed with care as the physiological responses and tolerances of different species have not been fully determined. It ought not to be used for surgical procedures without an additional local anaesthetic.

Status today

From a conservation aspect, the American alligator is probably better situated than any other crocodilian species. Habitat destruction and unrestricted hunting had so decimated stocks by the 1960s that the species became officially protected as an endangered animal in ten states (Alabama, Florida, Georgia, Mississippi, South Carolina, North Carolina, Texas, Louisiana, Arkansas and Oklahoma). Limited harvesting of alligators for skins was sanctioned in 1972, but even with this cull and probably some poaching taking place the stocks had risen to gratifyingly high numbers in the mid-1970s, when about 600,000 alligators (75 per cent of the total population) were living in Florida and along the coastal swamps of Georgia, Louisiana, South Carolina and Texas. As a result, the alligators of these areas were reclassified as not threatened, along with thriving populations in Alabama and Mississippi. In some areas of Texas, numbers doubled within five years, while around Miami they proliferated to such an extent that police were collecting alligators from swimming pools, golf courses, backyards and even downtown street corners so that they could be returned to the Everglades.

In 1980, the United States Fish and Wildlife Service permitted the export of alligator hides for the first time since 1969, and within a few years in Florida alone some 1,800 of these reptiles were being killed annually under the

Nuisance Alligator Control Program run by the Florida Game and Freshwater Commission. Overall in the United States, between 10,000 and 16,000 alligators were culled each year, plus another 1,000 slaughtered on alligator farms, which emphasises the small part these establishments play in the hide trade. The first skins from captive-bred animals were not in fact sold on the open market until 1978. All hides and meat offered for sale have to be officially tagged or labelled by the state authorities, and even the killing or sale of alligators requires a licence. Heads and feet can be sold as curios to tourists, while gall bladders and penises find a market in the Orient for their alleged medicinal attributes. Since the first commercial alligator farms were opened in Louisiana in 1954, the number of operations has gradually risen to between 20 and 30, about two-thirds of which are in Florida and virtually all of the rest in Louisiana (a solitary farm was functioning in Texas in the mid-1980s).

The Chinese alligator has been driven out of much of its original homeland along the Yangtze by building and agriculture, while the peasants regarded it for many years as a pest that was detrimental to fish-farming and duck-rearing. Consequently the alligators were killed whenever they were seen, and in the breeding season children were encouraged to smash their eggs. Indiscriminate use of pesticides and chemical fertilisers that seriously depleted the alligators' food resources was a further factor in the species' decline. More enlightened councils now prevail, and by 1986 a breeding programme was incubating 600 eggs a year with a 70 per cent hatchling survival rate, the total population of captive-bred Chinese alligators numbering about 1,000 (Anhui province, where most of the remaining non-captive representatives of the species live, probably has fewer than 300 wild Chinese alligators left).

Of the caimans, *Melanosuchus* has suffered the worst from persecution, this big crocodilian with a hide valued because of its largely osteoderm-free flanks having become rare over most of its former range by the 1980s. In French Guiana and Guyana it had been shot out virtually to extinction, and the species was declining rapidly in Peru. The black caiman is absent from Surinam, despite the fact that there is no commercial hunting in the country and the government is amenable to proposals for studies on crocodilians. Such a sizeable reptile is unlikely to be regarded as an acceptable neighbour by rural communities or agricultural enterprises, and with a commercially saleable hide the black caiman's prospects cannot be regarded as bright. Only in eastern Ecuador is it not in immediate danger of extinction — wildlife is fully protected in this state — and it has been estimated that the present *Melanosuchus* population is only 1 per cent of what it was originally.

Caiman itself was valued early in the 20th century for its fat (used as a fixing agent by the perfume industry) and as a source of oil for lamps or for ointment to treat wounds and rashes, but initially escaped hunting for its skin because of the bony platelets present in the belly scales. Once a means had been devised of tanning such hides, the future of these reptiles became a good deal less secure, and in the Pantanal area of Brazil the large *Caiman crocodilus yacare* (which has few osteoderms and therefore yields a valuable skin) has been wiped out in some places, although still fairly abundant here and there;

this subspecies is now seriously threatened in both Argentina and Paraguay, despite legal protection. Nonetheless, *Caiman crocodilus* remains common in Surinam and is protected in Venezuela, Brazil, Ecuador and Mexico, although the legislation is only weakly enforced. Perhaps surprisingly, the spread of cattle ranches in tropical South America seems if anything to have increased the amount of habitat available to this species.

The little smooth-fronted caiman (*Paleosuchus*) is so small and so heavily armoured that the commercial value of its hide is negligible: the principal danger to this diminutive denizen of the South American rainforests is habitat destruction. Unfortunately, logging and ranching operations are making such substantial inroads into the forests of this region that *Paleosuchus* faces a very uncertain future.

The New World crocodylines are in anything but a flourishing condition. American crocodiles (*Crocodylus acutus*) have not been recorded from the Florida east coast since the 1930s, and elsewhere in Florida they are now restricted to the islands of Florida Bay, parts of the Florida Keys, and mainland shores south of Cape Sable. The Everglades population is slowly being built up towards a maximum density of 2,000 individuals, the most the area can support. In Jamaica the American crocodile is restricted to the south coast of the island (reported occurrences on the northern shore are almost certainly of escaped or released former captives) and the population does not exceed 2,000 animals, while in Mexico *Crocodylus acutus* no longer breeds on the Pacific coast, although in Vera Cruz it is regarded as a tourist attraction — unfortunately it is not difficult for visitors to bribe the local people to take them on illegal hunting trips. It has largely vanished from Venezuela and is in abrupt decline in Peru, while stocks in Belize, Costa Rica, Colombia, Guatemala, El Salvador and Nicaragua have fallen precipitately. Only in Panama and on Hispaniola are reasonable numbers still present, with a dense population of around 3,000 individuals occurring at the large Dominican salt lake of Lago Enriquillo (some 35 m/115 ft below sea level) and a smaller group of 70 crocodiles at Etang Saumatre in Haiti; in addition, a few American crocodiles still survive along the southern coast of Hispaniola, but the species has been exterminated from 70 per cent of its former range in this littoral environment. What remained of the United States population received official protection in 1975, and the species was listed by the United States Fish and Wildlife Service in 1980 as endangered in Central and South America, thus putting a stop to United States trade in *Crocodylus acutus* skins.

The Orinoco crocodile (*Crocodylus intermedius*) is in an even worse case. Easier to hunt than caimans because it frequents rivers or lakes readily accessible by boat, and possessed of a commercially valuable hide, this species has diminished to a pathetic remnant of its former relative abundance. By 1976, in addition to the Colombian population of about 300 adults, there were only another 1,000 or so individuals in Venezuela.

Morelet's crocodile (*Crocodylus moreleti*), commercially hunted since the 1930s but still very common in the 1950s, is now rare throughout most of its range, largely as a result of hide-hunting (the belly skin has no osteoderms and tans well), but in isolated colonies juveniles are still quite abundant (adults represent only 5–10 per cent of populations). There are few roads in Belize, and virtually all the hunting is carried out by natives, shooting crocodiles at night with the aid of a flashlight and selling the hides to a local dealer for about 5 US dollars per 1 ft (30 cm). A licensed European exporter buys them for around 7 US dollars per 1 ft to pass on to a Belgian holding company for 10–15 US dollars per 1 ft, the skins ending up in Italy for processing to make bags, belts and shoes. A 2-m (6½-ft) Morelet's crocodile yields products worth a total of around 2,500 dollars, of which the retailer gets 1,135 dollars and the contractor 1,100 dollars, the tanner, foreign broker and leather workers accounting for most of the rest. Not much more than 2 per cent of the profit remains in Belize. A *Crocodylus moreleti* captive-breeding programme is under way in Atlanta zoo, Georgia, and there are other stocks in Mexican zoos.

The Cuban crocodile (*Crocodylus rhombifer*) is in a particularly parlous state owing to agricultural development of its last remaining stronghold, the surviving semi-wild stock being held since the early 1960s in 'corrals' near a lake in the Zapata swamp with no real attempt to maintain their natural habitat. At one time they were interbreeding with what is left of the island's *Crocodylus acutus* population, but the remaining pure-bred *Crocodylus rhombifer* stock is now segregated. The future of *Crocodylus rhombifer*, however, probably depends largely on zoo stocks held by establishments in Jersey, Havana, East Berlin and Winnipeg.

The position of crocodilians in Latin America is precarious in the extreme. Large-scale commercial hide-hunting, mostly promoted by French and German tanneries, flourished in the 1920s and 1930s, but tailed off owing to increasing scarcity of crocodilians in the late 1940s. Nonetheless, in the 20 years between 1950 and 1970, an estimated 9 million caiman hides were exported, along with ½ million skins from *Crocodylus acutus* and 200,000 from *Crocodylus intermedius*. Between January 1976 and June 1978, a total of 1,180,153 hides was reported to have been legally exported from Colombia, the major South American centre of the hide trade. These figures alone suggest an insupportable drain on natural crocodilian populations, and smuggled hides are not accounted for. Much of this trade passes through the town of Leticia in extreme southwestern Colombia, the capital of the Colombian Amazon.

Smuggling of crocodile skins takes place along the Meta River from Venezuela into Colombia and thence up the Casanare. Settlers in the llanos could at one time get 6.25 US dollars for a 1.2-m (4-ft) skin at Puerto López, but by 1980 few adult crocodilians remained in the area and most skins offered for sale did not exceed 60 cm (2 ft). Colombian processors also legally re-import skins originally smuggled into Panama, often from caimans poached along the Colombian coast between Cienaga Grande and the River Magdalena, but again the hides are increasingly only from juveniles. Even in the Isla de Salamanca National Park, the caimans' mangrove habitat has been destroyed, although elsewhere along the lower and middle Magdalena valley a decline in manatees has led to a resurgence of riverside vegetation which provides small numbers of caimans with a measure of protection from hide-hunters. Most South American countries have passed protective wildlife legislation, but enforcement is often lax in the extreme. Prohibition on the taking of small crocodilians is widely disregarded, especially as tanneries now find flank skin, with its very small scales, particularly attractive.

In Africa the once abundant Nile crocodile is steadily losing its struggle to survive in the wild. Anthony Pooley concluded in 1981 that in the 30 years from 1950 to 1980 at least 3 million African crocodiles had been slaughtered for their skins. Mostly they would have been Nile crocodiles, although these are becoming so scarce that the West African long-snouted crocodile (*Crocodylus cataphractus*) and the dwarf crocodiles (*Osteolaemus*) are now being taken by hide-hunters, despite the commercially inferior skins of these species. In addition, crocodiles are drowned in the gill nets of fishermen, and in many areas suffer persecution on the grounds that they deplete fish stocks (which is untrue, as they prey primarily on the large predators of small food fishes, and also fertilise lakes and streams with minerals and phosphates from their excreta that help to promote a rich aquatic fauna and flora). Some African countries still regard crocodiles as vermin and even offer rewards for their destruction, and with stocks so decimated by hide-hunters even the demand for crocodile meat and eggs by local tribes is making serious inroads into remaining crocodile communities, especially now that firearms are readily available. Nowhere in Africa can crocodiles be said to have a flourishing future in the wild, and African crocodile farms have so far had limited success. Only in Zimbabwe (where 2,253 crocodiles were culled for hides in 1978–80) and in South Africa have these enterprises looked at all promising, but even in these two countries the scale of operation does not begin to meet the demand for crocodile skins. As a result, poaching, often with the aid of an official 'blind eye' in response to financial favours, is a highly profitable activity all over Africa.

In southern Asia, the mugger (*Crocodylus palustris*) has become rare throughout its former range save in Ceylon (Sri Lanka), where the local race (*Crocodylus palustris brevirostris*) is represented by large populations in national parks (wild stocks on the island are dwindling rapidly, however, since the Sri Lankan authorities seem to have little interest in protecting them). Elsewhere there is nominal protection for the mugger in southeastern Baluchistan (the Sarbaz River drainage), but this area of Iran is too remote for adequate implementation of legislation, while in Pakistan the species is approaching extinction. India has no local laws to prevent the sale of crocodile hides and other articles, with the result that a flourishing trade in poached skins is maintained, and in Burma and Bangladesh the mugger finally disappeared in the mid-1970s. The Nepalese population of this species is believed to be fairly numerous. Captive-breeding stocks of muggers exist in several zoos (e.g. Ahmedabad, Baroda, Bangkok, Jaipur, Hyderabad) and there is the official Indian crocodile-breeding project which depends on the collection of wild eggs for incubation; an important step was the setting-up in 1978, at the instigation of Dr H. R. Bustard, of the Central Crocodile Breeding and Management Training Institute, located beside the Mir Alam tank (opposite the Nehru Zoological Park in Hyderabad), where training is provided in crocodile husbandry.

The gavial (*Gavialis gangeticus*) had reached such a low ebb by 1975 that it was estimated only 60 or 70 wild individuals remained. In India, an urgent rehabilitation programme was so successful that by 1986 this number had risen to around 1,500 wild animals and another 1,000 at various rearing centres. In Bangladesh, fewer than 20 gavials were believed still to exist in 1983, despite protective legislation that is apparently difficult to enforce, and the species is extinct in Burma.

Last strongholds of the saltwater crocodile in India include the Bhitarkanika Islands (Orissa), where about 500 existed in the mid-1980s, the Sundarbans (approximately 165 animals) and the Andaman Islands (some 330 survivors), all of these populations apparently showing steady increases; it is, however, extinct in Kerala, Tamil Nadu and Andhra Pradesh. The species was rare in Ceylon and fast disappearing from Burma in the mid-1970s. Sarawak had only about 1 per cent of its original saltwater crocodile population left by 1987, and the species had been wiped out in parts of Papua New Guinea, where commercial crocodile-hunting became established in the late 1940s and quickly eliminated a substantial proportion of the 2–3 m (6–10 ft) animals which yield the best skins. Eventually the remaining crocodiles retreated into the most inaccessible swamps, and local tribesmen had to be recruited to go in and locate them. By 1970, medium-sized crocodiles were hard to find anywhere in New Guinea, and the expatriate hunters had become skin-buyers while natives did all the actual hunting, which now perforce had to concentrate on smaller animals: a few wily older crocodiles of large size still remained, but they now constituted the surviving breeding population and had fortunately become exceedingly evasive. The dealers taught native tribesmen how to prepare skins for marketing, the villagers along the Fly River becoming more skilled in this respect than those on the Sepik. The protective legislation of 1977, which enabled villagers to profit from the conservation of crocodile stocks, came just in time; it succeeded in halting the seemingly inexorable decline of Papua New Guinea's crocodiles.

Saltwater crocodiles are exceedingly rare nowadays in Malaysia, where once these reptiles were relatively common, and have not bred on Singapore since the 1950s, while only an occasional individual now reaches the larger Solomon Islands, although a breeding population persists on one small island in the group. Not more than about ten adults were still to be found in Thailand by the 1980s (although about 6,000 are held there in captivity), stocks in the Philippines are greatly depleted, and in Indonesia this species is dwindling everywhere (almost to extinction in Java), sufficient nonetheless remaining in Irian Jaya to rebuild a viable population if excessive hide-hunting can be curbed. The saltwater crocodiles of northern Australia also declined substantially from an estimated population of over 1 million in the 1930s (perhaps to as few as 5,000 individuals), before protective legislation enabled numbers to increase to around 15,500 by 1982; large examples are still infrequently encountered, however, even though some authorities considered the area's *Crocodylus porosus* stocks to be in excess of 50,000 by the end of the 1980s.

The hide of the saltwater crocodile is particularly in demand, as dermal armour is minimal and the species grows to a very large size. Some idea of the rapidity with which stocks have been decimated is given by world-trade figures for saltwater crocodile skins, 100,000 having been traded annually around 1971 but only 20,000 in 1979. Considerable crocodile habitat still remains in northern Australia, where the coastal wetlands become swamps in the rainy season, and there seems no reason why these reptiles should not quickly re-establish their numbers, given proper protection, since farming is a relatively minor activity in this part of Australia and does not involve the saltwater crocodile's habitat. Unfortunately, feral water buffalo, the descendants of stock imported from Timor in the 19th century and released when settlements were abandoned, create channels that destroy the marshland habitat (they are now being herded by helicopter and sold for meat), and there must be economic incentives to fence swamp areas so that crocodiles can become a profitable commercial enterprise, not just a purely aesthetic conservation project. The first Australian national park established specially for crocodiles (in this case the saltwater species) was opened on the Ord River, near Wyndham, in May 1973 and covers 54,000 acres (22,000 ha). Nevertheless, in a particularly pessimistic 1986 report, H. Messel, G. C. Vorlicek, W. J. Green and I. C. Onley of Sydney University concluded that the Australian saltwater crocodile population had virtually no future outside national parks and only limited prospects within these reserves if net fishing was permitted to continue in them, as many crocodiles were being caught and drowned in the mesh, particularly in Kakadu National Park, where barramundi fishing is widely practised. A significant recovery of Australian *Crocodylus porosus* stocks nonetheless seems to have occurred in Arnhem Land (where 60 per cent of the Northern Territory's crocodile habitat is located, most of it under the control of aboriginal communities), notably in the Adelaide River system, in the tidal waters of the Alligator region, and in the Roper River system, but elsewhere population growth has admittedly been disappointing. Substantial losses of animals between 3 and 6 ft (1–2 m) in length occur every season, up to 70 per cent of this size group disappearing apparently as a result of intraspecific competition for the limited number of 'territories' existing along the rivers of the region, and with restricted habitat area a wastage rate of this magnitude makes population augmentation a very slow process. Helicopters are now extensively used in northern Australia for locating crocodile nests to recover eggs for incubating at rearing units.

Persecution of the saltwater crocodile in New Guinea meant that hide-hunters (or the local tribesmen who agreed to hunt on their behalf) had to transfer their attention to the smaller species of the island, *Crocodylus novaeguineae*. By the late 1960s, 90 per cent of skins exported from coastal localities and 99 per cent of skins originating at inland centres were of this species: it had been exterminated from many areas on the Fly and Sepik Rivers, and had become rare on Lake Murray where these reptiles had previously existed in substantial numbers. A survey in 1967 disclosed that there were no New Guinea freshwater crocodiles at all on the Fly below d'Albertis and the Avu River. The government-sponsored conservation project launched in Papua New Guinea in January 1977 which rewards tribespeople for collecting juvenile crocodiles for the official breeding establishments has resulted in quite substantial augmentation of *Crocodylus novaeguineae* stocks. This species is not found east of longitude 148 East because of an absence of suitable inland swamps, but in the extensive marshy plains of the New Guinea interior these crocodiles were formerly abundant and constituted a major source of food for the local population. In 1980, Indonesia declared *Crocodylus novaeguineae* to be a protected species in Irian Jaya, and by 1986 both the saltwater crocodile and the freshwater crocodile were increasing in numbers in Papua New Guinea.

The Mindoro crocodile seems unlikely to survive for very much longer in the wild since the Philippine government regards agricultural and industrial development as a major priority and elimination of the species' swamp habitats is proceeding virtually unchecked. Scattered populations, probably including no more than a few hundred individuals, were all that remained in 1980, when a captive-breeding programme was started at Silliman University, in Dumaguete City on Negros Island. By 1985 this scheme included 25 crocodiles, 11 of them hatched in 1984, and during July 1985 two three-year-olds were released into Calawit National Park, Northern Busuanga, in the hope that they would establish a breeding population. A Japanese company was preparing to open a crocodile-ranching operation in the Philippines in the late 1980s, and although planning to stock principally saltwater crocodiles they also anticipated breeding a small number of the indigenous Mindoro form.

Little enthusiasm has been shown by the Thai government for the protection of the Siamese crocodile (*Crocodylus siamensis*), and by the early 1970s it was estimated that the wild Thai population of this species numbered fewer than 40 individuals; it was also very rare on Sumatra and probably extinct on Java. Meanwhile, Utai Yangprapakorn had established a crocodile farm at Samut Prakan in 1950 which by 1970 contained 11,000 crocodiles of the saltwater and Siamese species. Thailand had a human-population growth rate of 3.3 per cent in the 1970s, which generated an intense demand for land. With the untreated skin of a crocodile only a few years old fetching 75 US dollars — at that time equal to about half the annual income of a typical Thai villager — it was not surprising that the native species of crocodile was being wiped out at an alarming rate. By 1970, however, the Samut Prakan farm was hatching 3,500 crocodiles a year, a substantial proportion of which were *Crocodylus siamensis*, and the survival of the species in captivity seemed to be assured. Furthermore, Indonesia declared the Siamese crocodile to be protected over the rest of its range.

In Australia, Johnston's crocodile was suffering severely from hide-hunters until protective legislation was passed by the state of Western Australia in 1962 and by the Northern Territory in 1964. Poaching took place thereafter through Queensland, but this state also outlawed hunting in 1974. An export ban on crocodile hides was imposed by the Australian government in 1974 and *Crocodylus johnsoni* was increasing again by 1982, with the population numbering somewhere between 100,000 and 200,000 in the late 1980s.

The false gavial (*Tomistoma schlegeli*) has been protected in Indonesia since 1980 and cannot be caught, killed or traded in this area without permission from the Director of Conservation. Unfortunately, the species has already declined precipitately in the wild, and in Sarawak was to be found in only one river system by 1987. Moderate numbers still apparently remain in a few rivers of eastern Sumatra and south Kalimantan, however, with sparse populations persisting elsewhere in Sumatra, Borneo, Malaysia and Sulawesi. The species appears to be extinct in Thailand.

International trade

International regulation of the trade in wildlife and wildlife products is the object of CITES, the Convention on International Trade in Endangered Species. Countries party to the Convention accept controls on international trade imposed by CITES to protect rare or threatened species, except where a signatory nation exercises its right to declare a reservation in respect of any particular species. Trade by CITES members with non-party states requires the party state to treat the non-signatory nation as if it had also been a member of the Convention.

The key to CITES protection is assessment of a species' rarity or endangerment and its assignment to an appropriate category. Appendix I to the Convention lists species threatened with extinction or which may be endangered by trade, and virtually all international trade in these animals is prohibited unless the exporting party grants an export permit specifying that the trade is not detrimental to wild stocks and the importing party produces a permit confirming that commercial gain is not the primary purpose of the transaction. Exceptions to this requirement for species listed in Appendix I are made in the case of captive-bred animals, which are treated as if they were Appendix II species, i.e. not currently threatened but likely to become so if international trade is not limited. Trade by CITES signatories in Appendix II species is permitted only if the exporting country issues an export permit certifying that the trade will not be to the detriment of the wild population.

All crocodilians are listed by CITES in one or other of these appendices, with those referred to Appendix I comprising *Alligator sinensis, Caiman latirostris, Caiman crocodilus apaporiensis, Melanosuchus niger, Crocodylus acutus, Crocodylus cataphractus, Crocodylus intermedius, Crocodylus moreleti, Crocodylus niloticus* (excluding some more flourishing populations, and with a number of national export quotas), *Crocodylus novaeguineae mindorensis, Crocodylus palustris, Crocodylus porosus* (except for the Australian, Papua New Guinea and Indonesian populations), *Crocodylus rhombifer, Crocodylus siamensis, Osteolaemus tetraspis, Tomistoma schlegeli* and *Gavialis gangeticus*.

By the late 1980s, Japan had become the world's largest consumer of crocodile skins, most of them from South American countries, although significant imports were also consigned from Asia (notably Singapore) and the United States. The demand for so-called 'classic' skins — those which lack flank and belly osteoderms, e.g. the American alligator, the various species of *Crocodylus*, the gavial and the false gavial — continues to be dominated by European importers: traditionally France, Switzerland, West Germany and Italy have been the major buyers of these skins, but in this market, too, the Japanese are playing an increasing part. Species principally involved in the 'classic' skin trade are the Nile crocodile (about 6,500 skins in 1984, including over 4,000 from ranches in Zimbabwe), the saltwater crocodile (principally from Papua New Guinea, which exported over 5,000 skins in 1984), and the New Guinea freshwater crocodile, 30,000 skins of which were marketed in 1984 (22,600 from Papua New Guinea and most of the rest from Indonesia).

The future

Despite their ecological value in wilderness areas, the threat some of the larger crocodilian species pose to human life and the generally unappealing appearance of these reptiles make them a ready target for persecution, especially if money can be obtained from their hides. Following human fatalities in Queensland in 1985–86, some 60 crocodiles were shot in the Cairns region, and fishermen in the Gulf of Carpentaria were shooting crocodiles on sight. Killing crocodiles was illegal in Queensland by this time, but no prosecutions were reported, and a former Queensland Minister of the Environment, Martin Tenni, stated in Brisbane that he wanted crocodiles completely wiped out.

In the face of human tragedies like those in Australia, crocodile conservationists have a major task to justify their beliefs in the value of these reptiles as an integral part of tropical and subtropical ecological systems and also as objects of special scientific interest in their own right, for these dragons of the Mesozoic are in truth the last of the ruling reptiles, the sole survivors of the scaly giants that once ruled the Earth. There is still much to learn from them, not least in the field of medical research: their resistance to disease and in particular the rarity of cancers in crocodiles merit close examination.

Crocodile-farming may well be the key, generating profits that will alone keep some species of crocodiles from dying out, although the availability of legally marketed skins will of course maintain a demand for crocodile products and thereby tend to encourage poachers. Ideally, reservations that preserve natural crocodilian habitat in which wild populations can breed must be an urgent priority, so that eggs and hatchlings may be collected from the wild and raised in captivity: possibly a more effective method of crocodile-farming than trying to maintain breeding pairs under artificial conditions.

Different solutions in different places may suit different species. But it would be tragic indeed if the last of the reptilian giants were allowed simply to disappear from the Earth — a unique race, 200 million years old, the last rearguard of a once mighty host.

Appendix I. Check list of principal crocodilian genera

(Living forms are marked with an asterisk)

Order Crocodylia

Suborder Protosuchia

Family Sphenosuchidae. *Pedeticosaurus, Platyognathus, Sphenosuchus*
Family Protosuchidae. *Baroqueosuchus, Eopneumatosuchus, Hemiprotosuchus, Lesothosuchus, Protosuchus, Stegomosuchus*

Suborder Archaeosuchia

Family Notochampsidae. *Microchampsa, Notochampsa, Orthosuchus*

Suborder Mesosuchia

Family Atoposauridae. *Alligatorellus, Alligatorium, Atoposaurus, Hoplosuchus, Karatausuchus, Shantungosuchus, Theriosuchus*
Family Goniopholididae. *Coelosuchus, Dakotasuchus, Eutretauranosuchus, Goniopholis, Kansajsuchus, Microsuchus, Oweniasuchus, Petrosuchus, Pinacosuchus, Pliogonodon, Polydectes, Shamosuchus, Sunosuchus, Symptosuchus, Vectisuchus*
Family Trematochampsidae. *Baharijodon, Trematochampsa*
Family Bernissartiidae. *Bernissartia*
Family Artzosuchidae. *Artzosuchus*
Family Notosuchidae. *Araripesuchus, Brasileosaurus, Notosuchus, Uruguaysuchus*
Family Libycosuchidae. *Libycosuchus*
Family Sphagesauridae. *Sphagesaurus*
Family Gobiosuchidae. *Gobiosuchus*
Family Hsisosuchidae. *Doratodon, Hsisosuchus*
Family Edentosuchidae. *Edentosuchus*
Family Teleosauridae. *Aeolodon, Gavialinum, Gnathosaurus, Haematosaurus, Heterosaurus, Machimosaurus, Marmarosaurus, Pelagosaurus, Platysuchus, Rhytisodon, Steneosaurus, Teleosaurus*

Family Pholidosauridae. *Anglosuchus, Crocodilaemus, Meridiosaurus, Peipehsuchus, Pholidosaurus, Sarcosuchus, Suchosaurus, Teleorhinus*

Family Dyrosauridae. *Atlantosuchus, Dyrosaurus, Hyposaurus, Phosphatosaurus, Rhabdognathus, Rhabdosaurus, Sokotosuchus, Tilemsisuchus*

Suborder Thalattosuchia
Family Metriorhynchidae. *Capelliniosuchus, Cricosaurus, Dakosaurus, Enaliosuchus, Geosaurus, Metriorhynchus, Neustosaurus, Purranisaurus, Teleidosaurus*

Suborder Sebecosuchia
Family Sebecidae. *Ayllusuchus, Ilchunaia, Sebecus*

Family Baurusuchidae. *Baurusuchus, Bergisuchus, Cynodontosuchus, Iberosuchus, Limnosaurus*

Family Peirosauridae. *Peirosaurus*

Family Wanosuchidae. *Wanosuchus*

Suborder Eusuchia
Family Hylaeochampsidae. *Hylaeochampsa*

Family Stomatosuchidae. *Chiayusuchus, Stomatosuchus, Stromerosuchus*

Family Aegyptosuchidae. *Aegyptosuchus*

Family Dolichochampsidae. *Dolichochampsa*

Family Crocodylidae

    Subfamily Crocodylinae. *Aigialosuchus, Akanthosuchus, Allodaposuchus, Asiatosuchus, Brachyuranochampsa, Charactosuchus, Crocodylus*, Deinosuchus, Dzungarisuchus, Kentisuchus, Leidyosuchus, Lianghusuchus, Manracosuchus, Megadontosuchus, Navajosuchus, Necrosuchus, Orthogenysuchus, Osteolaemus*, Oxysdonsaurus, Pallimnarchus*

    Subfamily Alligatorinae. *Albertochampsa, Alligator*, Allognathosuchus, Arambourgia, Balanerodus, Baryphracta, Bottosaurus, Brachychampsa, Brachygnathosuchus, Caiman*, Caimanosuchus, Ceratosuchus, Colossoemys, Dinosuchus, Diplocynodon, Eoalligator, Eocaiman, Eocenosuchus, Ferganosuchus, Hispanochampsa, Melanosuchus*, Menatalligator, Notocaiman, Paleosuchus*, Proalligator, Procaimanoidea, Prodiplocynodon, Purussaurus, Sajkanosuchus, Tadzhikosuchus, Wannaganosuchus*

    Subfamily Pristichampsinae. *Planocrania, Pristichampsus, Quinkana*

    Subfamily Thoracosaurinae. *Dollosuchus, Eosuchus, Eotomistoma, Euthecodon, Gavialosuchus, Holopsisuchus, Leptorrhamphus, Maroccosuchus, Thoracosaurus, Tienosuchus, Tomistoma**

    Subfamily Gavialinae. *Eogavialis, Gavialis*, Gryposuchus, Hesperogavialis, ?Ikanogavialis, Rhamphostomopsis, Rhamphosuchus*

Family Nettosuchidae. *Mourasuchus*

Appendix II. Living crocodilian species and their common names

Crocodylus niloticus: Nile crocodile, Mamba
   Crocodylus niloticus niloticus: African crocodile, Amsah, Champsae, Ethiopian crocodile, P'amsah, Sudanese crocodile, Timsah
   Crocodylus niloticus suchus: Central African crocodile
   Crocodylus niloticus chamses: West African Nile crocodile
   Crocodylus niloticus pauciscutatus: Kenya alligator, Kenya caiman, Kenya crocodile
   Crocodylus niloticus cowiei: South African crocodile
   Crocodylus niloticus africanus: East African crocodile
   Crocodylus niloticus madagascariensis: Madagascan crocodile, Madagascan alligator, Croco Mada
Crocodylus cataphractus: African gavial, African gharial, Long-nosed crocodile, African sharp-nosed crocodile, African slender-snouted crocodile, Faux gavial africain, Loricate crocodile, Subwater crocodile, West African long-snouted crocodile, Khinh
   Crocodylus cataphractus cataphractus
   Crocodylus cataphractus congicus
Crocodylus palustris: Makar, Äle Kimbula, Ali Kimbula, Bhakuna, Broad-snouted crocodile, Dhakor Muhma, Gohi, Gomua, Häle Kimbula, crocodile, Bony crocodile, Broad-nosed crocodile, Broad-nosed West African crocodile, Crocodile cuirassé, Crocodile nain, Rough-back crocodile
Crocodylus siamensis: Singapore small grain, Buaja, Buaya, Freshwater crocodile, Siamese crocodile, Siamese freshwater crocodile, Soft-belly
Crocodylus novaeguineae: Singapore large grain
   Crocodylus novaeguineae novaeguineae: New Guinea freshwater crocodile
   Crocodylus novaeguineae mindorensis: Mindoro crocodile, Philippine crocodile, Philippine freshwater crocodile
Crocodylus porosus: Singapore small grain, Baya, Buaja, Buaya, Estuarine crocodile, Gator, Gatta Kimbula, Gorekeya, Pita Gatteya, Rawing crocodile, Saltwater crocodile, Semmukhan Muthelei, Sea-going crocodile, Subwater crocodile
Crocodylus johnsoni: Johnston's crocodile, Australian freshwater crocodile
Crocodylus acutus: American crocodile, Caimán de Aguja, Central American alligator, Cocodrilo de Rio, Crocodile à museau pointu, Lagarto Amarillo, Lagarto Real, Llaman Caimán, South American alligator

Crocodylus moreleti: Morelet's crocodile, Mexican crocodile, Soft belly, Belize crocodile, Central American crocodile, Cocodrilo de Pantano, Lagarto de El Petén, Lagarto Negro, Lagarto Pantanero, Lagarto Panza

Crocodylus rhombifer: Cuban crocodile, Caimán Zaquendo, Cocodrilo Criollo, Cocodrilo Legitimo, Cocodrilo Perla, Crocodile Rhombifère

Crocodylus intermedius: Orinoco crocodile, Colombian crocodile, Venezuelan delta crocodile

Osteolaemus tetraspis: African caiman, African dwarf crocodile, Black crocodile, Bony crocodile, Broad-nosed crocodile, African broad-nosed crocodile, Crocodile cuirassé, Crocodile nain, Rough-back crocodile

    Osteolaemus tetraspis tetraspis: Cabinda, Croco Bnin, West African dwarf crocodile

    Osteolaemus tetraspis osborni: Osborn's dwarf crocodile, Pseudo Cabinda, Congo dwarf crocodile

Alligator mississipiensis: American alligator, Mississippi alligator, Pike-headed alligator, Gator

Alligator sinensis: Chinese alligator, T'o, Tou Lung, Yow Lung

Caiman latirostris: Overo, Yacaré Overo, Ururau, Yacaré de Hocico Ancho, Broad-nosed caiman, Jacaré de Papo Amarelo, Jacaré Verde, Jacaré de Hocico Ancho

    Caiman latirostris latirostris

    Caiman latirostris chacoensis

Caiman crocodilus: Spectacled caiman, Tinga

    Caiman crocodilus crocodilus: Baba, Babilla, Babiche, Cachirré, Caiman Blanco, Caiman de Brasil, Cascarudo, Common caiman, Jacaretinga Lagarto, Lagarto Blanco, Yacaré Blanco

    Caiman crocodilus fuscus: Brown caiman, American caiman, Cuajipal, Dusky caiman, Jacaretinga, Lagarto Chato, Lagarto de Concha, Lagarto Negro, Magdalena caiman, Pululo, Talulín, Wizizil

    Caiman crocodilus apaporiensis: Apaporis River caiman, Babilla, Cachirré, Ocoroché

    Caiman crocodilus yacare: Cascarudo, Red caiman, Yacare de Hocico Angosto, Yacare Negro, Southern spectacled caiman

    Caiman crocodilus paraguayensis: Paraguay caiman

    Caiman crocodilus matogrossiensis: Mato Grosso caiman

Melanosuchus niger: Black caiman, Caiman Negro, Jacare Açu, Jacaré Assu, Jacare Asu, Jacare Uassu, Jacaré Una, Yacare Assu

Paleosuchus palpebrosus. Cuvier's smooth-fronted caiman, Cachirré, Dwarf caiman, Jacaré Coroa, Musky caiman

Paleosuchus trigonatus: Schneider's smooth-fronted caiman, Jacaré Coroa

Tomistoma schlegeli: False gavial, false gharial, Baja (Baya) Kanulong, Bediai Sampit, Boeaja, Buaja, Buaya, Buaya Jolong-Jolong, Buaya Sa(m)pit, Buaya Senjulong, Buaya Sepit, Jolong-Jolong, Malay gavial, Malay gharial, Malayan fish crocodile, Senjulong

Gavialis gangeticus: Indian gavial, Indian gharial, Bahsoolia, Nakar, Chimpta, Lamthora, Mecho Kumhir, Naka, Nakar, Shormon, Thantia, Thondre

Bibliography

Buffetaut, E. (1979) The evolution of the crocodilians. *Scientific American*, **241**, 124–32.

Cott, H. B. (1961) Scientific results of an inquiry into the ecology and economic status of the Nile Crocodile (*Crocodilus niloticus*) in Uganda and Northern Rhodesia. *Transactions Zoological Society of London*, **29**, part 4, 211–356.

Finkelstein, D. (1984) Tigers of the stream. *Audubon*, **86**, May 1984, 98–111.

Gore, R. (1978) A bad time to be a crocodile. *National Geographic Magazine*, **153**, January 1978, 90–115.

Groombridge, B. (ed., 1983) *IUCN Amphibia-Reptilia Red Data Book*, part 1: Testudines, Crocodylia, Rhynchocephalia (International Union for the Conservation of Nature), 283–413.

Guggisberg, C. A. W. (1972) *Crocodiles: their natural history, folklore and conservation* (David & Charles), 204 pp.

International Union for the Conservation of Nature (1971) *Crocodiles: proceedings of the first working meeting of crocodile specialists*, vol. 1 (IUCN Supplementary Paper no. 32), 191 pp.

International Union for the Conservation of Nature (1986) *Proceedings of the seventh meeting of the Crocodile Specialist Group* (IUCN), 446 pp.

Luxmoore, R. A., Barzdo, J. G., Broad, S. R., and Jones, D. A. (1985) *A Directory of Crocodilian Farming Operations* (International Union for the Conservation of Nature Wildlife Trade Monitoring Unit), 204 pp.

Meyer, E. R. (1984) Crocodilians as living fossils, in N. Eldredge and S. M. Stanley, (eds.), *Living Fossils* (Springer), 105–31.

Neill, W. T. (1971) *The Last of the Ruling Reptiles* (Columbia University Press), 486 pp.

Nichol, J. (1984) *The Ganges Gharial* (Channel Four Television, London), 8 pp.

Pooley, A. (1983) *Discoveries of a Crocodile Man* (Collins), 213 pp.

Steel, Rodney (1973) Crocodylia, in O. Kuhn (ed.), *Handbuch der Palaeoherpetologie*, part 16 (in English, Fischer), 116 pp.

Index